The Other
Ariel

For Kim, Jake, and Nick

The Other
Ariel

LYNDA K. BUNDTZEN

SUTTON PUBLISHING

This book was first published in 2001 by
University of Massachusetts Press

This new edition first published in 2005 by
Sutton Publishing Limited · Phoenix Mill
Thrupp · Stroud · Gloucestershire · GL5 2BU

British Library Cataloguing in Publication Data
A catalogue record for this book is available from the British Library.

ISBN 0 7509 4123 5

Quotations from drafts and typescripts of the *Ariel* poems used by
permission of the Sylvia Plath Collection, Smith College Library Rare book
Room.

Quotations from Aurelia Plath's marginal notes to letters in the Sylvia
Plath Collection, Smith College Library Rare Book Room, used by
permission of Susan Plath Winston, Copyright Permissions Agent for the
Estate of Aurelia S. Plath.

Portions of this book appeared earlier in somewhat different form in
"Poetic Arson and Sylvia Plath's 'Burning the Letters,'" *Contemporary
Literature* 39, no. 3 (Fall 1998): 434–51. © 1998. Reprinted by permission
of the University of Wisconsin Press. In revised form. "Mourning Eurydice:
Ted Hughes as Orpheus in *Birthday Letters*," *Journal of Modern Literature* 23,
nos. 3–4 (Spring 2000): 455–69. © 2000 Indiana University Press.

Typeset in 11/13pt Photina.
Typestting and origination by
Sutton Publishing Limited.
Printed and bound in Great Britain by
J.H. Haynes & Co. Ltd, Sparkford.

Contents

Preface

In writing this preface, I become part of a tradition in Plath scholarship, a member of a group of scholars, biographers, and critics who have been discouraged by the executors of the estate of Sylvia Plath (and now the estate of Ted Hughes) from pursuing their research, scholarship, and interpretations. It is a distinguished company, including Jacqueline Rose, Linda Wagner-Martin, and Anne Stevenson among others. When I sent my initial request for permission to quote from the works of Sylvia Plath and Ted Hughes to their publisher, Faber and Faber, along with a copy of the manuscript, I was asked only for a line count and inventory of the citations made. After a month had passed, I received a letter informing me bluntly 'that permission cannot be granted.' There was no explanation as to why or what went into what was described as 'very careful consideration.' Believing with my publisher that I deserved clarification of this curt dismissal of a manuscript I had worked on since 1995, I requested an explanation. In reply, I was assured that 'the same consideration' is given to everyone's work – that is, that my manuscript had not been singled out for this peculiar punishment. Further, I was given a general rule: Faber and Faber and the estates of Plath and Hughes 'only grant permission when their material is used in a strictly literary context.' I was asked to understand their 'reasoning' that 'if we agreed to the quotations being published then we would be seen as giving our seal of approval to the comments you make,' and further, 'we do not feel that your views reflect our own or those of the Estates concerned and we cannot therefore grant permission.' The letter concluded by reiterating that 'we deal with many similar requests and they are all given the same consideration,' once again, I imagine, reassuring me that everyone is treated the same way. It is, of course, impossible to publish a critical study of works that cannot be quoted. Therefore, the impact of this denial was clearly to discourage *The Other 'Ariel'* from being published.

I was extremely surprised by several of these statements. I did not know that I needed to 'reflect' anyone else's views in order to express my own in print. A scholar-critic seeks publication in order to contribute new interpretations, arguments, and findings and to stimulate further research and informed debate. The expectation is that one's interpretations are open to disagreement, that there is a 'free marketplace' of ideas, and that not everyone will want to 'buy' a single scholar's work as definitive. My understanding of the thinking of the unidentified 'we' at Faber and Faber and the collective estates is that I should not have access to this marketplace of ideas because they disagree with me. Prior approval of one's ideas seems to be mandatory for publication on Plath and Hughes. I was also surprised by the criterion of 'strictly literary.' Quite apart from the overtly biographical content of *Birthday Letters* and, of course, many of Plath's 'confessional' poems, Faber and Faber had just published a book titled *Ariel's Gift* by Erica Wagner that was strictly biographical in its narrative – each chapter following the poems in *Birthday Letters* as episodes in the courtship and marriage of Plath and Hughes.

After discussing this murky 'clarification' with the director of the University of Massachusetts Press, I wrote yet another letter expressing our 'surprise and dismay' that permission should be denied to 'a serious work of literary criticism,' and asking for further clarification of the criterion of 'strictly literary context.' Since this seems to be a mandatory requirement, I respectfully requested an example of such a work, and asked about Erica Wagner's study, since it seemed to violate that absolute requirement. Finally, I offered to include on the copyright page a disclaimer to the effect that the views and opinions expressed by the author are not endorsed by Faber and Faber or the estates of the two poets. This would make clear that I did not have their 'seal of approval.'

I waited six weeks for a response. Representing the estates, Faber and Faber rejected the offer of a disclaimer, but followed the rejection by stating the hope that I 'could cut down [my] quotations to fall under the remit of "fair dealing"' adding, 'I hope this explains the situation clearly.' I was also informed that 'a strictly literary context' is one in which 'the works themselves are being discussed.' This gave me pause. When is one not talking about the work being quoted? Finally, I was informed that Erica Wagner's book was published 'because Ted Hughes approved the project' – as well he might, since Wagner agrees with his characterization of Plath, their marriage, and what went wrong.

I did feel set free, however, to investigate the whole issue of 'fair dealing' and 'fair use.' With the help of a librarian I found two useful documents: a one-page description of 'Anthology and Quotation Rates 1999' by the British Society of Authors, and from the Register of Copyrights at the Library of Congress a one-page definition of 'Fair Use.' The former documents states: 'Unfortunately, it is not possible to give very specific guidance on what constitutes 'fair dealing'; it is a matter of impression and common sense according to the circumstances.' Similarly, the Library of Congress document states that 'the distinction between 'fair use' and infringement may be unclear and not easily defined.' Given the generally unclear status of these terms, however, both documents provided me with some guidelines that I proceeded to apply as best I could, using my 'common sense.'

The Society of Authors suggests that in 'quotations for "purposes of criticism or review,"' it may be relevant to take into account the following:

the length and importance of the quotation(s);
the amount quoted in relation to your commentary;
the extent to which your work competes with or rivals
    the work quoted;
the extent to which works quoted are saving you work.

By way of example, the society recommends 'the use of a single extract of up to 400 words or a series of extracts (of which none exceeds 300 words) to a total of 800 words from a prose work, or of extracts to a total of 40 lines from a poem, provided that this did not exceed a quarter of the poem.' Adhering to these rules, I cut several of my extracts from poems by Ted Hughes and reviewed my quotations from his prose. I also paraphrased portions of his unpublished play 'The Calm,' because I believed that quoting them might be saving me work.

The Society of Authors document concludes: 'It does not mean . . . that a quotation 'for purposes of criticism or review' in excess of these limits cannot rank as 'fair dealing' in some circumstances.' I did not cut my quotations from Plath with such a liberal hand as I used on Hughes because of the character of my study, which is a very close analysis of a small group of Plath's poems. The amount of my commentary on individual poems in most instances far exceeds the number of lines quoted. I also turned to the Library of Congress document here, which specifies that 'reproduction of a particular work may be considered 'fair' when used for criticism, comment, news reporting, teaching, scholarship, and research.' Despite my quotation of one-third to one-half of some poems by Plath, I do not, in fact, 'reproduce' any of them, either in their complete form or in draft form, preferring to analyze individual lines and stanzas in a rigorous way. My intent is entirely that of criticism, comment, teaching, scholarship, and research. The Library of

Preface

Congress document goes on to raise questions of motive and effect. Is this publication for 'commercial' or 'nonprofit educational purposes'? Clearly, a scholarly study like mine is not calculated to be a best-seller. Even the publisher's promotional questionnaire for authors asks for one's Social Security number only as a courtesy – '*if there are any royalites.*' What 'effect of the use upon the potential market for or value of the copyrighted work' will I have? I strongly believe that I will encourage more research on Plath's manuscripts and enhance the value of the *Ariel* poems, and that the effect on readers of my study will be to send them back to a volume they may have set aside years ago. There is no appropriation of Sylvia Plath's intellectual property, but rather an extended critical commentary intended to increase the value of that property.

Finally, I did cut my quotation of unpublished portions of letters by Plath. Although I received no clarification of which views, comments, and opinions had met with disapproval (I *did* ask), I assumed that many of them were actually Plath's when she wrote to her mother, brother, and friends about her feelings toward Ted Hughes and Assia Wevill in the period when she was writing the *Ariel* poems. I have therefore paraphrased unpublished excerpts from these letters, only occasionally borrowing words and phrases. Although I frequently express my doubts about Plath's accusations against Hughes, attributing them to her heightened sense of being wronged, I believe that the estates would prefer her accusations remain unspoken. The effect of my paraphrase may be to arouse unwanted (by the estates) curiosity, I am afraid, but their inclusion in summary form still seemed necessary to establish the state of mind in which Plath composed the *Ariel* poems, since in many instances that state of mind shaped her creative process in distinctive ways.

Lynda K. Bundtzen
Williamstown, Massachusetts

Acknowledgements

I begin by expressing my gratitude to the members of my National Endowment for the Humanities summer seminar for high school teachers in 1995. With their unbounded energy and enthusiasm, they rekindled my scholarly interest in Sylvia Plath. The 'Plathheads,' as they came to call themselves, include Jan Adkins, Birthe Dahl, Sandra Glynn-Lippe, Jane Kehoe Higgins, Eileen M. Kelleher, Kelli Kuberski, M.A. Mahoney, Jeanne E. Martinelli, Kelly Moore, Sue Mullen, Leslie Renee Proud, Theresa A. Squires, Mary Scanlon, Greg Standish, Marianne Werner, and Anne Wilson.

I was also inspired by the publication of Janet Malcolm's book *The Silent Woman*, which persuaded me to think again about the problems faced by Plath scholars and to propose the seminar on Plath to the National Endowment for the Humanities. Her participation in one of those classes and another at Williams College on Sylvia Plath was appreciated by my students as well as myself.

The librarians and archivists at the Mortimer Rare Book Room of Smith College were essential to me in my work as both a scholar and teacher of Plath. Barbara Blumenthal has welcomed me and my students on several occasions and made presentations of the Plath collection which have sparked their intellectual curiosity. I am especially grateful to Karen V. Kukil, associate curator of Smith College's rare books collections. Her friendship as well as expertise on Sylvia Plath have been invaluable.

Williams College provided me with research support and sabbatical leaves that permitted me to complete my manuscript. I am also grateful for the stipend from the Oakley Center for the Humanities and Social Sciences of Williams College, where I was a Herbert H. Lehman fellow in 1997–98.

My colleagues at Williams have been wonderful readers and resources for my work. Professors of English Lawrence Graver and Lawrence Raab were early readers of my manuscript and provided me with both criticism and praise. I am very indebted to Professor of Classics Meredith Hoppin for the help she gave me in pursuing classical sources for my mythology on bees, and Professor of English Alison Case, who set me off in pursuit of the folk custom 'telling the bees.'

I also thank beekeeper and family friend Dennis Austin for answering all of my practical questions about bees and beekeeping, for showing me his hives, and supplying me with his book collection on bees. Without his help, I probably would have only a literary sense of bees and beekeeping.

Finally, I thank my husband, Kim, who encouraged me to follow my inclinations and go ahead with this project initially, and provided me with sympathetic support at every stage of its progress.

Introduction

Although the 'other' *Ariel* of my title has now been published, 'restored' to conform with Sylvia Plath's 'original selection and arrangement,' the publishing history of this famous volume needs review in order to comprehend the critical impact this 40-year-long delay has had on our understanding of Plath's work. The first British edition of Sylvia Plath's *Ariel* was published in 1965 by Faber and Faber as a 'Choice of the Poetry Book Society.' The book jacket quotes A.E. Dyson's review in the *Critical Quarterly* predicting that these poems would be 'among the handful of writings by which future generations will seek to know us and give us a name,' and A. Alvarez's personal testimony from *The Review* that 'it was only by her determination both to face her most inward and terrifying experiences, and to use her intelligence in doing so – so as not to be overwhelmed by them – that she managed to write these extraordinary last poems.' When the first American edition appeared in 1966, the critical blurbs cited on the back matched – perhaps exceeded in their cumulative force – the praise lavished on the volume in England. George Steiner claimed that 'Plath's poems have already passed into legend' and 'reference to Sylvia Plath is constant where poetry and the conditions of its present existence are discussed' (*The Reporter*); the *Times Literary Supplement* pronounced *Ariel* 'one of the most marvelous volumes of poetry published for a very long time'; and A. Alvarez is quoted again, warning the timorous reader that 'poetry of this order is a murderous art' (*The Review*), thereby promoting the melodramatic critical judgment of Plath and her

1

work expressed in the foreword to *Ariel* by Robert Lowell, the preeminent American poet of the sixties: his name beneath Sylvia Plath's on the cover is printed as large as hers.

Lowell's foreword also begins on the cover, drawing the browser in with his authoritative approval and election of Plath into the pantheon of fellow confessional poets. Lowell is unreserved in his praise for *Ariel*'s importance and uniqueness:

> There is a peculiar, haunting challenge to these poems. Probably many, after reading *Ariel*, will recoil from their first overawed shock, and painfully wonder why so much of it leaves them feeling empty, evasive, and inarticulate. In her lines, I often hear the serpent whisper, "Come, if only you had the courage, you too could have my rightness, audacity and ease of inspiration." But most of us will turn back. These poems are playing Russian roulette with six cartridges in the cylinder, a game of "chicken," the wheels of both cars locked and unable to swerve. Oh, for that heaven of the copyist, those millennia of Egyptian artists repeating their lofty set patterns! (viii)

Lowell immediately lifts Plath into an American style of originality that makes poetry dangerous and new – no 'humble copyist' she! Her inimitable 'audacity and ease,' her fusing of poesy with suicidal risk-taking makes Plath resemble other American icons of the sixties – like James Dean – who lived fast and died young.

Newsweek borrows Lowell's metaphor for the title of its review, 'Russian Roulette' (June 20, 1966), and adds to the inflated and inflamed critical rhetoric by describing *Ariel* as 'a symphony of death and dissolution' (110). Not to be outdone, *Time*'s review article, 'The Blood Jet Is Poetry' (June 10, 1966), describes Plath as 'a literary dragon who in the last months of her life breathed a burning river of bale across the literary landscape' (56). *Time* also reprints 'Daddy,' one of Plath's most unforgiving and personal poems, with a photo of Plath as a child with her mother and brother. I remind the reader of the feverish publicity surrounding the appearance of *Ariel* in 1965–66, first because it explains why so few sober-minded questions were asked about how this posthumous volume came into being: Who selected these poems? Were they 'selected' at all, or is this everything Plath left behind? Or, rather, are these poems *the best* of what she left behind? Did Plath select these poems prior to her death? Is there more to come? Who came up with the title? Why are the poems ordered as they are? Who was responsible for editing the poems – and from what manuscripts, typescripts, and poems already published in little magazines? Why does the British edition of *Ariel* differ from the American edition?[1] In the excitement of *Ariel*'s reception, such questions seemed impertinent. Second, I want to remind my reader that, in terms of literary history, Ariel is legendary – assuredly one of the important volumes of contemporary poetry.

But who 'authored' *Ariel*?

While it would be an exaggeration to argue that Plath's estranged husband and fellow poet Ted Hughes 'authored' *Ariel*, we know now that it represents his, not Plath's, overall narrative intentions. One of the surprising revelations of Ted Hughes's publication of Plath's *Collected Poems* in 1981 was that Plath had compiled her own volume, titled ''Ariel' and Other Poems,' and that it was significantly different from the *Ariel* Hughes put together for publication in 1965 for British readers and in 1966 for American readers. His brief description of this volume may be found in his editorial notes for 1963, where Hughes simply lists the forty-one poems for 'Sylvia Plath's own prepared collection of poems' (*CP* 295).[2] By 1981, however, Plath was no longer regarded with quite the same critical fervor. As Marjorie Perloff points out in a lengthy article comparing Plath's version of *Ariel* with the one authorized by Hughes, 'the literary landscape had changed and interest in Plath's poetry had appreciably declined' ('The Two *Ariels*' 309). And no one, except Perloff, seemed interested in trying to reconstruct Plath's intentions for the volume. Although both Helen Vendler in the *New Yorker* and Kathe Pollitt in *The Nation* notice Hughes's remark that Plath planned a 'somewhat different volume'' (*CP* 15) from the *Ariel* that made her famous, neither prolongs the interrogation. Pollitt simply muses, 'Would it have made a difference to her reputation, I wonder, if Plath's pattern [for *Ariel*] had been preserved?' (55)

Plath's version of *Ariel* was kept intact in a typescript housed at the Smith College Library Rare Book Room and is now in print, also published in facsimile and along with facsimile drafts of two poems, the title poem 'Ariel' and 'The Swarm,' which was included in Hughes's American edition of the volume, but not the British. The 'restored' *Ariel* includes Plath's commentary on several of these poems for a BBC broadcast and a Foreword by her daughter Frieda Hughes. Before addressing the arrival of this 'new' edition and what it might mean for future interpreters of Plath's work, it would be useful to discuss the differences between Hughes's *Ariel* and Plath's. As Frieda Hughes acknowledges at the end of her Foreword, 'each version has its own significance though the two histories are one' (xxi). Whereas Ted Hughes's *Ariel* ends with poems composed days before her suicide in February 1963, Plath ends her version with a sequence of bee poems written between October 3 and 9, a week when Hughes was packing up to leave Plath and their two children in their Devon home. The poems Hughes appended to Plath's bee poems are described by Perloff as 'death poems,' while the bee poems are allegorical, multilayered, overdetermined with possible meanings. Because Plath's final word in the poem 'Wintering' is 'spring,' Perloff and others have read Plath's original plan for *Ariel* as ending with her imagined survival and rebirth beyond the difficult winter she was about to confront alone. I will argue, however, that the allegory of the bee poems has a more complicated narrative than this suggests; and, further, that the manuscripts for the 'Other *Ariel*' – unavailable to Perloff when she first

approached this problem of *Ariel*'s authorship and integrity –
add additional layers of prophetic ambiguity to the bee
sequence.

Plath completed the final poem for the 'Other *Ariel*' on
November 14, 1962, and in a letter to her mother dated
December 14 claimed that she had finished her second volume
of poetry. Plath did not begin composing again until six weeks
later, and Hughes concedes that 'she herself, recognizing the
different inspiration of these new pieces, regarded them as the
beginnings of a third book.' These differently inspired poems
replace works he omitted from her pattern that were 'more
personally aggressive.' Why? As Hughes explains his selection
in 1981: 'The collection that appeared was my eventual
compromise between publishing a large bulk of her work –
including much of the post-*Colossus* but pre-*Ariel* verse – and
introducing her late work more cautiously' (*CP* 15). Perloff
and other feminist critics, however, have seen Hughes's motives
as self-protective and defensive. Most of the poems Hughes
omitted were attacks on him. Although he explained these
omissions in a variety of ways and on several occasions, often
supporting his alterations as a strategy for making the true
villain of her narrative – Otto Plath – emerge more forcefully, it
is impossible to ignore his sense of marital betrayal. These are
poems meant to hurt.

Plath's dated manuscripts for the *Ariel* poems – all of them –
are written on the back of old typescripts and manuscripts of
poems and plays by Hughes and on the reverse of her
typescripts for *The Bell Jar*. Her poems are literally 'back talking'
– in passionate dialogue, argument, and conversation with
these parallel textual bodies on the underside of her
compositions. There is a strange sense of literary
companionship and collaboration at times between these paper
bodies, when a reader turns over a manuscript to read the
reverse text and discovers an interchange. At times her ink
bleeds through onto her husband's work, indelibly staining it
with her own anguish. At others Plath appears to be

challenging the poetic stance of her husband or else finding inspiration in what is written on the reverse for her own imagery. As Susan Van Dyne interprets this 'back talking,' Plath is also gazing backward, engaged in an effort to revise her life and over-writing old selves with a refigured identity. Van Dyne, however, sees 'no inevitable progression in these poems,' and therefore Plath's original plan for *Ariel* is less important than the multiple 'ways Plath's poems revised her life' (*RL* 3). My own sense of this idiosyncratic writing process is that it is similar to the drama of what poet Louise Glück terms a 'conscious diagnostic act' and 'swearing off' invested in each volume she creates (17).

In the chapters that follow, I describe the unusual nature of Plath's textual body for the 'Other *Ariel*' and what it tells us about the conception of these poems. We need, I believe, to at least consider what Plath originally intended. To reconstruct her intentions for the volume, I focus first on the manuscripts for the excised poems and their violation of the marital relationship with Hughes. Plath trespasses on private, intimate ground shared with her poet husband. These are poems in which it is difficult to discern very much distance between the biographical Plath and her personae. I then turn to the allegorical complexity of the bee poems and the question why Plath wanted them for her conclusion. Finally, because the 'Other *Ariel*' remained unpublished for over 40 years, its condition one of limbo in the Smith College Library Rare Book Room where it remained in dialogue with the textual bodies on which it was composed, I also explore the arguments initiated by Plath on these manuscripts. Then, because this dialogue continues even to the present with the publication of Hughes's *Birthday Letters*, many of them borrowing Plath's titles and engaged in answering her with his own version of their shared story, I include these poems as part of an ongoing conversation between two poets, husband and wife, on the nature and limits of the confessional mode. As this suggests, I do not wish simply to offer an alternative to the *Ariel* published in 1965-66, but hope ultimately to multiply *Ariel*'s narratives and interpretive possibilities, to enrich our understanding of its making and its literary history.

This scholarly response to *Ariel* will probably be perceived as unwelcome by Frieda Hughes – despite my best efforts to represent her 'mother's vision and experience at a particular time in her life during great emotional turmoil' (xx), which is how Ms. Hughes herself aptly describes these poems in her Foreword to the restored edition of *Ariel*. I expect Ms Hughes's Foreword only to add more controversy to *Ariel*'s literary history, since it refuses to celebrate the publication, instead drawing attention to the contentious past. Ms Hughes immediately advises the reader that her Foreword is 'purely personal' (xi). She seems oddly resentful about overriding her father's version of the volume with Plath's own – as if she has been harassed into taking sides in a parental fight and honoring her mother's poems at the expense of her father's best intentions. In exasperation over the way her unfairly 'vilified' father was criticized for altering the volume, Ms Hughes reminds her reader that, after all, 'the extracted poems were included in the *Collected Poems* for all to see' (xvii). Ms Hughes also suggests that critics of her father's editing are only interested in the 'sanctity' of Plath's suicide (xviii), and that '*Ariel*'s notoriety came from being the manuscript on her desk *when she died*, rather than simply being an extraordinary manuscript' (author's italics, xviii) – as if this is the true explanation for her mother's fame. The tone of Ms Hughes's Foreword thus implies that she would like all interpretation to cease, and that Plath's 'own words describe her best' (xx), with no commentary, no critical fabrication. In my own judgment, because *Ariel* is the extraordinary volume Ms Hughes acknowledges it to be, I doubt this will happen.

ONE

A Rare Body

Towards what [A. Alvarez] calls 'the Plath industry throbbing with busy-ness in the Universities,' and towards that 'vast potential audience,' I feel no obligations whatsoever. The scholars want the anatomy of the birth of the poetry; and the vast potential audience want her blood, hair, touch, smell, and a front seat in the kitchen where she died. The scholars may well inherit what they want, some day, and there are journalists supplying the other audience right now. But neither audience makes me feel she owes them anything.

Ted Hughes, from *The Observer*, November 21, 1971

What Ted Hughes calls 'the anatomy of the birth' of Plath's *Ariel* poems is now available to scholars in the Sylvia Plath Collection at the Smith College Rare Book Room,[1] but working there, I also feel haunted at times by a stronger presence – if not her 'blood, hair, touch, smell,' something closely akin. This may be symptomatic of the somewhat perverse way two of Plath's distinctive traits as an artist assume their final embodiments in this collection.[2] First, Plath's compulsion to exploit her body as a creative resource in the last poems, whether she freezes it into statuary, as in the rigor mortised body of the woman in 'Edge,' or lets it take fiery flight as in 'Lady Lazarus' and

'*Ariel*,' finds fulfillment at Smith in a 'rare' textual body now tended with assiduous care: 'my gold beaten skin/Infinitely delicate and infinitely expensive' ('Fever 103°," *CP* 232). Acutely aware of both the delicacy and expense of the Plath collection, the librarians are a bit like the hospital staff tending the woman in 'Tulips':

> They have propped my head between the pillow and the sheet-cuff
> Like an eye between two white lids that will not shut.
> Stupid pupil, it has to take everything in.
> The nurses pass and pass, they are no trouble,
> They pass the way gulls pass inland in their white caps,
> Doing things with their hands, one just the same as another,
> So it is impossible to tell how many there are.
>
> My body is a pebble to them, they tend it as water
> Tends to the pebbles it must run over, smoothing them gently.
> (*CP* 160)

The Rare Book Room has as many protocols, rules, and forms to complete as a hospital for patients and visitors. Except for the occasional hum of a copier, the atmosphere is hushed, soothing, quiet. The window blinds are closed. There is no weather in the Rare Book Room – a controlled environment. One signs a visitor's book and may then view parts of the textual body after filling out a slip for each one. Each limb and organ has been treated to prevent infection and decay, and only pencils 'must be used for taking notes in this room' to prevent potential wounds by pen and ink. A sign at each table reads: 'Fountain pens and ballpoint pens are a hazard to rare books.' Manuscripts are smoothed and sterilized in plastic covers. One opens a white folder like a 'sheet-cuff,' and often there is the lively pink flash of Smith College memorandum paper, pilfered by Plath when she taught there for one year (1957–58) and much beloved by Plath for composition. Every time, its vibrant color reminds me of the living mind and body invested in this corpus.

Plath's textual body is also hopelessly entangled with that of her husband, Ted Hughes. Many of the manuscripts and typescripts for her final poems are written on his backside, so to speak: Plath recycles old manuscripts and typescripts by Hughes, and often she seems to be back talking, having the last word in argument. As she describes the impossibility of separation from Hughes in 'The Courage of Shutting-Up,' composed on the verge of his leavetaking from their Devon home in October 1962, it is conceived as the transformation of surgical incision to indelible marking: 'A great surgeon, now a tattooist,/ Tattooing over and over the same blue grievances' (*CP* 210). Plath cannot cut herself off from Hughes, cannot surgically amputate her life from his; she can only tattoo his papery body with images of her grief for his deceptions, his desertions, his infidelities: 'The snakes, the babies, the tits/ On mermaids and two-legged dreamgirls' (*CP* 210). The friction between the two bodies is palpable at times, as text clashes with text, and one intuits Plath's purposeful coercion and filleting of Hughes's poems and plays as she composes. Even some of Plath's phrases—

> And here is an end to the writing,
> The spry hooks that bend and cringe, . . .
> ('Burning the Letters,' *CP* 204)

> The tongue stuck in my jaw.
> It stuck in a barb wire snare—
> ('Daddy,' *CP* 223)

> . . . small, mean and black

> Every little word hooked to every little word
> (*Three Women: A Poem for Three Voices*, *CP* 178)—

11

allude to Hughes's sometimes indecipherable handwriting, clotted with a thicket of curlicues, hooks, flourishes, and backward snarelike strokes that might literally tongue-tie a feminine voice, stuttering to assert itself in the presence of a stronger masculine one: 'Ich, ich, ich, ich' ('Daddy,' *CP* 223).

Ironically, Smith paid for one corpus, but received tattered (and tattooed, to borrow from Plath) remnants of another body of work. As one of the librarians opined, 'We really must do something about cataloging what we have of Hughes.' If Plath's 'rare' body is skillfully re-membered for public viewing, Hughes's seems hopelessly dis-membered and disorderly in its dress.[3] Her words are on top and one peeks at the other side, often finding her ink has bled through, indelibly splotching and staining Hughes's work.[4] One also cannot help but interpret Hughes's book cover for *Winter Pollen*, his 1995 collection of critical essays (some of them on Plath), in light of this practice by his wife. His photograph on the cover is defaced on one side by Plath's manuscript for 'Sheep in Fog' covering him from pate to cheek to chin – an acknowledgment of how thoroughly he has been 'over-written' (humbly 'effaced') by his wife? How hopelessly his own immortal body of work is inscribed/entombed with that of his wife?

This brings me to a second trait of Plath as an artist that haunts the Mortimer Rare Book Room: her sometimes total absorption in money issues, a preoccupation often regarded as beneath the artistic temperament, but for Plath inextricably tied to her ambition. As she writes to A. Alvarez about three poems she hopes he will accept for publication in *The Observer*, 'Money money. You know' (July 21, 1962). Her American entrepreneurial spirit smiles in the Rare Book Room. In looking at these materials, I sometimes think of Gatsby's lists (and their precedents in Benjamin Franklin), which plot out his time for self-improvement and material success – 'Study electricity, etc.' and 'Practice elocution, poise and how to attain it' – and leave nothing to spontaneous choice: 'Rise from bed' at 6:00 a.m. and 'Bath every other day' (174). Plath, too, has endless lists for self-improvement, some of them methodically plotting out her days and, toward the end of her life, bearing poignant witness to the failure of such lists to defend her from chaos – something they were originally intended to do. In therapy after her breakdown and suicide attempt in 1953, her psychiatrist advised her that perfectionists like herself need a sense of accomplishment, and one way of achieving this was lists.[5] Checking things off as they were done gave Plath a sense of satisfaction for many years, so that the sudden appearance of items left undone in the final months is symptomatic of trouble. One series of 'to do' lists shows 'wash hair' rolling over from one day to the next and the next and the next. Alvarez remembers her on Christmas Eve with her 'tent' of hair giving off a 'strong smell, sharp as an animal's' (*Savage God* 31) as he climbed up a flight of stairs behind her.

Other lists patiently keep track of how many poems have been accepted at various journals and how much she has been paid, and even calculate how much per line. Then there is the extraordinary care Plath took to make her manuscripts marketable. Did she have an eye on transforming all of the gleanings of her creative process of inspiration, revision, and final form into cash? I suspect she did. She was delighted when the Lilly Library bought manuscripts of earlier poems by both herself and Hughes, gloating to her mother in a letter, 'We've made a good bit off our scrap paper' (November 20, 1961, *LH* 437). In a letter to her old college friend Marcia Brown, dated January 2, 1963, she complains (and this is a habitual lament in the final months) about Ted's prodigal expenditure of the wealth she helped to create through 'utter scrimp' and self-sacrifice. While he is 'living on brandy & not a worry in the world,' easily turning his manuscripts into hard cash – 'over $100 for a couple of handwritten pages' – she will be consigned to poverty, 'lucky' if she receives $2,800 a year for alimony. Hughes was himself somewhat amazed at 'the wad' of Plath's manuscripts and typescripts he found after her death. After he pulled together the collection of poems for the British and American editions of *Ariel* (1965–66), he says,

> it left me with a wad of poems I had no particular thought of publishing, beyond the fact that I had no intention of destroying them. This wad wasn't exactly the 'mass' that some people seem to have been expecting, though it depends how you look at it. Considering the quality, I suppose it was a 'mass.' What made it look more was the fact that from the first *Ariel* poem she suddenly started saving all the draft pages, which she had never bothered about before. She not only saved them, she dated them carefully. ('Publishing Sylvia Plath,' *WP* 167)

The saving of every scrap of draft, combined with meticulous dating, was a new practice by Plath and suggests to me that she knew both the potential monetary value of this 'mass' and also that the writing process itself – on recycled manuscripts and typescripts – would provide invaluable information about how to read these poems.

Each of the *Ariel* poems has its own folder at Smith, where the creative process can be tracked from conception to birth. Most often this occurred in the space of one day. In the *Collected Poems*, Hughes dates twenty-five poems composed in the month of October 1962, from 'The Detective' on October 1, to 'Lady Lazarus,' which was created over three days, October 26–29. '*Ariel*,' composed on Plath's birthday, October 27, is completed in one day. The great five-poem bee sequence takes but one week, October 3–9. What is somewhat deceptive about this extraordinary inventiveness in a compressed period of time is that many poems do evolve slowly, going through several manuscript and typescript drafts before assuming a 'final' form. Only by examining the multiple manuscripts and typescripts does one gain a sense of what must have been

Plath's intense working schedule, the long hours, beginning perhaps in the early morning, but surely extending well into the day: 'These new poems of mine have one thing in common. They were all written at about four in the morning – that still, blue, almost eternal hour before cock crow, before the baby's cry, before the glassy music of the milkman, settling his bottles' (Sylvia Plath's typed notes on 'New Poems'). Plath knew she was writing great poems – 'I am writing the best poems of my life; they will make my name' (letter to Aurelia Plath, October 16, 1962, *LH* 468); and this – knowing her true value – may well be the motive for saving every scrap of her genius, every moment when inspiration strikes:

> . . . Miracles occur,
>   If you care to call those spasmodic
>   Tricks of radiance miracles. The wait's begun again,
>   The long wait for the angel,
>   For that rare, random descent.
>   ('Black Rook in Rainy Weather,' *CP* 57)

Who knew when the angel/muse might leave again? To keep a record of its arrival and its departure might be to preserve important testimony.

Yet I intuit and want to give priority (at least for the present) to Plath's pecuniary motives, if only to complicate or perhaps ironize the critical narratives that have elevated her writing ecstasy in the final months to something like aesthetic sainthood.[6] As Hughes, for example, describes what happened in his foreword to Plath's *Journals*, 'One can compare what was really going on in her to a process of alchemy. Her apprentice writings were like impurities thrown off from the various stages of the inner transformation, by-products of the internal work.' Emerging from this alchemy is what Hughes calls 'a real self,' and '*Ariel* and the associated later poems give us the voice of the self. They are proof that it arrived. All her other writings, except these journals [which don't really count in this scheme except as artless autobiography], are the waste products of its gestation' (*J* xiii, xiv). I am not the first to notice about this narrative that Plath is not permitted to have any but the purest artistic impulses when she finally produced the *Ariel* poems. For Jacqueline Rose, the impact of Hughes's editing of her work, coupled with his forewords and introductions to the *Journals*, her short stores in *Johnny Panic and the Bible of Dreams* (*JP*), and her poems, has been to impose 'concepts of writing and poetic language' which determine 'not only what *can*, but also what aesthetically *should*, and *how* it should, be read.' Further, 'There is, therefore, a set of decisions being taken here as to whether, and to what extent, Plath can be allowed to be *low* – low as in nasty, low as in the degradation of culture' (*Haunting* 73–74, 82), and low, too, in terms of her desire to make money by writing 'potboilers' for novels and short stories for the *Ladies' Home Journal*.

Commodity Fetishism in the Rare Book Room

To my mind, Plath would have been absolutely pleased at the condition of her body at Smith, which includes everything high and low, both the by-products of the creative process – what Hughes calls the 'waste' – and the final artifacts: commodity fetishism in the Rare Book Room, or another version of sainthood. She is catalogued and neatly pocketed and filed, right down to miscellaneous scraps of paper (one small leaf reads simply, 'Writer's Block' and is underlined), check stubs from 1960–62, cardboard inserts with her notes, and all of this at a very large charge – the collection bought from Sotheby's at an undisclosed price. The librarians say the amount is a closely guarded secret. The Rare Book Room has its Plath relics, too – baby furniture she enameled, a 1960 collage of magazine images from the 1950s,[7] even her old typewriters. The elm plank Plath used as a writing table for the *Ariel* poems is also there, originally fashioned 'with a plane' by Hughes as 'a perfect landing pad/For your inspiration' ('The Table,' *BL* 138), though dismissed with disdain as merely 'a curio' for the 'peanut-crunchers' who visit the archive as a shrine.

Perhaps Plath divined what Jacqueline Rose and Mary Lynn Broe have described about the history of Plath's archival body: its marketability. Rose claims that 'money can also be seen as the sub-text of the archive' (*Haunting* 86), because evidence of wrangling over what, when, and by whom parts of it will be published or made available to scholars, and who will profit thereby, is everywhere. Broe bluntly revises a line from Plath's poem 'Kindness,' titling a 1994 article 'Plathologies: The 'Blood Jet' Is Bucks, Not Poetry,' and decries the 'hucksterish quality' (50) that has accompanied the piecemeal publication of her work. She goes on to speculate, as others have, about what awaits disclosure in 2013, when the Smith vault opens up and more writings by Plath are revealed. What secrets do they have to tell about Plath's final days?

What also should be noted here is that the process of acquisition is ongoing at Smith. Far from being a dead body, Plath's archive continues to grow, to acquire new limbs. Letters to her many correspondents are collected here, as is the rancorous correspondence between and among such actors in her posthumous drama as Peter Davison, Anne Stevenson, and Olwyn Hughes over the writing and publication of Stevenson's biography of Plath, *Bitter Fame*. A 1996 acquisition includes several letters exchanged between Olwyn Hughes (Ted Hughes's sister and the literary executor of the Plath estate for many years) and Plath's mother, Aurelia, all saved by her. The letters from Olwyn are sometimes annotated with Aurelia's furious responses and have their own story to tell. In response to Olwyn's efforts in one letter (November 29, 1968) to persuade Aurelia to permit American publication of *The Bell Jar*, Aurelia writes on the back, 'I have sufficient faith in Ted's gifts and his ability to support two of his children adequately without recourse to the income from the writings of a discarded, deceased wife.' On a three-by-five card dated December 29, 1968, Aurelia writes, 'Olwyn – I am not only to endure the suffering you inflict upon me, I am to sanction it!' Just beneath, another date, January 11, 1968, and Aurelia writes: '(not sent, didn't answer letter *re "Bell Jar"*).' Olwyn is spared such revelations of Aurelia's true feelings in other ways as well. The mother's letters are occasionally filed as either a 'draft' or an 'exact copy.'[8] An 'exact copy' of a letter sent deletes some of the more historionic outbursts from the draft that – like her annotations – reflect Aurelia's anguish over the possible publication of *The Bell Jar* in the United States.[9] Olwyn's principal motive appears to be pragmatic – what a nice inheritance Aurelia's grandchildren will receive if she consents to the American publication of *The Bell Jar*.

Eventually Aurelia does appear to come around, and by October 30, 1971, is thoroughly pacified by 'the real wealth that is coming to the children through the success of my daughter's publications. The delay in publishing *The Bell Jar* just whetted the public's curiosity – back in 1963–64 there would not have been the sale there is now.' Even more, she is now willing 'to accept income from publications of my girl's writing – my working prospects have changed so suddenly, threatening my financial earning power and the hope of financial independence in retirement, that I shall be very glad to accept my share of my daughter's work-reward.' After initially telling Olwyn that 'I wish to heaven nothing more would be printed about Sylvia!' (September 15, 1971), when Olwyn writes her that one of Plath's old boyfriends, Gordon Lameyer, is proposing to publish her correspondence with him together with his commentary, Aurelia seems softened by Olwyn's promise of one third of the royalties.[10]

Of course, by this time Aurelia is also beginning to think about a publication of her own: *Letters Home*. And Olwyn is hard at work on her own editions of Plath's poems. The Rainbow Press will produce three volumes, conceived, by virtue of their limited number and costly presentation, as 'rare books.' These include *Lyonnesse* (1971), *Crystal Gazer and Other Poems* (1971), and *Pursuit* (1973). All of these collections are somewhat strange in the selection of poems brought together – an issue I will explore later – but *Pursuit* is of special interest as the only place where 'Burning the Letters' was printed before it appeared in *The Collected Poems*. *Pursuit* came out in an edition of one hundred copies with a signed etching and illustrations by Leonard Baskin, and it is autographed with a poem by Ted Hughes in at least one copy.[11] It has the appearance, then, of a memorial volume by a loving husband, but includes 'Burning the Letters' – the only poem Plath wrote in August 1962 and commemorating her immolation of Ted Hughes's papers, an angry reprisal for his suspected infidelity. The poem is an anticipatory ritual of sorts, marking Plath's entry into her most prolific period of writing. Its long absence from the Plath canon and singular appearance in *Pursuit* are symptomatic of the rather freakish way in which Plath's textual body has been dissected for publication and served to readers.[12] Olwyn's comment to Aurelia that parts of *The Bell Jar* can be cut if she finds them too painful (May 28, 1968) also hints at a governing principle for looking at Plath's work: find the original anatomy and trace its burials and amputations.

The Body of *Ariel*

Excision of material painful to survivors was clearly a motive for some editorial decisions. Ted Hughes, writing as an editor of her *Journals*, describes what Plath's husband Ted Hughes did to save himself and 'her children' (why not 'our children,' or, if maintaining editorial distance, 'their children'?) from potential hurt:

Sylvia Plath's journals exist as an assortment of notebooks and bunches of loose sheets, and the selection just published here contains about a third of the whole bulk. Two other notebooks survived for a while after her death. They continued from where the surviving record breaks off in late 1959 and covered the last three years of her life. The second of these two books her husband destroyed, because he did not want her children to have to read it (in those days he regarded forgetfulness as an essential part of survival). The earlier one disappeared more recently (and may, presumably, still turn up). (*WP* 177)

Later, editor Hughes quizzically muses, 'Looking over this curtailed journal, one cannot help wondering whether the lost entries for her last three years were not the more important section of it. Those years, after all, produced the work that made her name. And we certainly have lost a valuable appendix to all that later writing' (*WP* 178).[13] The lucid and detached editor Hughes criticizes the impetuous and emotional husband Hughes for an unnecessary appendectomy on Plath's corpus. Or, is this a case of a split personality governing the publication of Plath's work, with Hughes the editor as Jekyll undermined at every turn by Hughes the husband as Hyde?

Since Plath died without a will, all of her work was handled by Ted Hughes, who was quite candid, albeit belated in his candor, about his editorial tampering. He made no claims to being a scholar in the way he managed her work; indeed, some of his remarks show contempt for scholarly conerns:

All these people [i.e., both scholars and an 'inferior audience' enamored with the sensational] are basically telling Sylvia Plath's executors just what their editorial obligations are and were. It seems her complete opus should be published (should have been published long ago) in complete detail, preferably with all the fragments and variants and cancellations of her bristling manuscripts – some of these otherwise being a loss to literature. To a scholar, it is a simple business, and merely needs his/her diligence and care.

As I am aware of them, my obligations are not so simple as a scholar's would be. They are, first, towards her family, second, towards her best work. Just like hers, in fact – a point to be considered, since I feel a general first and last obligation to her. ('Publishing Sylvia Plath,' *WP* 163)

In the same editorial response to an *Observer* review by A. Alvarez of Plath's *Crossing the Water* (1971) and *Winter Trees* (1972) that is critical about delays in publishing her poems, Ted Hughes describes a manuscript for Sylvia Plath's *Ariel* – the 'Other *Ariel*' – that has never made its way into print:

She left behind a carbon typescript, its title altered from *Daddy* to *Ariel*, its pages littered with minor corrections, containing about thirty-five poems, beginning as now with 'Morning Song' and ending with the Bee poems (without 'Stings'). It began with the word 'love' and ended with 'spring,' as she pointed out. . . . The last of the poems in that manuscript had been written on 2 December 1962. After writing nothing for nearly two months she began again on 28 January 1963 and writing on five days up to 5 February produced twelve more poems. (*WP* 164–65).

Hughes added, he says, 'about nine' of these twelve final poems, even though he acknowledges 'she herself regarded those last poems as the beginning of a new book' (*WP* 167).

Plath's typescript for the 'Other *Ariel*' is one part of the collection at Smith. Her table of contents is as follows, with my inclusion of bracketed dates of composition and italicized titles for poems deleted by Hughes for publication in *Ariel*:

The Other *Ariel*

ARIEL and Other Poems
Sylvia Plath

MORNING SONG	[February 19, 1961]
THE COURIERS	[November 4, 1962]
THE RABBIT CATCHER	[May 21, 1962]
THALIDOMIDE	[October 11, 1962]
THE APPLICANT	[October 11, 1962]
BARREN WOMAN	[February 21, 1961]
LADY LAZARUS	[October 23–29, 1962]
TULIPS	[March 18, 1961]
A SECRET	[October 10, 1962]
THE JAILOR	[October 17, 1962]
CUT	[October 24, 1962]
ELM	[April 12–19, 1962]
THE NIGHT DANCES	[November 6, 1962]
THE DETECTIVE	[October 1, 1962
ARIEL	[October 27, 1962 (Plath's birthday)]
—— DEATH & CO.	[November 12–14, 1962 (insertion; last poem composed for the 'Other *Ariel*')]
MAGI	[1960]
LESBOS	[October 18, 1962 (not in British *Ariel*)]
THE OTHER	[July 2, 1962]
STOPPED DEAD	[October 19, 1962]
POPPIES IN OCTOBER	[October 19, 1962]
THE COURAGE OF SHUTTING-UP	[October 2, 1962]
NICK AND THE CANDLESTICK	[October 29, 1962]
BERCK-PLAGE	[June 30, 1962]
GULLIVER	[November 6, 1962]
GETTING THERE	[November 3, 1962]
MEDUSA	[October 16, 1962]
PURDAH	[October 29, 1962]

A Rare Body

This is somewhat different from Hughes's description. It consists of forty poems, not 'about thirty-five'; the table of contents actually lists forty-one poems, but parenthesizes 'The Swarm,' which is set off from the final bee sequence, perhaps reflecting Plath's indecision about whether to include it in the volume. She certainly includes 'Stings,' though, so Hughes appears to be forgetful about which bee poem is missing.[14] Chronologically, the latest poem included in the 'Other *Ariel*' is 'Death & Co.' composed November 12–14, 1962, and *not* December 2. Hughes, I believe, is alluding to 'Sheep in Fog,' which is one of *his* additions to *Ariel* (and, indeed, replaces the attack on him in 'The Rabbit Catcher'). Plath started it on December 2, but revised its final stanza and dated her revision January 28, 1963, when, as Hughes notes, she began composing again after a two-month hiatus.[15] Virtually all of the 'minor corrections' in the typescript are excisions of Plath's beloved exclamation marks, suggesting that at some point either she decided or was warned that these poems were too emphatic, too 'loud.'[16] The volume begins, as it does in Hughes's version of *Ariel*, with 'Morning Song' and the phrase 'love set you going,' but ends with the bee poems and 'Wintering' and its final word, 'spring.'

For an American audience unlikely to keep up with the editorial column in *The Observer*, this revelation in 1971 that Plath had quite a different volume in mind from the *Ariel* published here in 1966 went unnoticed until the publication of The *Collected Poems* in 1981. Even so, the news is buried. In Hughes's editorial 'Notes: 1963' to this volume, he lists the forty-one poems (including 'The Swarm') of 'Sylvia Plath's own prepared collection of poems, titled *Ariel*' (*CP* 295). The import of Hughes's transformation of this volume has not registered fully,[17] despite Marjorie Perloff's lengthy article 'The Two *Ariels*: The (Re)Making of the Sylvia Plath Canon,' first published in the *American Poetry Review* in 1984, where she argues that Hughes thoroughly mutilated the narrative discernible in Plath's version of *Ariel*. For a variety of reasons, not least of which is that Hughes's version has the irrefutable evidence of Plath's death to verify his ending to her story in *Ariel*, the 'Other *Ariel*' has received very little attention.

I will return to Perloff's description of Plath's narrative, but at this stage pose the question of precisely what were Hughes's motives for tampering with *Ariel*. In the *Observer* editorial of 1971, Hughes describes several decisions he made about the creation of *Ariel*, all motivated by the knowledge that 'I knew what I was offering, and I knew it was the last' (*WP* 166). He reminds Alvarez that in 1965 Plath was certainly not a well-known poet: 'When I finally got a typescript of her manuscript to publishers, in England and the States, neither of them wanted it,' and 'even its most ardent and vocal supporters wanted the manuscript cut by half, or at least to 'about twenty poems.' They felt the full collection might provoke some outraged backlash.' He then wonders:

A Rare Body

Was the whole book simply unacceptable, did it overdo itself? I was anxious that the collection should not falter in any way, and that the work should be recognized, yet I saw quite plainly that very few knew what to make of it. And I know what a person becomes while writing a review. So I had already started rearranging the collection, cutting out some pieces that looked as if they might let in some facile attacker, cutting out one or two of the more openly vicious ones, and a couple of others that I thought might conceivably seem repetitive in tone and form. Two or three I simply lost for a while in the general fog of those days. I would have cut out 'Daddy' if I'd been in time (there are quite a few things more important than giving the world great poems). I would have cut out others if I'd thought they would ever be decoded. I also kept out one or two that were aimed too nakedly (I kept them out in vain, as it happened. They were known and their work is now done.) I added two pre-*Ariel* poems, 'Little Fugue,' because I think it is good enough to stand with the others, and belongs, and 'Hanging Man' not because it is good – though it is – but because it describes with only thin disguise the experience that made *Ariel* possible – a definite event at a definite moment (like everything in her poems). Also, I added about nine of the last poems, because they seemed to me too important to leave out. The uncertainties around this cutting and adding were naturally very thick. I'm still not sure whether *Ariel* would not be a better book if I had kept out everything that followed the Bee poems, as in her version. . . . But I no longer remember why I did many things – why the US edition is different from the English, for example. But again, I think most of it was concern for certain people. I don't think I overestimated the possible injuries. (*WP* 166–67)

After perusing this lengthy list of various forms of amputation and reconstructive surgery, motivated by such a variety of impulses, one cannot help but wonder what Hughes means by his statement, 'I feel a general first and last obligation to her." At best, he seems very conflicted. At worst, and this was the immediate conclusion of Perloff when she saw his changes, most of the poems deleted by Hughes save only himself from painful scrutiny: 'The poems that make only too clear that Hughes's desertion was the immediate cause of Plath's depression are expunged' ('Two *Ariels*' 313). Indeed, 'The Hanging Man' seems inserted primarily to divert attention from immediate to past experience – to Plath's traumatic shock treatments in 1953 as 'what made *Ariel* possible,' and not the more recent desertion and infidelity of Ted Hughes. As for Hughes's efforts to protect people, surely Otto Plath, long dead, could no longer be hurt by 'Daddy,' so if anyone's feelings might be hurt by its verbal abuse, wouldn't it be Hughes himself, who is 'the model' of Daddy, 'the man in black with a Meinkampf look // And a love of the rack and the screw' (*CP* 224)? Or, if Hughes's concern was for Aurelia Plath's feelings, why did he leave in 'Medusa,' which caused great pain to Plath's mother? Or was this poem one of those he felt would never be 'decoded'? As he notes, Plath had already been sending these lethal poems out to journals, and we can only wonder how many of them he might have cut if they had not already been in print.[18]

All of this might be a very unfair assessment of Hughes's motives, though. While the possibility of depriving the world of an admittedly 'great' poem such as 'Daddy' might appear to Plath scholars as either blasphemous or self-protective, its inclusion in *Ariel* clearly hurt Aurelia Plath, who did not want 'Daddy' to be published.[19] Hughes may have wished to protect her even more than himself, to save Aurelia from what she describes as the 'horrors and indignities that transpired' after it was published in the *Time* review of *Ariel*.[20] It is also clear from many of Hughes's poems in

Birthday Letters – whether we agree with him or not – that he sees the origin of Plath's suicidal despair of 1963 in her earlier 1953 breakdown and in her prolonged mourning for the dead father, Otto Plath. 'The Hanging Man' and 'Little Fugue' are logical choices for inclusion based on those beliefs. Finally, Hughes's comment that 'very few knew what to make of it' (*Ariel*) is borne out by some of the correspondence with poetry editors (also part of the collection at Smith). Not everyone was as receptive as Alvarez to the type of poetry Plath began to write in the summer of 1962.

Retrospectively, it is inconceivable to me that the poetry editor of the *New Yorker* would return poems like 'Ariel,' 'Purdah,' 'Fever 103°,' or 'Lady Lazarus' and accept a poem like 'Amnesiac.' Even so, Howard Moss tells Plath in a letter dated November 7, 1962, that he and his staff like the second section of 'Amnesiac' but have no sense of its relation to the first. He goes on to ask her if they can print the second section alone. Always eager to get into print, Plath cut the first section (which is now published separately as 'Lyonnesse'), at least to my mind, making the poem much less interesting. 'Amnesiac' is now just a poem about a deserting husband, indeed, about Hughes: 'Sweet Lethe is my life./I am never, never, never coming home!' (*CP* 233). In its original form, with the indictment of a 'big God' who could wipe out whole civilizations with a blink of an eye, the poem had some heft as a satiric representation of masculine power, the unfeeling nature of how it is exercised.

Moss also appears rather obtuse in his handling of Plath's 'Elm.' He is worried about whether readers will understand that the voice in the poem belongs to Elm and insists the title be changed to 'Elm Speaks' (letter of September 26, 1962). Even more, he fusses over the dedication to Plath's friend and fellow poet Ruth Fainlight and fears that readers will worry about who 'she' is in the first line (letter of June 27, 1962). It is hard to imagine even an unsophisticated reader of poetry so dense as to ignore all the cues in the poem indicating that the speaker is the tree, or to somehow mistake the speaker for Ruth Fainlight. Plath acquiesced to Moss's quibbles, as usual 'delighted' for 'Elm' to be accepted for publication by the *New Yorker* under any terms. She even praises Moss's change of title, astoundingly preferring it to her own. ('Yes, I think I do'), in her eagerness to have this 'wild and bloody' poem in print (letter to Howard Moss, October 10, 1962), In his role as editor of *The Observer*, A. Alvarez, by contrast, immediately appreciates Plath's 'wild and bloody' poems and praises them as her finest work – 'by a long way'. He is especially taken with 'The Rabbit Catcher,' which he deems 'flawless' (letter to Plath dated July 24 [1962]).

Plath's dual ambition for fame and fortune, then, has been served well by Hughes's version of *Ariel*. There is little evidence to suggest that she worried excessively (or at all) about her artistic intentions being violated when it came to getting published and, even more, getting paid. And if Olwyn Hughes's limited editions of oddly selected poems (including the 'leftovers' from Plath's original plan for *Ariel*) were a savvy way to create additional income for Plath's children, I don't think she would have objected. Despite Aurelia Plath's belief that her daughter would never have wanted to publish *The Bell Jar* in America under her own name, she had already sent a copy of the novel to American publishers as 'Mrs Ted Hughes.' If she had maintained the fictitious authorship of Victoria Lucas in the United States, one suspects it would not have lasted for very long. After her death, the real worry was not the potential scandal but, as Olwyn Hughes warned Aurelia Plath, 'stoppage of all income in case of a pirated edition' (letter of April 9, 1971). Plath virtually ensured eventual publication of all her final poems because of her systematic circulation to magazines.

From the perspective of the textual scholar, the literary historian, and critic, however, Plath's fame depends rather heavily on editorial decisions that openly violate her intentions about what the 'Other *Ariel*'s' themes and narrative were to be. For me, the clearest evidence for this is a contrast with the planning that went into her first volume, *The Colossus*. In letters to her friends and her mother, Plath is constantly changing the title for this volume. The process of culling and adding poems to the collection is ongoing as well. On June 12, 1959, she writes to Ann Davidow Goodman, listing the myriad and wildly incongruous subjects she tackles: 'cadavers, suicides, Electra complexes, ouija boards, hermits, fat spinsters, thin spinsters, ghosts, old men of the sea, and, yes, fiddler crabs and mammoth pigs,' From these, she hopes to put together a volume that has changed its title no fewer than six times. It is currently titled 'The Devil of the Stairs,' but in earlier forms took its title from the poems: 'The Lady and the Earthenware Head' and 'The Bull of Bendylaw.' In the archive at Smith there is a note in which she describes the latter volume as 'a celebration' of a motley assortment of 'birds, beasts, and fish (sows, bulls, owls, snakes, frogs, rooks, fiddler crabs), people (housewives, landowners, parents, factory workers, the dead, lovers, spinsters, suicides, beggars, hermits, pregnant women, sculptors), and places (Winthrop Bay, Boston, Point Shirley, Benidorm, Roch Harbor, Hardcastle Crags) and the various moods of joy, sorrow, humor and irony, energy and weariness, which are part of the human condition.' Animals, people, places, and moods? As this ponderous compendium suggests, Plath had no clear unifying principle for *The Colossus*. She may have discovered its theme much later, when she decided to end it with the seven-part 'Poem for a Birthday.' According to her biographer Linda Wagner-Martin, she is reported to have told her Knopf editor, Judith Jones, that the 'collection had a theme, the person who is 'broken and mended,' beginning with the smashed colossus and ending with the self' (184). When Knopf wanted to cut all of the final 'Poem for a Birthday,' Plath at least retrieved two parts, 'Flute Notes from a Reedy Pond' and 'The Stones,' both suggestive of rebirth and mending.

About the 'Other *Ariel*,' Plath is much more assured. On

December 14, 1962, she writes to Aurelia, 'A. Alvarez, the best poetry critic here, thinks my second book, which I've just finished, should win the Pulitzer Prize' (*LH* 490), and in a postscript, 'I'm dedicating the second one I've just finished to Frieda and Nick, as many poems in it are to them' (*LH* 491). Before closing '*Ariel' and Other Poems* for her title to this new volume, she toys with '*Daddy' and Other Poems*, '*A Birthday Present' and Other Poems*, '*The Rival' and Other Poems*, and '*The Rabbit Catcher' and Other Poems*, reflecting a certain hesitancy about what the dominant narrative of the volume is. The choice of 'Ariel' as her title poem, however, composed on her thirtieth birthday, October 27, 1962, supports all of the critical narratives which valorize the primacy of artifice over confession, of poetry over biography, of the poet over the woman. This does not mean that biography simply disappears as a narrative issue, but that the volume contains conflicting narratives, even while Plath works toward the release and triumph of an artistic identity over the anguish in her personal life. 'Ariel,' with its reverberations of Shakespearean magic and biblical revelation, tells the critic that the poet is staking no mean claim to greatness. Likewise, the concluding sequence of five bee poems, I will argue, is intimately related to this hoped-for triumph of Plath's muse, Ariel.

The other titles Plath ponders tell us of the presence of competing stories central to Plath's self-conception. The importance of 'Daddy' as an organizing principle reminds us of the Freudian and psychoanalytic exploration of identity in Plath's work and the effort in many ways both to write an emphatic conclusion to this story and to include Ted Hughes and their marriage in its catastrophe:

> If I've killed one man, I've killed two—
> The vampire who said he was you
> And drank my blood for a year,
> Seven years, if you want to know.
> (*CP* 224)

Not surprisingly, the 'seven years' correspond to the years of her marriage. When she says, 'Daddy, daddy, you bastard, I'm through' (*CP* 224), it ends a masochistic relationship not only with her father but to her husband as well. If 'A Birthday Present' had remained the title poem, perhaps the narrative drive toward metaphysical revelation, the desire to unveil even devastating truths and to penetrate a world of appearances that hides the real, would have been interpreted as the dominant impulse of these poems:

> Only let down the veil, the veil, the veil.
> If it were death
>
> I would admire the deep gravity of it, its timeless eyes.
> I would know you were serious.
> (*CP* 208)

In turn, if 'The Rival,' or especially 'The Rabbit Catcher,' had been Plath's choice for a title poem, the primacy of the marital breakup would have been understood as the controlling narrative. Indeed, the poems that Hughes omitted, among them 'The Rabbit Catcher,' and then added, transformed a story Perloff describes as one of 'struggle and revenge, the outrage that follows the recognition that the beloved is also the betrayer, that the shrine at which one worships is also the tomb' ('Two *Ariels*' 330), into one that we have been reading since 1966 'as a text in which, as Charles Newman puts it, 'expression and extinction [are] indivisible,' a text that culminates in the almost peaceful resignation of 'Years' or 'Edge.' The poems of *Ariel* culminate in a sense of finality, all passion spent' (330). What Perloff alludes to here is Hughes's addition of twelve poems to Plath's original ending, most of them written in the final weeks of Plath's life and presaging her suicide. The contents of the American *Ariel* authorized, if not authored, for publication by Hughes are as follows, with

poems in italics indicated as additions, and dates for the new
poems in brackets:

MORNING SONG
THE COURIERS
SHEEP IN FOG   [December 2, 1962,
                                           January 28, 1963]

THE APPLICANT
LADY LAZARUS
TULIPS
CUT
ELM
THE NIGHT DANCES
POPPIES IN OCTOBER
BERCK-PLAGE
ARIEL
DEATH & CO.
LESBOS
NICK AND THE CANDLESTICK
GULLIVER
GETTING THERE
MEDUSA
THE MOON AND THE YEW TREE
A BIRTHDAY PRESENT
MARY'S SONG   [November 19, 1962]
LETTER IN NOVEMBER
THE RIVAL
DADDY
YOU'RE
FEVER 103°
THE BEE MEETING
THE ARRIVAL OF THE BEE BOX
STINGS
THE SWARM
WINTERING
THE HANGING MAN   [June 27, 1960]

LITTLE FUGUE	[April 2, 1962]
YEARS	[November 16, 1962]
THE MUNICH MANNEQUINS	[January 28, 1963]
TOTEM	[January 29, 1963]
PARALYTIC	[January 28, 1962]
BALLOONS	[February 5, 1963]
POPPIES IN JULY	[July 20, 1962]
KINDNESS	[February 1, 1963]
CONTUSION	[February 4, 1963]
EDGE	[February 5, 1963]
WORDS	[February 1, 1963]

Anyone familiar with these final poems written in the last days of Plath's life would have to assent to Perloff's accusation that Hughes has virtually ensured that Plath will be understood as governed by despair and the inevitability of death by her own hand: '"The woman is perfected" in more ways than one' (330).

Unwilling to dismiss Hughes's tampering as innocent, as 'simply completing Plath's own story, carrying it to its final conclusion' (330), Perloff relentlessly compares Plath's original plan to Hughes's. He replaces 'The Rabbit Catcher' with 'Sheep in Fog,' thereby ridding the volume of what Perloff regards as an 'explicit reference to the broken marriage,' and diverting the reader to 'a much less personal lyric that belongs to the cycle of death poems of January-February 1963' (319).[21] By cutting poems so clearly embedded in biographical circumstance, Perloff argues, Hughes gives us 'a Sylvia Plath who is victimised by her time and place rather than by a specific personal betrayal' (326). Perloff finds this strategy exemplified in Hughes's decision to replace 'Purdah,' 'one of Plath's most forceful statements about power' (326) and the sexual politics of marriage, with 'Mary's Song,' a poem Perloff disparages for its 'empty and histrionic references to the Nazis, the gas chambers, and the holocaust' (326).

Finally, and perhaps most important, we lose sight of the narrative that might be best understood as 'You can't keep a good woman down.' Perloff delineates a situation like those Plath avidly read abut in her favourite 'women's slick,' the *Ladies' Home Journal*, in its ever-popular feature 'Can This Marriage Be Saved?' Why, Perloff asks, have critics stressed the importance of Otto Plath's desertion by death when Plath was a child, when 'in April 1962, just three months after the birth of her second child, Nicholas, Plath found out that her husband was having an affair'? (315) An affair with 'the wife of a mutual friend' (316) makes it a double betrayal, and 'when we bear in mind that Nick was only [a few] months old at the time and demanded regular night feedings, that Frieda was just two, and that Plath, who had feverishly remodeled the old Devon farmhouse, had not yet regained her strength, we can sense how devastating the discovery must have been' (316). Why worry about 'the coldness of January 1963' as a factor in Plath's suicide, as if frozen plumbing had killed her, when the brute reality of being abandoned with an infant and a toddler by her husband and their father looms over these final months? (317) In Perloff's account, it is to add insult to injury when Hughes cleanses the 'Other *Ariel*' of its 'move toward rebirth' (313) in the final bee sequence. Perloff intuits a narrative continuum, a wholeness that begins with 'Morning Song,' a poem about the birth of Plath's daughter Frieda, and ends with Plath's own birth as a poet separate from Hughes, the husband and male poet she worshipped (315): 'Between these two poles – the pole of the 'Love' for a man that produces babies and the pole of rebirth as an isolate itself, a rebirth that produces the honey of poetry – the narrative of *Ariel* I [Plath's version] unfolds' (318). In Perloff's version of *Ariel* I's narrative, Plath's fertility is the matrix for the volume's conception and eventual triumphant completion, and the queen bee is the central figure representing Plath's dramatic and ultimately successful struggle to survive it. Love for another begins the volume, and a recovered self-love ends it.

A Rare Body

While Perloff's account is persuasive – perhaps because it is so singleminded in its argument that Hughes engaged in a cover-up, erasing his role as villain in Plath's original version of *Ariel* – there are also, I believe, several conflicting impulses at work in Plath's composition and arrangement of the 'Other *Ariel*' that do not support this seamless and melodramatic women's story. Perloff did not have access to the manuscripts, and is therefore not aware of the way in which several of the excised poems are in dialogue with Hughes's play manuscript for '*The Calm.*' Here the *Ariel* muse finds expression – as in Shakespeare's play – in conjuring a vengeful tempest on the reverse side of Hughes's play, where a deadly calm holds his characters captive on an island. Perloff also tends to see these poems, which constitute a strong personal attack on Hughes, as tonally and thematically in concord with the allegory embedded in the bee sequence at the end, and she places primary emphasis on the queen bee – also a vengeful figure – as Plath's creative identity. As we shall see, Plath's identity is distributed less certainly in the bee sequence: at times she is the beekeeper, at others one of the female workers, and at still others she is invested in the mind of the hive, a communal organism that does not think individually. The queen is herself not in control of her fate, despite her central importance to the life of the hive. Plath portrays the queen as also a captive and scapegoat of the hive. While the bee sequence expresses hope for the poet's survival, despite being played false in her personal life, it is not the unambiguous rebirth Perloff wants to celebrate. Instead, the bee poems fuse the rhythms of beekeeping, the secretive workings of the female hive, with the interior drama of the woman poet, unsure whether she will last through the winter, ambivalent toward her own power, and fearful of the power of the new queens.

Once again, the bee sequence manuscripts unavailable to Perloff also multiply the ambiguities of Plath's narrative intentions in the 'Other *Ariel*.' Here, the *Ariel* muse is often striving to overcome the desire for vengeance. The mood in

'Wintering' is contemplative and inner-directed, and in the manuscripts even more quizzical and uncertain of the hive's survival through the months of hibernation. The first draft for 'Edge' – one of the poems added by Hughes and described by Perloff as one of the death poems that mutilated Plath's narrative – is composed on the verso of a draft of 'Wintering,' the poem originally intended to end the 'Other *Ariel*.' As Susan Van Dyne explains in *Revising Life*, 'The final vision of the "perfected woman" literally overlays the hopeful prophecy of the end of "Wintering"' (10). While it may be going too far to say that the dead woman of 'Edge' cancels out the hopeful flight of the bees in 'Wintering' and thereby inexorably alters our understanding of Plath's narrative design with a signifier of impending doom, this manuscript evidence should, I believe, take us back to the bee poems to determine how confidently the prophecy of spring rebirth is stated.

Releasing 'Dainty Ariel'

Although Hughes is assuredly guilty of deleting Plath's ending with the addition of what Perloff calls the 'death poems,' there are many readers who regard these poems as fulfilling a suicidal trajectory implicit in the volume as a whole. Adding them is thus less a betrayal than a completion of what Plath intended. Ironically, Hughes, I suspect, would agree, at least provisionally, with the theme of rebirth and what Perloff describes as the birth of an 'isolate self' in *Ariel*, although in his *Birthday Letters* he will define this 'newborn' as inherently self-destructive: 'your own self in flames' (148) and 'a child-bride/On a pyre' (149). In earlier critical assessments, Hughes is less morbidly inclined, delineating the emergence of a 'real self' from the camouflage of 'her lesser selves, her false or provisional selves,' and claiming enthusiastically, 'I never saw her show her real self to anybody – except, perhaps, in the last three months of her life.' Its appearance is both stunning and cause for celebration: 'When a real self finds language, and manages to speak, it is surely a dazzling event – as *Ariel* was' (Foreword, *J* xiv, xv). Unlike Perloff, Hughes ignores the bee poems as significant harbingers for rebirth, instead tracing the origin of Plath's new self to the composition of 'Elm' in April 1962. As in Prospero's release in *The Tempest* of his 'tricksy spirit,' Ariel, also from a tree, the genie is let out of the bottle, and Plath's voice is set free. As Hughes describes this moment, it is one of heroic struggle. In the manuscripts for 'Elm,'

> we see a struggle break out, which continues over several pages, as the lines try to take the law into their own hands. She forced the poem back into order, and even got a stranglehold on it, and seemed to have won, when suddenly it burst all her restraints and she let it go.
>
> And at once the *Ariel* voice emerged in full, out of the tree. From that day on, it never really faltered again. During the next five months she produced ten more poems. The subject matter didn't alarm her. Why should it, when *Ariel* was doing the very thing it had been created and liberated to do. In each poem, the terror is encountered head on, and the angel is mastered and brought to terms. The energy released by these victories was noticeable. According to the appointed coincidence of such things, after July her outer circumstances intensified her inner battle to the limits. In October, when she and her husband began to live apart, every detail of the antagonist seemed to come into focus, and she started writing at top speed. (*WP* 188)

Where Plath's abandonment by Hughes is a key event in the narrative described by Perloff, here it is fortuitous, even fortunate ('the appointed coincidence of such things'), and might even be said to contribute to the Promethean fire, the Herculean labors he ascribes to Plath's Prospero-like effort to release the *Ariel* identity.[22] The 'subject matter' of some of these poems is Hughes's infidelity, and there is a lot of evidence, both in the poems and in her letters, that it was more devastating than alarming. Unlike Perloff, then, Hughes privileges a narrative in which mundane matters like sexual betrayal ultimately must be dismissed in favour of aesthetic values, for 'a real self, as we know, is a rare thing' (Foreword, *J* xv). For the moment I would like to note that the voice, this rare and real self, the Ariel persona are all, in some ways, disembodied phenomena as described by Hughes, set free not only from the humdrum melodrama of Sylvia Plath, beleaguered wife and mother, but also from the ink-stained pages of their creation.

Getting the Work into Critical Dress: Myth or Confession?

Against the feminist readings of Plath's *Ariel* narrative as a woman's story and, even more, a woman poet's story, Hughes sustained and promulgated his mythic view of Plath's poetic identity – not only in his occasional essays, but also in his support of Judith Kroll's 1976 *Chapters in a Mythology: The Poetry of Sylvia Plath*, the only critical study that I believe received such endorsement by the man who controlled Plath's estate. Hughes clearly made himself available to Kroll as the ultimate authority on Plath and did everything he could to assist her imposition of a mythic structure and narrative on Plath's work, derived from the White Goddess mythology of Robert Graves. A typical passage in Kroll reads: 'The White Goddess myth, when Plath first encountered it, seemed to her to order her experience; and it continued to do so, and was more and more completely appropriated by her, so that she increasingly saw her life as defined by it' (42). How does Kroll know this? Her note reads, 'Ted Hughes, in conversation, remarked that Plath felt The White Goddess 'gave shape to what had happened to her' (n. 19, 220). In Kroll's chronology (xv), the importance of hearing Laura Riding (Graves's muse and collaborator on the White Goddess mythology) read her work in April 1962 is virtually equivalent in significance to such major milestones in Plath's life as marriage, births, deaths, awards, and publications. Ironically, Laura (Riding) Jackson is crushingly unsympathetic to Kroll's work:

> Miss Kroll plunges us into a far-advanced tailoring of certain ideas, that have been in prolonged critical vogue in this century, to the poetic work of Sylvia Plath; and the movement is, then, from the getting the work into critical dress, to an extraction of a person Sylvia Plath from the critical histrionism. After this, the literary-stage figure and the private-life figure are coupled in a twinship that dispels reality from both the literary and the personal scenes. The offered analytical clues to the posed mystery gather themselves up into a ballooning synthesis of explanations that floats overhead throughout the book, as if to remind readers that, while it is all perfectly explicable, it is better viewed, better understandable, as a mystery. (75–76)

Far from being flattered, Jackson sees the effect of Kroll's appropriation of White Goddess 'critical dress' as mystification of both Plath's life and her art, and regrets that 'Miss Kroll saves herself from the critic's highest but most dangerous privilege, that of self-sacrifice to the ardours of independent judgment, by relying on Sylvia Plath's husband, Ted Hughes, for the keys to the main matters on Sylvia Plath's work.' Jackson recommends that the critic begin 'with the human location of the work,' for 'what is literary criticism, properly, but understanding a work as a human work, the purposeful linguistic production of a certain human somebody?' (77, 75)

These critical disputes over whether or not the *Ariel* we know is authentic – truly authored by Plath – or a contrived volume reflecting the 'impure' intentions of a guilty husband, conniving to cover his guilt, and whether we should read her poems as either confessional and firmly embedded in biographical circumstance, or, in Kroll's words, as 'the articulation of a mythic system which integrates all aspects of her work' (2), only appear to be local and specific to Plath. Larger questions quickly emerge about what is good and bad art, and what is good and bad in terms of critical elucidation of poetic texts generally. Hence, Kroll reminds us of a New Critical position when she cautions that 'biographical detail, then, does not explain the impact of her poems as works of art (in reading a really *bad* sensationalistic confessional poem, we can readily perceive that the subject matter shocks, fascinates, and moves us, while on the other hand, we see quite clearly that the poem has no value as art)' (49). A 'good' poem stands on its own, with no need of 'biographical detail' to make it work. Indeed, if such detail seems necessary for understanding the poem, the poet has failed in her task, failed to set her work free for purely aesthetic contemplation. Similarly, if the critic is confronted with a 'good' poem (i.e., one not dependent on sensational biographical information) and can say nothing about its complex verbal structure, its formal wholeness and completeness, and so on, then the critic, too, has failed in her work. Finally, then, if Hughes deleted 'personally aggressive' plems, perhaps he was 'purifying' *Ariel* and protecting the 'immortal' body of Plath's work from being sullied with 'really *bad* sensationalistic' blots. To insist, as Perloff and others have, on resuscitating these poems, and restoring the biographical context for reading all of the *Ariel* poems, might be deemed a strategy that ultimately diminishes her achievement.

Plath herself, when she introduced many of these poems for a BBC radio reading, was careful to distance herself from the speakers and content. Hence, about 'The Applicant,' which has been read as a disillusioned assessment of her marriage, Plath advises, 'In this poem, . . . the speaker is an executive, a sort of exacting super-salesman. He wants to be sure the applicant for his marvelous product really needs it and will treat it right' (n. 182, *CP* 293). When she reads 'Daddy,' no mention is made of Otto Plath or Ted Hughes. Instead, she coolly distances herself from 'a girl with an Electra complex. Her father died while she thought he was God. Her case is complicated by the fact that her father was also a Nazi and her mother very possibly part Jewish. In the daughter the two strains marry and paralyse each other – she had to act out the awful little allegory once over before she is free of it' (n. 183, *CP* 293), and 'Lady Lazarus,' that ringing indictment of father and husband as controlling figures in Plath's ritualized death and rebirth, is about 'a woman who has the great and terrible gift of being reborn. The only trouble is, she has to die first. She is the Phoenix, the libertarian spirit, what you will. She is also just a good, plain, very resourceful woman' (n. 198, *CP* 294). Plath, I believe, knew she was writing dangerous poetry, and these critically detached assessments of her personae simultaneously encourage her interpreters toward a New Critical aesthetic appraisal and deflect any readers who might dismiss the poems as out-of-control and too personal tirades. Of course, Plath probably also expected the literary milieu in London to be fully aware of and curious about the scandalous triangle with Hughes and Assia Wevill, and further, to know how to read the poems' covert narrative. Plath's highly controlled descriptions, then, can be understood at still another level as posed, cosy assurances to anyone who really wants to know that she is just fine, thank you, fully in control of her writing, and additionally 'a good, plain, very resourceful woman.'

There is, finally, no way of settling these disputes over authenticity and what is good or bad in terms of these poems. If we mythify and disembody this 'real self,' this voice, this Ariel persona, we are guilty of a cultural mystification that disempowers the 'certain human somebody' and the 'human location' of Sylvia Plath. Even Jacqueline Rose's elegant disclaimer about what she is doing in *The Haunting of Sylvia Plath* – 'I am never claiming to speak about the life, never attempting to establish the facts about the lived existence of Sylvia Plath' (ix), seems a dismissive sublimation of a poet who tells us, 'The world is blood-hot and personal / Dawn says, with its blood flush' (*CP* 264). And, of course, Rose managed to convince no one who figures in Plath's poems of the disinterested nature of her interpretations, of her immersion in texts, not lives. Nevertheless, the dangers of interpreting Plath's poetry solely in terms of her life and her death were readily apparent from the beginning. In Mary Kinzie's 1970 description of critical reception to Plath, she notes 'the frequency of the claim that Sylvia Plath's poetry is inseparable from her life, or that she erased the boundaries between art and experience. In its most extreme form, the feeling is that her aesthetic, after all, is nothing more than the chronicle of a nervous breakdown' (Newman 290). Instead of drawing attention to Plath's skills as a poetic craftsman, *Ariel* 'has become an artifact of sensibility in which the craft of the poetry is frequently lost amidst speculation about how one ought to confront life' (Newman 290–291).

Parallel Bodies, Concealed and Hidden Narratives

In a 1988 paper, 'Sylvia Plath: The Evolution of "Sheep in Fog,"' Hughes offers a view of Plath's manuscripts as

> essentially a parallel body of poetry. They are a transparent exposure of the poetic operations to which the finished work is – well, what is it? In one sense, that final version conceals all these operations. It exploits them, plunders them, appropriates only what it can use, and then, finally for the most part, hides them. But

having seen these drafts [for 'Sheep in Fog'], we do not respect the poem less. We understand it far better, because we have learned the peculiar meanings of its hieroglyphs. These drafts are not an incidental adjunct to the poem, they are a complementary revelation, and a logbook of its real meanings. (*WP* 206)

While for Hughes the 'parallel body' of Plath's manuscripts in this essay is only that of the *Ariel* poems themselves, I include for discussion in the chapters that follow the parallel textual bodies underlying the 'Other *Ariel*' poems – the manuscripts and typescripts by Hughes and the typescript for *The Bell Jar* on her cherished pink Smith memorandum paper that Plath chose to recycle for the 'Other *Ariel*.' Since the 'Other *Ariel*' never moved from the limbo of its archival state to final publication, it is a hypothetical volume, a parallel body in and of itself to the *Ariel* authorized by Hughes, and the 'logbook of its real meanings' must include all of the manuscript material.[24]

In addition, I occasionally extend the notion of parallel bodies to include other dated materials, both those already published, like the *Journals* and *Letters Home*, and documents available in the Smith and Lilly archives – such as Plath's Tablet Diary, more letters, and lists – as offering 'complementary revelations' about the composition of the 'Other *Ariel*.' The biographical information available for certain dates and events is an especially helpful context for interpretively situating many poems. Further, I want to explore the relation between Plath's 'rare body' and its posthumous and piecemeal presentation in various publications, attending especially to the appearance of poems originally intended as part of the 'Other *Ariel*' in editions created by Olwyn Hughes for the Rainbow Press. The impact of these editions has been to obscure biographical context and the potential meaning of some poems, or to divert readers from their original sites of meaning in the narrative of the 'Other *Ariel*.'

Finally, because I believe that Plath's poetic practice set a precedent for a peculiar kind of collaboration and conversation between ostensibly different textual bodies, I want to look at several of Ted Hughes's *Birthday Letters*, when they continue the dialogue and collaboration she originally created. Hughes is not simply breaking a long silence, offering his 'side' of the story, but also, I would argue, revising his aesthetic appraisal of Plath's achievement in the *Ariel* poems. As we shall see, some of his poem-letters specifically challenge her decision to tell all, to sacrifice their intimacy for poetic fame; others reprove her for mistaking sacrifice for grief, rage for mourning; and several letters argue with what Hughes regards as fictions Plath derived from her therapy in Freudian psychoanalysis and superimposed on their marital narrative. These are not simply letters from a husband to a dead wife, but one poet addressing another in poems that speak – often eloquently – to Plath's poems, extending the over-writing, the back talking, the quarrel, and the dialogue she initiated.

As this suggests, for me the choices are not myth or confession, good or bad art, real versus false selves, because there is a way in which Plath's carefully preserved manuscripts defy these modes of critical dress. Similarly, I am less worried about the highly contested issues of whether Plath erased the boundary between art and life, or took risks in her art that led fatally to her death, than about the way this mass of material refuses to be tamed by such single-minded critical narratives. The archival body tells several stories about Plath's aspirations, and some of them are noble – 'high,' if you will. But there are also moments of outright derisions, unsurprisingly directed at her husband's artistic ambitions, that both make a mockery of pretensions to the eternal beauty of 'great' art and offer transgressive – confessional – alternatives to his aesthetic.

In the chapters that follow, I focus on two groups of poems from the 'Other *Ariel*.' Chapter 2 explores seven of the group of twelve poems Hughes deleted from the 'Other *Ariel*' and three others Plath did not include: 'Event' (first titled 'Quarrel'), an early version of 'Stings [2],' and 'Burning the Letters.' I include these three because they are early companions to the poems attacking Hughes. 'Event' was written May 21, 1962, the same day as 'The Rabbit Catcher,' and together they respond to a visit by Assia and David Wevill that first aroused Plath's jealous suspicion. 'Stings [2]' and 'Burning the Letters' are the only poems Plath composed in August. By this time Plath was aware of the other woman's identity, aware of Hughes's betrayal, and in a state of indecision about her marriage. Based on an event in June, 'Stings [2]' describes an attack by Plath's bees on Hughes. Together with 'Burning the Letters,' based on an event in July, when Plath invaded Hughes's attic study and burned his papers, these two poems anticipate Plath's effort to give poetic shape to her desire for vengeance. The parallel bodies of manuscripts for this entire group of poems also reflect, I believe, Plath's struggle to overcome a strong reticence about making her marriage to Hughes, when it began to fall apart, a subject of her poetry. It was one thing to celebrate her perfect man and perfect marriage as she had in earlier poems, and quite another to admit publicly that it was all lies: 'A ring of gold with the sun in it? / Lies. Lies and a grief' ('The Couriers,' *CP* 247). These are poems that come alive especially when the biographical context is fully restored. I am uncertain whether this dependency on biographical detail defines them, in Kroll's words, as 'really *bad* sensationalistic confessional poem[s],' but I would argue that their power to fascinate and move a reader is considerably enhanced when Plath's situation as she wrote them is fully acknowledged as playing a role in the creative process. Hughes's responses to this invasion of the 'private property' he shared with Plath also form an extensive parallel body to these texts and manuscripts, and include correspondence, essays, and editorials addressed especially to the attacks of feminist critics, and poems in *Birthday Letters* that often admonish Plath for trading their intimate life together for posthumous fame and making her family – Otto, Aurelia, her children, as well as himself – the victims of intense critical scrutiny.

Chapter 3 focuses on the sequence of bee poems Plath wrote between October 3 and October 9, 1962, and intended as her conclusion to the 'Other *Ariel*.' Her intentions for the volume as a whole are obviously at stake here. Why did Plath see this sequence of poems as so crucial that she placed them as her ending? Why did she choose bees, beekeeping, and the beehive, with their allegorical complexity and extensive literary history, as her metaphorical mode of expression? The bee poems have also provoked extensive, primarily feminist critical commentary, and I will review what has been said, while also exploring the parallel bodies of the manuscripts and archival material as providing 'complementary revelations,' and, I believe, concealed and hidden narratives, to the dominant one described by feminists. These poems also come alive in new ways when situated in a biographical context, but their power to fascinate and to move is much less dependent on such knowledge. In some ways, too, I will be in conversation with myself here. When I wrote about Plath's investment in beekeeping in 1980, before the publication of the *Collected Poems*, before knowing when they were written or where she wanted them placed, I saw them differently than I do now and imposed a critical dress not entirely fitting the 'rare body' I admire now. Finally, I will once again look at the *Birthday Letters* by Hughes, which extend the allegory initiated by Plath and revise the ending she planned for the 'Other *Ariel*.'

Chapter 4 explores the publication of *Birthday Letters* as a conclusion to the conversation and dialogue between these two poets. Here I am especially concerned with the way Hughes expresses grief for his dead wife – in poems that restore her briefly to vivid life and then dissolve her into shades. There are, I believe, many indications that Hughes is adopting an Orpheus identity to mourn for Plath, who in turn is conceived as his Eurydice. Additionally, while much has been made of their biographical import, these poem-letters also address Plath as a poet who created a self-destructive mourning narrative to enact her grief for a dead father. Hughes's poetics of mourning is, I will argue, critical of Plath's and offers a different ritual for achieving closure to his sense of loss. By the end of the volume, his poem-letters have freed him of his bereavement and restored a memory of Plath that Hughes will oppose to her image in literary history as the wounded and endlessly grieving daughter of Otto Plath.

TWO

Private Property

I hope each of us owns the facts of her or his own life.
Ted Hughes, letter to The Independent, *April 20, 1989*

. . . the muse has come to live here, now Ted has gone . . .
Sylvia Plath to Ruth Fainlight, October 22, 1962

<And the open gate stencilled Private>
<These freedoms astonished me>
These freedoms flew through me
Sylvia Plath, 'Snares,' draft 1a

Of the twelve poems Hughes chose to delete from the 'Other *Ariel*' for the American edition of *Ariel*,[1] seven of them wantonly trespass on the privacy of the Plath-Hughes marriage. Described as 'more personally aggressive' by Hughes in his introduction to the *Collected Poems* (15), these poems violate taboos against exposing the intimate and familial to public scrutiny. Plath tramples on the propriety of marriage, the shared private property, if you will, of what passes between man and wife, between her and Ted. The peculiar literary history of these poems, I believe, is directly related to Ted Hughes's sense that in them Plath had abused their marriage. He handled them in such a way as to suggest an investment in them as private property: only reluctantly did he relinquish control over them, and one suspects that some of them might have met the fate of the destroyed journals if Plath had been less vigilant about making their existence known to the editors of little journals or to the audiences of the BBC, which sponsored her early public reading of the poems. Hughes's decisions, whatever their motive, aroused critical suspicion. What was interpreted as Hughes's initial suppression of these poems, their eventual publication in collections that might be construed as disguising the intimate nature of their contents, and the controversies occasionally incited by their appearance suggest ambivalence, if not hostility, on Hughes's part over critical pressure to divulge the full extent of Plath's poetic legacy.

The following list indicates Plath's plan for placing each of these seven excised poems in the 'Other *Ariel*' and is followed by the date of composition:

    no. 3 'The Rabbit Catcher' (May 21, 1962)
    no. 9 'A Secret' (October 10, 1962
    no. 10 'The Jailor' (October 17, 1962)
    no. 14 'The Detective' (October 1, 1962)
    no. 22 'The Courage of Shutting-Up' (October 2, 1962)
    no. 28 'Purdah' (October 29, 1962)
    no. 32 'Amnesiac' (October 21, 1962)

Beginning with 'The Rabbit Catcher,' composed on May 21, 1962, Plath moves in a new poetic direction. As her biographer Anne Stevenson remarks, 'For the first time . . . Sylvia was using her own husband and offspring for material in a confessional way' (244), and in a way that Ted Hughes would ultimately find 'humiliating.' Eventually 'The Rabbit Catcher' provoked a scandal pitting the critic Jacqueline Rose's freedom of speech against Ted Hughes's right to privacy. In 1992, thirty years after Plath wrote 'The Rabbit Catcher,' Hughes objected publicly to an interpretation of the poem by Rose that felt like an intrusion on Plath's, and by extension his own, sexual life: 'I was taken aback, therefore on first reading [Jacqueline Rose's] typescript [for *The Haunting of Sylvia Plath*], when I came across her detailed interpretation of Sylvia Plath's 'The Rabbit Catcher.' Here, Professor Rose distorts, reinvents etc. Sylvia Plath's 'sexual identity' with an abandon I could hardly believe – presenting her in a role that I vividly felt to be humiliating to Sylvia Plath's children' (April 24, 1992, *TLS*). It is hard not to read Hughes as the ultimately offended party, but in an effort to 'wake [Rose] up' to the emotional state of the surviving children (by then admittedly adults in their thirties) and how they might feel having their mother's 'sexual identity' interpreted as unstable – not clearly heterosexual in orientation – and as enmeshed, in Rose's view, in the practice of 'oral sex' in the poem (*The Haunting* 138), Hughes 'asked [Rose] to imagine how it would be, to interpret some local mother's 'sexual identity,' . . . as she had . . . in one of those pride and honour societies of the Mediterranean.' Rose was unsympathetic to Hughes's efforts to awaken her sensitivity to Plath's children and their feelings and, in fact, had gone on public record two weeks earlier as believing that Hughes was not only refusing permission to quote from Plath's work but also threatening her very life with such a query, using 'illegitimate pressure' by suggesting that what she had done was 'grounds for homicide' in some cultures (April 10, 1992, *TLS*).

One senses throughout this controversy that what Plath did in the writing of 'The Rabbit Catcher' and what Rose does in contending legally with the estate (with Ted and Olwyn Hughes) over her reading of Plath is precisely captured in the notion of 'Private Property: No Trespassing.' In the late 1960s, when A. Alvarez wrote a memoir of Plath for *The Observer*, later published as the prologue to *The Savage God*, Hughes wrote to him after the publication of the first half, accusing him ultimately of exposing 'her infinitely humiliating private killing of herself' (Malcolm 127), but along the way, accusing Alvarez of trampling on him as well, taking advantage of his friendship to trespass on his private life with Plath:

> You saw little enough of us. Both of us regarded you as a friend, not a *Daily Mirror* TV keyhole, rat-hole journalist snoop, guaranteed to distort every observation and plaster us with these know-all pseudo-psychological theories, as if we were relics dug up from 10,000 B.C. Of our marriage you know nothing. . . . It is infuriating for me to see my private experiences and feelings reinvented for me, in that crude, bland, unanswerable way, and interpreted and published as official history.
>
> (Malcolm 125)

'The Rabbit Catcher' was one of the poems Plath sent to Alvarez in July 1962, and without Hughes's knowledge. In doing so, Plath made Alvarez her confidant and gave him access to private feelings expressed in the poem of which even her husband may have been unaware. Similarly, by opening the gates to wider public viewing of their intimate relations in poems such as 'The Rabbit Catcher,' Plath would later make her husband and their marriage prey to interpretive poachers like Rose. As Hughes explains, 'This is a fair example of how an "interpretation" (her misreading of my appeal to her better feelings) becomes a 'fact' that is now 'accepted' and even exploited, quite noisily, as publicity scandal, by new biographers . . . drifts through literary gossip, settles as an assumption into various corners of critical opinion ('violates' my 'identity,' in fact)' (*TLS* April 24, 1992). Ironically, Hughes realizes here that his wife's portrait of him as the hunter of the poem, sexually ensnaring her in a marriage with no exit but death, is now being confirmed by Rose's supposed fear of the latent menace in his 'appeal to her better feelings.' His 'identity' as the violent rabbit catcher of the poem's title, he claims, is now strangely corroborated by Rose's belief – now a 'fact' – that he means to do her harm. In Hughes's view, then, one misreading breeds another and another, where Rose's distorted interpretation of Plath's 'The Rabbit Catcher' leads fatally to misreading his intentions and ultimately to more gossip for biographers to report as if it were true.

Virtually all of Hughes's efforts to reclaim the private domain of his marriage exposed in these poems similarly managed to backfire, which may be why he chose to respond with outright venom in *Birthday Letters* to feminist critics and readers who have been his most persistent antagonists. He assails them as scavengers, grave robbers, and cannibals. In 'The Dogs Are Eating You Mother,' Hughes describes these hyenas as grave robbers who dig up Plath's body and 'batten / On the cornucopia / Of her body' (*BL* 195). Plath's gravestone, inscribed 'Sylvia Plath Hughes,' has been defaced several times of the 'Hughes' identity and name by feminist pilgrims paying perverse homage to their martyr. This act, in Hughes's view, also robs her children of their shared identity with their mother. Addressing their daughter Frieda and son Nicholas, Hughes warns them that if they try to protect their mother, they will be cannibalized 'as if you were more her' (*BL* 195). Hughes's advice here presumably derives from his own bitter experience of being savaged by literati, and from his belief that 'what she was' has been utterly misinterpreted by hyena critics and biographers who have made both him and Plath their 'spoils':

> Let them
> Jerk their tail-stumps, bristle and vomit
> Over their symposia.
> (*BL* 196)

For Hughes, academics who labor over Plath's corpus are nothing more than jackals in a feeding frenzy.[2] In 'Freedom of Speech,' there is not a symposium but a 'reunion' on Plath's 'sixtieth birthday' of all who have benefited from her work: 'your court of brilliant minds, / And publishers and doctors and professors' (*BL* 192). When these guests are not spewing gobbets of Plath's body, they are all laughing and grateful because Ariel is very much alive, happily sitting on Plath's knuckle like an exotic bird, while 'You feed it grapes, a black one, then a green one, / From between your lips pursed like a kiss' (*BL* 192). Even the stars 'shake with laughter' (*BL* 192), as if in joyful celebration of Ariel's immortality and place in the poetic firmament. Only Plath and Hughes 'do not smile.' Why? The year of Plath's sixtieth birthday is 1992, also the year of Rose's publication of *The Haunting of Sylvia Plath* and the controversy over her freedom of speech versus what Hughes believed to be a slur on Plath's sexual identity and a violation of his own.

Ironically, all these situations mimic the one in Plath's first version of 'Stings,' 'Stings [2],' composed in August 1962 and concerning an incident of June 15 (*LH* 457). Unprotected, Hughes tried to move a beehive and its queen, and was assailed by the female workers:

> What honey in you summons these animalcules?
> What fear? It has set them zinging.
> Zinging & Zinging on envious strings, & you are the center.
> (*CP* n. 178, 293)

By August, when these lines were written, Plath was headed towards imagining a poetic vengeance on her husband that would ultimately mobilize a hive of feminist critics and 'set them zinging' on Hughes.[3] As Hughes depicts this incident in 'The Bee God,' he is the 'target' of bees who are religious zealots – 'Fanatics for their God, the God of the Bees' (*BL* 152), and this God is none other than Otto Plath: 'When you wanted bees I never dreamed / It meant your Daddy had come up out of the well' (*BL* 150). As with so many poems in *Birthday Letters*, Plath is portrayed as unwittingly conspiring with a fate that demanded the sacrifice of herself and everyone she loved. Virtually all of her actions are seen by Hughes as a desertion of him, her children, and her mother in pursuit of her dead father, 'The Minotaur.' For them she chose a dead end, while she entered a labyrinth that

> Brought you to the horned, bellowing
> Grave of your risen father—
> And your own corpse in it.
> (*BL* 120)

In turn, virtually all of Plath's words, her poems, are seen by Hughes as exposing these same loved ones to public infamy and censure. Father, mother, and husband are sentenced to decapitation by Plath, alternately a steel-helmed Athena and an Aztec goddess of human sacrifice in Hughes's 'Brasilia':

> Your great love had spoken.
> Only the most horrible crime
> Could have brought down
> The blade of lightning
> That descended then. Dazzled,
> All coughed in the ozone.
> Even the dogs were stunned. And the same flash
> Snatched you up into Heaven.
> (*BL* 178)[4]

'Every day since, throughout your Empire,' the poems that ensure Plath's apotheosis also lead to public accusation and 'execution' of those she found guilty. As if Plath were still alive to feel the sting of his reproof, Hughes indicts her pen and its damning sentences:

> A dumb creature, looping at the furnace door
> On its demon's prong,
> Was a pen already writing
> Wrong is right, right wrong.
> ('The Blackbird,' *BL* 162)

As we shall see, to many of the excised poems, Hughes wrote responses that attempt to right and rewrite these wrongs, or at least to complicate the immortality of his supposed guilt with an equally immutable sense of his personal loss.

'You were weeping with a rage / That cared nothing for rabbits'

Plath composed 'The Rabbit Catcher' (originally titled 'Snares') immediately following Assia and David Wevill's weekend visit to Court Green, Devon, May 18–20, 1962. According to Anne Stevenson, Plath's jealous perception of Assia as a sexual rival devastated her: she conceded defeat even before a battle was joined. Stressing Plath's inherently self-destructive nature, Stevenson and her collaborator, Olwyn Hughes,[5] believe that 'the poet almost wills the worst to happen' (*BF* 244), that Plath is herself culpable for fabricating fatality out of faint intuitions. Citing the line 'And we, too, had a relationship—,' they note how 'the relationship is curiously set in the past, and its ending is compared to the noose of a rabbit trap that kills her' (245).

Olwyn Hughes's access to her brother no doubt provided Stevenson with the actual incident behind the poem and, perhaps through her, Ted Hughes's interpretation of the antagonism feeding Plath's poetic conception: 'It originated during a walk she and Ted had taken some months before. Coming upon a line of snares along a clifftop, Sylvia had wildly rushed around tearing them up. As a countryman, Ted Hughes was sympathetic to the simple economics of village life and saw nothing admirable in Sylvia's harming the rabbit catcher's livelihood. It was one of the small incidents, after they came to Devon, that made Ted realize how different their attitudes toward country life were' (244).[6] In draft 2b of the poem, Plath describes her attempt to foil the hunter as ultimately impotent: 'The pegs were too deep to move, but I buried the prop sticks.' Only briefly she nettles her foe, hoping at least 'It might cause him a morning's anger' (2b-1). How different Plath's and Hughes's feelings were on this occasion is fully dramatized in Hughes's own 'The Rabbit Catcher,' which explicitly alludes to Plath's imagery in an 'I saw'/'you saw' counterpoint of two opposing visions:

> . . . I saw
> Country poverty raising a penny,
> Filling a Sunday stewpot. You saw baby-eyed
> Strangled innocents, I saw sacred
> Ancient custom. You saw snare after snare
> And went ahead, riving them from their roots
> And flinging them down the wood.
> (*BL* 145)

Remarkably, what Hughes does not see is an attack on their marriage, even though his diction suggests a trust broken. Plath has violated what is sanctified and sacred in country customs, what is precious and precarious in her husband's English heritage, and in her recklessness, then, shows how little she values and honors what her husband holds dear.

For Hughes, the day intended as a family outing, 'an exploration,' is marred at its outset by Plath's black mood, which may be, he suggests in the image of 'the moon's blade,' the result of her menstrual cycle:

> What had I done? I had
> Somehow misunderstood. Inaccessible
> In your dybbuk fury, babies
> Hurled into the car, you drove.
> (*BL* 144)

Whatever the causes, the wife's rage forces Hughes into the role of guardian, protecting Plath from doing something extreme, irretrievable: 'She'll do something crazy,' he thinks (*BL*

144). The drama here is tritely prosaic in its representation of a husband tyrannized by his wife's ill temper: 'I simply / Trod accompaniment, carried babies, / Waited for you to come back to nature' (*BL* 144). Only at the end of the poem does Hughes lift the episode from a domestic dispute to a moment of poetic revelation for Plath. At the same time, however, Hughes transforms her into the rabbit catcher, and makes her poetry – this new verse she would write – the snares. Like snares,

> Those terrible, hypersensitive
> Fingers of your verse closed round it and
> Felt it alive. The poems, like smoking entrails,
> Came soft into your hands.
> (*BL* 146)

The surprise here is that Hughes denies that the poem is really about him. Only briefly does he acknowledge that Plath may have 'caught something' in him. This is a strategy typical of Hughes's *Birthday Letters* – to diminish his own importance in a mythic drama where Plath is struggling to give birth in poetry to her 'doomed self,' laboring to bring forth a sacrificial being like the rabbit here.[7] Like the entrails massaged into life by her hands, Plath's new poems are ironically moribund at birth.

'His body blocked off my vision – stolid & faceless'

The manuscripts for Plath's 'The Rabbit Catcher' tell a rather different story about what the snares, the rabbit, and the hunter mean, although Hughes's sense that Plath has suddenly 'caught' something new in her verse and overcome a blockage is, I believe, borne out. The occasion for composition, immediately following the visit from Assia and

David Wevill, when Plath felt her marriage to be in danger, is, I would argue, more important for understanding the poem than the actual incident described by Hughes. Together with 'Event' (originally titled 'Quarrel' and also composed on May 21, 1962), 'The Rabbit Catcher' depicts marriage as a tight place from which there is no escape: 'There was only one place to get to' (*CP* 193) in 'The Rabbit Catcher,' and in 'Event' the couple is caught in the 'rift' of a cliff, while she, like a stuck phonograph needle, moves monotonously 'in a ring / A groove of old faults' (*CP* 194–95). Even though Stevenson tells us that Hughes 'was appalled when he read 'Event' soon after it was written' (*BF* 244), Plath eventually sent it off together with 'The Rabbit Catcher' and 'Elm' on July 21 to A. Alvarez at *The Observer*, also a visitor at Court Green in the spring of 1962. Overall, the Stevenson biography depicts Plath as violating a marital trust by sending off such personal revelations to a family friend.

Of course, Plath waited two months before sending off these poems. By July 21, intent on retaliatory action, Plath might not have cared if Hughes 'was appalled.' Her marriage was on its way to disintegration under the pressure of what is alternately presented by biographers – depending on whose side they are on – as Ted Hughes's infidelity or Sylvia Plath's self-destructive jealousy.[8] Plath apparently chose not to show 'The Rabbit Catcher' to Hughes (*BF* 244), and although Alvarez thought it 'flawless' (letter to Plath dated July 24 [1962] and tried to get the poem into print, it did not appear until 1971, in the limited Rainbow Press edition of 'hitherto uncollected poems,' *Lyonnesse*, and then, also in 1971, in the Faber and Faber and Harper and Row editions of *Winter Trees*.[9] *Lyonnesse* is a most peculiar collection, including poems such as 'Metamorphoses of the Moon,' written prior to 1956 and classified in the *Collected Poems* as 'juvenilia,' but also a poem as late as 'Gigolo,' composed on January 29, 1963. Indeed, the only salient feature to the choice of poems for this volume is that most of them have never been collected: the 'hitherto uncollected' is not completely accurate.[10] One might be misled into believing that each poem was composed as a discrete and independent entity. Poems such as 'The Rabbit Catcher' and 'The Detective,' which are part of the poetic narrative in the 'Other *Ariel*,' are obscurely placed in a volume with poems that gush romantically over the early relationship between Plath and Hughes: 'Epitaph for Fire and Flower' (1956) was begun on Plath's honeymoon in Spain and idealizes both love and lovers, and 'Wreath for a Bridal' (1956) is a poem that celebrates their marriage in June 1956.

All interpreters of 'The Rabbit Catcher,' however, regard the poem as an indictment of marriage in general and, more specifically, Plath's own. Whereas Stevenson clearly does not view Plath as remotely feminist in inspiration, other critics and biographers have read the poem as feminist in impulse, although to varying degrees, from Linda Wagner-Martin pinpointing a moment of disillusionment in a woman's life – 'Now what she sees, in place of her ideal marriage, is the snare used for catching rabbits' (205) – to Rose's sweeping sense of Plath's 'radical feminist story' about 'the question of gender and power' (*Haunting* 142, 141). As Rose develops this 'story' – one that Hughes tried to suppress – the following lines define sex itself as a snare, a 'lure' to women that offers only masochistic and deathly pleasures:

> I felt a still busyness, an intent.
> I felt hands round a tea mug, dull, blunt,
> Ringing the white china.
> How they awaited him, those little deaths!
> They waited like sweethearts. They excited him.
> (*CP* 194)

Rose asks, or rather challenges her reader to disagree, 'How can we not read those 'little deaths' as orgasm as well as death, the death of the rabbits in their trap; how can we not read it, therefore, as saying that sexuality is the trap? This would give to Plath's poem as one of its meanings that complaint against (hetero)sexuality which has been most strongly articulated by Adrienne Rich' (139–40). The rhetorical leaps Rose makes from orgasm 'therefore' to sexuality in general, and then to heterosexuality, depend on the phrase 'little deaths,' and one might easily not want to go this far or this quickly toward reading Plath as a feminist.[11]

What is perhaps surprising is that the first draft (1a) of 'The Rabbit Catcher' makes no mention of either a marital relationship or a man.[12] A few phrases survive from this effort in the final poem, but the real story being told there is a struggle to overcome blockage, inhibition, reticence. As Janet Malcolm describes draft 1a:

> On the first page of the draft and on a part of the second page, the poem is unrecognizable – disconnected lines, most of them scratched out. There is the sense of a mind stirred by something, a mind activated but not able to move forward, like a car spinning its wheels in a rut, unable to get a purchase. Suddenly the car surges forward. 'It was a place of force,' Plath writes, and the rest of the poem follows the well-known first line essentially as we know it. The change from going nowhere to somewhere happens so quickly that the reader of the draft is stunned, and all the more moved. (128–29)

For Malcolm, the draft tells a story about poetic inspiration suddenly seizing Plath, and if not on the famed wings of poesy, 'the car surges forward.' For me, the 'change' is not so much 'from going nowhere to going somewhere' as a change to going somewhere new – Plath writing a different kind of poem, only with grave difficulty opening the door into her marriage as its painful subject. Of course, if we know the final poem, the following lines, many crossed out, already create an incipient analogy between marriage and rabbit snares, or a similarity between the 'old constancy' and the ball and chain of marital fidelity:

> . . . loops of metal, ankle-high
> With an old constancy.
> I, too, moved on wires,
> A flat personage in the gorse
> Dragged and chastised <many crossed-out words, including
> 'hard stars,'
> 'desires,' 'A force' – then followed by> certain fears.

Perhaps the 'I' here is walking on a high wire, fearful of making a mistake, falling. This 'I' is also a 'flat personage' – suggesting that she had been robbed of a 'round' personality? 'Dragged and chastised' to the point where she dares not speak or protest? In draft 2b, it is clearly a man's brutish intimidation that stops her: 'his body blocked off my vision – stolid & faceless' (2b-1). 'Vision' may also be understood metaphorically as poetic insight being blocked.

Plath composed this draft on the back side of an early typescript of *The Bell Jar*. In *Revising Life*, Susan Van Dyne argues convincingly that Plath recycled episodes from *The Bell Jar* not capriciously but deliberately, and indeed, Plath's choices here seem pertinent to the themes of 'The Rabbit Catcher.' The episodes on the back of draft 1a's two pages include Esther Greenwood's awakening from a siege of ptomaine poisoning with Betsy and Janeen (Doreen in the novel) at her bedside. The former depicts Esther sipping restorative broth and thinking, 'I felt purged and holy and ready for a new life.' Esther has, of course, literally purged herself on the poison she consumed at the *Ladies' Day* banquet, but also regurgitated the images of the perfect housewife created for mass consumption by *Ladies' Day*.[13] The latter birthing episode is, as I argue in *Plath's Incarnations* (124ff.), part of an extended allegory in *The Bell Jar* concerning the woman artist and the usurpation of her creative powers by men. If these two underlying narrative bodies about marriage and motherhood collaborate or converse with the epidermal 'surface' of 'Snares,' they encourage Plath, as she composes, to purge herself of feminine inhibitions about what wives properly should and should not do, and further, to regain control of her own fertility, symbolized in the woman's power to give birth.

Draft 1b of 'Snares' opens with the line that will ultimately be Plath's first in 'The Rabbit Catcher,' 'It was a place of force,' and here she also arrives at the phrase 'extravagant, like torture,' to define the speaker's sense of entrapment in a relationship that is exaggeratedly brutal but also luxuriant in its excess. Both of these lines seem inspired by the birthing scene, where Esther is told that the mother is given a drug to make her forget the pain and Esther sees her hoisted on what 'looked like some awful torture table with these metal stirrups sticking up in midair at one end and all sorts of instruments and wires and tubes I couldn't make out properly at the other' (reverse draft 1b, 3). For Rose, these underlying narratives are simply 'the hidden truth of the poem' (142) about marriage and heterosexuality that Plath is writing. Indeed, the ink leaks through like blood, sweat, and tears, testimony perhaps for Rose's reading of the poem as almost another *L'histoire d'O* – Plath's critique of her marriage as sexual bondage. The snares themselves are like the vagina in childbirth: 'Zeros, shutting on nothing, / Set close like birth pangs' (*CP* 194).

What I would suggest, however, is another type of bondage that may be more crucial to understanding this May 21 breakthrough and anticipation of the October miracle. It is the impact of marriage on Esther's budding ambitions as an artist that she finds most threatening. Buddy Willard smugly confides his belief that Esther won't want to write poems once she becomes a wife and mother. If 'The Rabbit Catcher' is about marriage, it is also about the way marriage enthralls a woman's creativity. In the first draft of this poem, Plath's efforts to disenthrall herself from marital constraints are part of the writing process. Hughes was, after all, more than a husband; he was also her poetic mentor. Their marriage was a collaboration of two writers, but an unequal one, in which Hughes's early success ensured his dominant position. For Plath, the treatment of him as her intimate tormentor in marriage (as in 'The Rabbit Catcher') was a strategy for releasing herself from a relationship in which he exerted a great deal of influence over her subject matter. Indeed, one of the more remarkable collections of scrap paper in the Smith College archive testifying to this influence includes lists of poem subjects assigned by Hughes, in his handwriting, with Plath's annotations or dots by many of them, indicating that she had tried, for example, 'Moon & yew' (recognizable as 'The Moon and the Yew Tree') or 'The stones of the city – their patient sufferance (requisitioned as they are)' (recognizable as 'The Stones'). The top corner of one list reads, in Plath's hand, 'The Pheasant,' 'Rabbit Snares,' 'Sheep by Moonlight & Christ tree,' and 'Owl Mobbed by Birds.' It is not clear whether she came up with her own additional poetic subjects, or whether she is transcribing more suggestions from her husband, but this is, at least, where 'The Rabbit Catcher' has its origin, as just another possibility among the many offered by her teacher-poet husband.

The poem's original title, 'Snares,' also captures the already mentioned visual texture of Ted Hughes's handwriting. In 'Daddy,' Plath explicitly equates here impotent efforts at speech in German with being ensnared in her father's language:

> I never could talk to you.
> The tongue stuck in my jaw.
>
> It stuck in a barb wire snare.
> Ich, ich, ich, ich,
> I could hardly speak.
> (CP 223)

Confirming Hughes's sense that Plath could not tell the difference between husband and father in her final months, this line is virtually lifted from a letter she wrote to Aurelia about Hughes, not Otto Plath, telling her, 'I hate and despise him so I can hardly speak,' and in a letter on October 12, 1962, the date of composition of 'Daddy,' she tells Aurelia, 'Every morning, when my sleeping pill wears off, I am up about five, in my study with coffee, writing like mad – have managed a poem a day before breakfast. All book poems. Terrific stuff, as if domesticity had choked me' (*LH* 466).

This sense of being silenced – 'choked' in her domestic role – and then permitting herself to speak dovetails neatly with what Plath called the 'out loud' nature of her new poems. As she announces in her October 30 BBC reading of new poems, 'They are poems written for the ear, not the eye: they are poems written out loud.' Their kinship with speech as opposed to writing was a breakthrough for Plath, away from the literariness of *The Colossus* to the emphatic utterance of *Ariel*. Meanwhile, Plath was assuredly responding to what she saw as 'a new spirit . . . at work in American poetry.' In a broadcast for the BBC Third Programme (January 10, 1963), Plath claims, 'The shift in tone is already history – the flashing elaborate carapace of [Robert Lowell's] *Lord Weary's Castle* dropped for *Life Studies* – walking the tightrope of the psyche naked.' The same might be said for the shift between the 'carapace' of *The Colossus* and the about-to-be-naked psyche of the *Ariel* poems. Early in 1962 Anne Sexton had also sent Plath a copy of her groundbreaking *All My Pretty Ones*, and even as Plath's American publication of *The Colossus* in May was strikingly inconspicuous, Sexton's work received growing attention and success. *The Colossus* was usually noticed in 'omnibus' reviews with several other volumes and received no attention in places such as the *New York Times Book Review* or the *New York Review of Books*. The contrast with critical acclaim for Sexton's work may well have prompted Plath to take risks in her poetry like Sexton's that simultaneously transgressed barriers against publicly saying anything negative about her marriage. If Ted 'was appalled' at 'Event,' 'The Rabbit Catcher' was even more of a slap in the face. When she sent it out, though, maybe, like Esther, she 'felt purged and holy and ready for a new life' – as if she had cleansed herself of an old dependency (an 'old constancy') on Hughes for his poetic approval.

The poem is about an imposed constriction of Plath's voice far more pervasive than having her 'mistaken' American views of British 'ancient custom' challenged by a native-born Englishman, which is how Hughes portrays the conflict in his own version of 'The Rabbit Catcher.' Draft 1a reflects Plath's sense of impotence: it is so heavily crossed out that not a single line survives into the final draft. It begins with 'A <great> long wind pushing things about,' as if Plath were looking for a force capable of shifting the poetic landscape. After more natural description – 'The green hill <running off> like the water beyond it,' and more terms for the wind, <cresting and staying>, 'Shuffling its lights,' she writes:

> White clouds putting the sun out
> These grew freedoms
> And the open gate stencilled Private
> These freedoms astonished me.
> These freedoms flew through me.
> Though the wind met objects, the hill & the sea
> Though the wind met objects & quickly
> Deflected itself . . .

Although none of these lines remains in the final poem, one senses a surge of uncontrollable power in this wind, an inspiring creator-destroyer not unlike Shelley's West Wind or Coleridge's storm blast in 'Dejection: An Ode.' The antecedent for 'these' is not completely clear, but 'These grew freedoms' that fly through her and astonish her before an 'open gate.' 'Open' is a surprising choice here, followed as it is by

'Private.' Ordinarily, a sign saying 'Private' also means 'no trespassing,' not open to the public, property that is closed to everyone but the owner and his family. Indeed, Plath is fumbling with the risk of flying through that gate, opening up the familial, the private, to public view.[14]

At the end of this first draft is a sudden blockage: ' . . . & in my heart / Snares nastier / crueller than in the dirt / Pushing me like a wind, & stopping me, like a rock.' What began as a notion of astonishing freedom turns into a silencing force so strong it is felt as coming from within – 'in my heart.' In the successive revisions, however, the poem projects these snares onto a landscape, onto a rabbit catcher, and eventually onto the husband and the marital relationship. Plath's strategy is to see the source of blockage as coming from without rather than as generated by her own emotional inhibitions. The torture of snares closeted 'in my heart' in draft 1a is therefore transposed to tortuous terrain with 'gorse' like 'black spikes' (another allusion to Hughes's handwriting?) and where the wind gags '[my] mouth with my own blown hair,' literally 'Tearing off my voice.' The rabbit catcher also begins to take form as an ominous presence in the snare-minded landscape, the furtive intelligence behind entrapment – 'The paths narrowed into the hollow / And the snares almost effaced themselves' – and she feels, but can neither see nor hear, his 'still busyness, an intent' to kill. The rabbit catcher is an early version of the 'man in black' in 'Daddy.'[15] Like Daddy, his silencing powers are godlike. In draft 1b the snares are 'Zeros, shutting on silence. // The absence of shrieks oppressed me. / The absence of shrieks was like the silence of God.' Only gradually is this power given human form, domesticated and anglicized in the lines alluding to the custom of taking tea: 'I felt hands round a tea mug, dull, blunt, / Ringing the white china' (*CP* 194).[16]

While 'Event,' the companion piece to 'The Rabbit Catcher,' is resigned in tone ('Love cannot come here'), like many of the poems written in the spring of 1962 ('The Moon and the Yew Tree,' 'Little Fugue,' and 'Elm'), 'The Rabbit Catcher' is fraught with dread. Like a panicky rabbit, the speaker tries to hide, but all 'paths narrowed into the hollow,' and the hunter, knowing his prey, shrewdly hides snares 'set close' and fatally designed for 'Sliding shut on some quick thing.' Plath's identification with the rabbits is visceral, her own panic mimicking their fear: 'The constriction killing me also' (*CP* 194). Yet finally, I would argue, the sense of identification with an animal caught in a snare is transformed into intellectual submission. The Rabbit Catcher's 'mind like a ring / Sliding shut on some quick thing' (*CP* 194) is a simile that suggests the pounce of a man of reason on the woman's flight of fancy – or perhaps the killing pronouncements and judgments of a writer husband already secure in his fame, at home in British high culture.[17] The suffocation Hughes alludes to in his version of 'The Rabbit Catcher' may have nothing to do with Plath's mythic rebirth, but may simply refer to Plath's sense of being fenced in by the constraints of Hughes's British heritage. Laughing apologetically on the BBC in October 1962, Plath told an interviewer, 'I think as far as language goes I'm an American, I'm afraid, my accent is American, my way of talk is an American way of talk.'

'Word after word is lit!'

The *Collected Poems* shows only one poem written during the month of August: 'Burning the Letters' (August 13, 1962).[18] Although Plath did not choose it for the 'Other *Ariel*,' indicating that for her it was not a 'book poem,' it is of special interest for the way it addresses what Van Dyne calls 'one of [Ted Hughes's] most famous statements of his own poetics, "The Thought-fox"' (*RL* 9), and thereby complicates the marital struggle with questions about aesthetics. In contrast to 'The Rabbit Catcher,' in which poetic power has 'an efficiency, a great beauty' akin to the masculine hunter's snares, where killing is a silent form and a form of silencing—

The absence of shrieks
Made a hole in the hot day, a vacancy.
The glassy light was a clear wall,
The thickets quiet.
(*CP* 193–194)—

'Burning the Letters' makes a case for the poetic efficacy of shrieks, the animal's death cry as immortal utterance:

The dogs are tearing a fox. This is what it is like—
A red burst and a cry
That splits from its ripped bag and does not stop
With the dead eye
And the stuffed expression, but goes on
Dyeing the air,
Telling the particles of the clouds, the leaves, the water
What immortality is. That it is immortal.
(*CP* 205)

While this immortal 'music' is not exactly – indeed, exactly *not* – the 'full-throated ease' of Keats's nightingale, Plath makes a similar if cruelly perverse claim for the fox's cry as transcendent expression, superseding the efficacy of the printed word. She turns a purposely deaf ear to poetic lyricism in favor of something crude and sensational. We know Plath means her immortal fox to challenge what she derides as Hughes's poetic taxidermy – 'the dead eye / And the stuffed expression' of his 'Thought-Fox' – because it makes its first appearance on the reverse side (draft 1, 2) of a recycled typescript of Hughes's poem. Her ink bleeds through onto his poem, 'dyeing' it with her agony, spilling onto his page and sullying its silent beauty.[19] Hughes's poem contrarily invokes a more conventional solitude and silence as the moment of poetic inspiration. He opens, 'I imagine this midnight moment's forest,' and before him is 'this blank page where my fingers move' ('The Thought-Fox' 14). Plath's handwriting mars his 'neat prints into the snow,' and thereby defies her husband's poetic authority. Her mockery of his 'Thought-Fox' is evident in 'stuffed expression,' nastily implying that Hughes's poem, his creation of a fox, is a stuffy and bombastic little piece with about as much life as one of Norman Bates's birds. Her own fox is immortal because of its pain, and by extension, Plath makes a case for private anguish as the basis for her new poems. She stakes the immortality of her verse on the sincerity of its feeling, on the impact of a cri de coeur. One discarded line baldly states, 'This is what it is to be loveless!' (draft 1, 1)

The aesthetic alternative in Hughes's poem is that the poet reveals nothing about himself except as a poet. 'The Thought-Fox,' to the extent that it has a content, is about all of those elements prized by Eliot, Pound, and Auden, Hughes's own poetic mentors: the impersonal voice, the crafting of sensuous images, the cultivated representation of the poet as a mind that creates and not a man who suffers or chooses poetic display of his suffering. 'The Thought-Fox' is one of those tricky little self-reflective pieces about the process of recreating the poem's writing of itself. The title suggests its cerebral origin, and when we come to the final stanza,

> Till, with a sudden sharp hot stink of fox
> It enters the dark hole of the head.
> The window is starless still; the clock ticks.
> The page is printed.
> (14),

we suddenly realize that the whole poem celebrates the imagination's ability to evoke an animal's presence in language. All of the animal's foxy grace resounds to the brilliance and concentration of the poet who created it – even, or perhaps most of all, its 'sudden sharp hot stink.' The fox's 'neat prints into the snow' magically become the poet's writing on the blank whiteness of the page at the end. Voilà! A poem has been made. Initially Plath responds in kind, with a splash of red ink, a writerly gesture: the cry of the fox 'goes on / Dying the air, <like a drop of> red ink in a glass of water' (draft 1, 3). By draft 3, the cry is independent of ink and paper, standing apart as simply a 'red burst.'

The youthful Hughes leaves himself open to the charge of smugness in the way he boasts about 'The Thought-Fox.' Indeed, one cannot help but speculate that Plath chose to attack this poem precisely because of the way Hughes invested it with claims to poetic immortality. On October 6, 1961, a year earlier, in the first of a series of BBC broadcasts designed for schoolchildren on how to write poetry, Hughes read the poem as part of a lesson titled 'Capturing Animals.' While he begins with childhood memories of trapping animals, as Hughes warms to his subject, we know he will end with the idea of 'capturing' as an artist captures the essence of animals, the essence of Fox, as it were, to use a 'stuffed expression.' He highly prizes his achievement in this poem:

> If I had not caught the real fox there in the woods I would never have saved the poem. I would have thrown it into the wastepaper basket as I have thrown so many other hunts that did not get what I was after. As it is, every time I read the poem the fox comes up again out of the darkness and steps into my head. And I suppose that long after I am gone, as long as a copy of the poem exists, every time anyone reads it the fox will get up somewhere out in the darkness and come walking towards them.
>
> So, you see, in some ways my fox is better than an ordinary fox. It will live forever, it will never suffer from hunger or hounds. I have it with me wherever I go. And I made it. And all through imagining it clearly enough and finding the living words. ('Capturing Animals' 20–21)

It is hard not to read the final lines of Plath's 'Burning the Letters' as throwing down the gauntlet, as spattering the blood/ink of her fox, the hunted and truly captured animal, onto Hughes's rigorously artificed fox and defying his intellectual and, yes, 'high' culture version of literary immortality with something literal, real, and downright low. Her emphatic 'This is what it is like,' followed by the extended trope of the fox torn by hounds, and then the repetition 'What immortality is. That it is immortal,' is flat-out assertion, insistently stomping on Hughes's subtlety, his cleverness, his 'mind like a ring.' She does not mean to dazzle with her brilliance, nor to condescend as to a child. As she explains earlier in the poem, 'Love, I am not subtle' (*CP* 204).

Ironically, 'Burning the Letters' was initially interpreted either as super-subtle in its meaning,[20] or as a grossly literal representation of an actual incident.[21] It was either so extraordinarily encoded with allusions to 'moment[s] of breakthrough and enlightenment' in Zen Buddhism (Kroll, *Chapters* 276), or simply negligible in the context of the literary value of Plath's later *Ariel* poems. I would argue that its subtlety – or perhaps cunning is a better word – paradoxically depends on its literal-mindedness, its insistence that textual and real bodies are the same: 'I open the pages, white wads that would save themselves. / Spirit after spirit gives itself up!' (draft 1, 2), and later, 'I flake up papers that breathe like people' (*CP* 204). Plath knew, I believe, that her fox was not subtle, not a product of sophisticated thinking about what constitutes poetic immortality. She means to be both coarse and low in her fury, and not a poet so much as a woman scorned, invading her husband's study, destroying his 'property,' by burning his letters: 'So I poke at the carbon birds in my housedress.' Violating all sense of propriety, she is consoled with having destroyed both his words and the words of others' writings to him: 'they have nothing to say to anybody. I have seen to that' (*CP* 204). The detail of the housedress makes her the 'little woman,' not the rival poet/wife, and the 'So there!' implicit in her satisfied assertions is meant as a retort to the condescensions she has suffered. She is cleaning house, and it's about time:

> And at least it will be a good place now, the attic.
> At least I won't be strung just under the surface,
> Dumb fish
> With one tin eye,
> Watching for glints,
> Riding my Arctic
> Between this wish and that wish.
> (*CP* 204)

Even the self-demeaning metaphor here seems appropriate, as if a house-wife were trying to challenge her poet husband with less than perfectly realized artistic form. To paraphrase, 'At least now I won't be treated like the dumb fish waiting, even hoping, to be caught, looking for a lure, a sign, from you, upstairs in the attic, while I live in cold uncertainty down here.' In draft 1, 'the cold, pure arctic' was, in fact, 'the space between your speaking, your thinking of me' – a sense of cold estrangement, or being taken for granted, in the husband's attitude toward her. The metaphor in this dramatic situation also suggests his 'higher' state of being, his clear atmosphere, his warm and ambient space, while she lives beneath his feet, a subhuman fish in a state of Arctic suspension.

The date of composition for 'Burning the Letters' is August 13, but the six heavily reworked drafts before the final, typed copy imply that the poem may have been composed over a longer period of time. It is based on an incident biographers place in early July: while Ted Hughes was away from the Court Green home in Devon he shared with Plath and their children, she invaded his attic study, gathered assorted papers and 'stuff,' and burned them. As she describes the act in her first draft, it is one of exasperation and vicarious control, as if to say, 'Even if you are not around, I can take possession of your things': 'And there was nobody for me to go to / So I burned the letters & the dust puffs & the old hair' (draft 1, 2). The most vivid account available is Clarissa Roche's, in her memoir 'Vignettes from England.' Roche was not a witness, but was Plath's confidante in November, after Plath and Hughes had separated and he had left her and the children in Court Green. Roche retells the incident as she remembers hearing it from Plath:

> When the moon was at a certain stage, she had skimmed from his desk 'Ted's scum,' microscopic bits of fingernail parings, dandruff, dead skin, hair, and then, with a random handful of papers collected from the desk and wastebasket, she had made a sort of pyre in the garden and around this she drew a circle. She stepped back to a prescribed point, lit the fire with a long stick of a torch and paced around, incanting some hocus-pocus or another. Flames shot up toward the moon, and smoke sketched the weird shapes in the mist. Then fragments of letters and manuscripts fluttered like moths, hovered and, after the heat abated, floated to the ground. One charred piece settled at Sylvia's feet. It had been reduced to an ash save for a corner. She picked it up and by the light of the moon read 'A ——,' the name of a friend. Sylvia now knew the woman with whom Ted was having an affair. (85)

Here the incident sounds as if Plath meant to cast a spell, to exorcise a demon. Whether Plath embellished what happened in order to entertain Roche, who also describes Plath as a witty raconteur, or whether Roche is the source of these spellbinding details, we still have the poem, and 'Burning the Letters' has none of this quality of a witch's ritual being performed. In fact, many of Plath's revisions have the effect of taming the potential melodrama in the incident.

Other evidence for what happened is confusing. Aurelia

Plath, visiting her daughter from June 21 to August 4, leaves no account of the incident immortalized by the poem. Nor do the letters from Plath to her mother after she concluded her visit refer to this episode. Biographers have supplied other details, the sources for which seem vague. In her 1987 biography, Wagner-Martin places the incident on the night of July 10, following Plath's interception of a 'mysterious phone call for Ted': 'And when Ted's conversation was over, she tore the telephone wires from the wall. She turned her rage inward as she stoically, blankly, dressed Nick and carried him to the car. Leaving Frieda with Aurelia, she drove the twenty-five miles to [her friend's] the Compton's. When she arrived, both Elizabeth and David were worried about her behavior; distraught, she wept and held on to Elizabeth's hands, begging 'Help me, help me.' . . . Sylvia fed Nick and the two of them spent the night in the Comptons' living room.'[22] The following day, Plath is described as returning home, and in the evening she made a pyre of Hughes's 'letters, drafts of work, and papers, and the manuscript of what was to have been her second novel, the book about her great love for Ted' (208). Biographers Ronald Hayman and Paul Alexander agree with this order of incidents, although Alexander claims that there were at least three bonfires that summer – one destroying a novel conceived as 'the sequel to *The Bell Jar*,' a second in which she burned all of Aurelia's letters to her ('upwards of a thousand') and then the third, the burning of papers from Hughes's attic study (286).[23] Stevenson oddly reverses the chronology, claiming that the phone incident occurs after the burning of the letters, and also refutes the notion that Plath burned anything of her own: 'There is no documentary evidence that such a novel existed' (*BF* 251). What provokes Plath to burn Hughes's papers is left so murky in Stevenson's narrative that it makes no sense at all:

On July 9 she and her mother drove to Exeter for a day's shopping. On the way home Sylvia exulted, 'I have everything in life I've ever wanted: a wonderful husband, two adorable children, a lovely home, and my writing.'

Days later, while Ted was in London, she invaded his attic study, hauled down what papers she could find – mostly letters – and made a bonfire in the vegetable garden. The mother watched, appalled. (250)

Adding more confusion to the motive, Stevenson then places the phone incident 'soon after the bonfire' (251). To this, Ronald Hayman adds that Aurelia 'was holding Nick and trying to keep Frieda inside the house' and 'did her best to stop Sylvia from starting a bonfire' (161).

Perhaps the best evidence for when Plath knew for certain who her rival was comes in the poem 'Words, heard, by accident, over the phone,' composed on July 11, 1962: one line reads, 'Now the room is ahiss,' suggesting the whispered intimacies between Hughes and the 'other woman,' but also Assia's name. The words in this poem are clearly feces, 'plopping like mud' from the 'bowel-pulse' of conversation, and the phone is itself a 'muck funnel' (CP 202–3). In 'Burning the Letters,' words are set on fire and become a vehicle for revenge and purgation: 'Word after word is lit!' (draft 1, 2). While the 'letters' in Plath's title refer directly to Hughes's personal correspondence, her delight in destruction extends to words and letters – to writing itself.

The first draft of 'Burning the Letters' begins on a page topped by three crossed-out lines from the first version of 'Stings [2]' about the bees 'zinging' Hughes in a June incident. The typescript for Hughes's poem 'Toll of Air Raids' is on the back, and may well have been chosen for its analogy to the air attack of the bees. Plath's last line reads, 'Watch it. You are in a cat's cradle, my love, my love, my pet.' Cat's cradle is a little girl's game, and the sense here is of flying fingers happily weaving and 'zinging' back and forth like stinging bees, with Hughes caught in the middle, tangled in knots of string.[24] Then two lines precede Plath's new title, indicating that the inspiration comes from the distinctive character of Hughes's handwriting: 'I made a fire. And your handwriting / Black & spry.' This later becomes 'And here is your handwriting, the spry hooks the lies' (draft 1, 2), and finally, 'And here is an end to the writing, / The spry hooks that bend and cringe, and the smiles, the smiles' (*CP* 204). The sense of smirking duplicity attributed to his writing, coupled with the substitution of Hughes's textual body for his actual body in the vengeance she imposes, makes Plath less the witchy voodoo queen of Roche's account than a vulgar harridan who has had enough of high culture, enough of linguistic sophistry. She wants to burn it all. The reverse of the third page of draft 1, is a typescript of Hughes's poem 'A Fable,' and the first line reads, 'A man brought to his knees in the desert' – what Plath would probably like to do to Hughes. That she conceives of his writing as a body on which she inflicts pain is evident in a line she plays with in drafts 2 through 4: 'the letters crawling, like hands on a skin of white' (draft 4) are desperately trying to escape – 'by hands & hooks,' or 'hand over hand' to crawl their way out of the fire. But the butt of her rake stirs and unfists the crumpled papers so that everything will burn in 'my little crematorium' (draft 2, 2).

One can only speculate as to why Plath chose not to include this poem in the 'Other *Ariel*.' My own suspicion is that she knew it was too low and too anti-literary. Of all the late poems, the body of his poem is the one most dependent for its meanings on knowledge of others' bodies. It is, as Freud might say, anaclitic in the way it leans on the writing body of Hughes and Assia Wevill's embodiment as burning paper. The frustrated desire in pyromania is also apparent in Plath's urge to play with the fire and to reach in and touch these paper bodies: 'My fingers would enter although / They melt and sag, they are told / *Do not touch*' (*CP* 204). The lines describing Assia confound her sexual and textual bodies, the sound of her voice and name with its signature:

And a name with black edges
Wilts at my foot,
Sinuous orchis
In a nest of root-hairs and boredom—
Pale eyes, patent-leather gutturals!
(*CP* 205)

In the image of the hairy orchid, Assia's crumpled and burning letter (invaginated folds of paper) resembles female genitals, and the hissing is both her name and the sound of the fire. In page three of draft 1, Plath misspells gutturals as 'gutterals' (a Freudian slip?), at once alluding to Assia's German accent and suggesting it belongs to a guttersnipe. As for Hughes, the poem celebrates an act of poetic arson and scorns Hughes's writing at every level – from its physical appearance to its poetic pretensions – as dissembling, pompous, and useful only as recycled scrap for her own poetic process.

According to Stevenson, this was also not the first time Plath systematically went about destroying her husband's poetic property. In a fit of jealous rage, she vandalized Hughes's work as an act of 'preemptive revenge' (206) for a liaison that never materialized except in her fantasy. Hughes was interviewed for 'a series of children's programs' early in 1961 (the same ones described earlier and including 'Capturing Animals') by a woman producer with 'a lilting Irish voice, which Sylvia instantly associated with flaming red hair and lascivious intentions.' When Hughes was late returning, and motivated only by the sound of the producer's telephone voice, Plath created 'a scene of carnage. All of his work in progress, his play, poems, notebooks, even his precious edition of Shakespeare, had been torn into small pieces, some "reduced to fluff"' (206).[25] The Shakespeare is described as 'his most treasured book,' and Stevenson goes on to claim that 'Ted could neither forget nor forgive this desecration' (206). The language suggests that Plath's crime was directed not only at her husband, but also at culture – a 'desecration' of an artist's work in progress, of a rare book, of Shakespeare. As in 'Burning the Letters,' Plath insists on venting her fury on textual bodies, literalizing poetry as a substitute victim for her husband, whom she would probably like to tear into, reduce to fluff.

This incident not only haunts 'Burning the Letters' but also seems to haunt Hughes. In *Birthday Letters*, one of the most moving poems, 'The Inscription,' revolves around 'The red Oxford Shakespeare/That she had ripped to rags when happiness/Was invulnerable' (173). After they separate, Plath visits Hughes in the fall of 1962 in his new flat in Soho. Even while begging for 'reassurance' that their marriage is not over, she jealously sniffs for evidence of his infidelity, inspecting his apartment 'Like a dog/That had seen a rat vanish, that smelt a rat' (172). Suddenly, she sees the precious volume of Shakespeare she thought she had destroyed

> Resurrected.
> Wondering, with unbelieving fingers,
> She opened it. She read the inscription. She closed it
> Like the running animal that receives
> The fatal bullet . . .
> (173)[26]

As Hughes describes Plath's wound, it is one 'she had given herself, striking at him / Had given herself' (173). The scorpion-like, self-stinging circularity returns to the original incident: if she had not shredded his Shakespeare in an effort to strike out at him, she would not suffer the fatal bullet of the inscription now, identifying a woman who has not merely replaced the book but taken her place, she fears, in her husband's affections.

Hughes also returns frequently to this image of Plath as a wild creature, often a fox like the one in 'Burning the Letters.'

Private Property

In 'The Dogs Are Eating Your Mother,' Hughes asks his children to think of the way hounds run foxes to the ground and tear them to shreds when they contemplate what hyena feminists have done to their mother's gravestone. Similarly, the moment of illumination in 'Epiphany' revolves around an opportunity he had to buy a fox cub that, in its challenge to being tamed, resembles Plath. At their first meeting, for example, she was something of a vixen who bit him and left a 'swelling ring-moat of tooth-marks / That was to brand my face for the next month' (*BL* 15). He is tempted to buy the fox cub in 'Epiphany,' but being a new father in a cramped London flat, he resists:

> What would we do with an unpredictable,
> Powerful, bounding fox?
> The long-mouthed, flashing temperament?
> That necessary nightly twenty miles
> And that vast hunger for everything beyond us?
> How would we cope with its cosmic derangements
> Whenever we moved?
> (*BL* 114)

The fox's unpredictability, its sharp temperament, and its 'derangements' all suggest an analogy to Plath's 'vast hunger' as she is portrayed in *Birthday Letters*. Only retrospectively, with regret, does Hughes recognize that he 'failed' his marriage when he turned away from the problems of raising a fox cub:

> If I had grasped that whatever comes with a fox
> Is what tests a marriage and proves it a marriage—
> I would not have failed the test.
> (*BL* 115)

Loving guardianship of a creature wild and precious, of a wife who is akin to the fox, is how he depicts his marital relationship to Plath – and his abrogation of that responsibility.

This comparison of Plath to a fox reappears in Hughes's correspondence with Anne Stevenson about *Bitter Fame*. He revisits the episode when Plath shredded his papers and Shakespeare, expressing regret for not asking Stevenson to delete 'one phrase in particular':

> When Sylvia's destruction of my papers etc. has been described, it is said 'this could never be forgotten or forgiven,' or words to that effect. . . .
>
> The truth is that I didn't hold that action against [Sylvia] – then or at any other time. I was rather shattered by it, and saw it was a crazy thing for her to have done. But perhaps I have something missing. She never did anything that I held against her. The only thing that I found hard to understand was her sudden discovery of our bad moments ('Event,' 'Rabbit Catcher') as subjects for poems. But to say I could not forgive her for ripping up those bits of paper is to misunderstand utterly the stuff of my relationship to her. It is factually untrue, in other words. So in future, in any new edition or translation, I would like to have that phrase cut out. Let the episode speak for itself.
>
> All those fierce reactions against her – which she provoked so fiercely – from people who thought, perhaps, sometimes, that they were defending me – were from my point of view simply disasters from which I had to protect her. It was like trying to protect a fox from my own hounds while the fox bit me. With a real fox in that situation, you would never have any doubt why it was biting you. (Malcolm 143)

Hughes's reluctance to understand Plath's 'sudden discovery of our bad moments' as poetic ore to be mined reflects his later editorial choices when he puts his version of *Ariel* together, deleting virtually all of the poems from the 'Other *Ariel*' that were explicitly about their bad moments. Yet Hughes also appears to be acknowledging Plath's fox in 'Burning the Letters' here – conceding its eloquence as poetic statement (if not its craft) and perhaps, ironically, its immortality over that of his own thought-fox. This may be a belated apology for the earlier hubris in the boast that he has 'captured' the fox by giving it the permanence of art in his poem. In his 1961 talk Hughes says, 'An animal I never succeeded in keeping alive [after capturing it] is the fox' (19). This is prelude, of course, to the claim he will then make that poetry is the better strategy for 'keeping alive.' A real fox, however, defies poetic sophistry. It desperately wants to escape, and in the frenzy of its capture will not abide its own survival, its own salvation, especially not at the hands of its captor. Its desperation and ferocity speak for themselves – as do Sylvia Plath's.[27]

Finally, in a 1995 poem published in the *New Yorker*, 'The Error,' Hughes provides chilling evidence that Plath's fire of July 1962 continued to burn and to inflict pain.[28] The overall conceit of the poem is that Plath's 'grave opened its ugly mouth' (156) and spoke to Assia, but that she made an 'error in translation':

> You must have misheard a sentence.
> You were always mishearing
> Into Hebrew or German
> What was muttered in English.
> (157)

The fire which yields up the name of Assia Wevill to Plath – 'The name of the girl flies out, black-edged, like a death card' (draft 1, 3) – eventually swallows up the woman herself, described as having 'selflessly incinerated yourself / In the shrine of her [Plath's] death' (157). He 'watched [Assia] feeding the flames' and once again, her life is crumpled paper:

Six full calendar years—
Every tarred and brimstone
Day torn carefully off,
One at a time, not one wasted, patient
As if you were feeding a child.
(157)

Six years after Plath's suicide, Assia Wevill killed herself and her daughter by Hughes, Shura, in a similar way to Plath, by gas and carbon monoxide asphyxiation. A discarded line from 'Burning the Letters' reads, 'This red earth loves the taste of ashes,' and following as it does the 'black-edged' name that 'presents itself' (draft 2, 2), one cannot help but hear – or mishear – the pun on Assia in 'ashes.' As Plath goes on to boast, 'I am slating the earth / It is red with women' (draft 2, 2).[29]

Like 'The Rabbit Catcher,' 'Burning the Letters' was published initially in one of Olwyn Hughes's editions of Plath's uncollected poems for the Rainbow Press titled *Pursuit* (1973). The oddity of its appearance here is that the title poem for this volume is about Plath's sexual longing for Hughes after their first meeting. '*Pursuit*' makes its first appearance in a letter Plath wrote to Aurelia on March 9, 1956 (*LH* 222–27), that devotes several rhapsodic exclamations to her love for Richard Sassoon, a lover from her Smith days: 'I am being refined in the fires of pain and love. You know, I have loved Richard above and beyond all thought; that boy's soul is the most furious and saintly I have met in this world; all my conventional doubts about his health, his frail body, his lack of that 'athletic' physique which I possess and admire, all pales to nothing at the voice of his soul, which speaks to me in such words as the gods would envy' (*LH* 223). No mention is made of her February 25 first meeting with Ted Hughes, and therefore the poem – with its epigraph from the French Racine – might be read by her mother as longing for her lover, the Parisian Sassoon. The passionate overstatement accords with the letter:

> His ardor snares me, lights the trees,
>   And I run flaring in my skin;
>   What lull, what cool can lap me in
> When burns and brands that yellow gaze?
> (*LH* 226)

Plath's *Journal*, however, makes it clear that the sexually predatory panther of 'Pursuit' is Hughes. A mutual friend tells her on March 10, 1956, that 'Ted threw stones at your window last night' (*J* 130), and she begs for his arrival:

> Please let him come . . . Please, please. . . . Oh, he is here; my black marauder; oh hungry hungry. I am so hungry for a big smashing creative burgeoning burdened love: I am here; I wait; and he plays on the banks of the river Cam like a casual faun.

> March 10. Postscript: Oh the fury, the fury. Why did I even know he was here. The panther wakes and stalks again, and every sound in the house is his tread on the stair. (*J* 131)

The final lines of 'Pursuit' echo the journal entry: 'The panther's tread is on the stairs, / Coming up and up the stairs' (*CP* 23).[30]

In an uncanny and bizarre way, then, the volume *Pursuit* commemorates the beginning and the ending of Plath's great love for Hughes. Leonard Baskin, who designed and illustrated the volume, also chose to include 'Faun,' the only previously collected poem (in *The Colossus*), as if he wanted to complement Plath's early representation of Hughes as a predatory panther with her other early depiction of him as a playful and 'casual faun,' a Pan-like creature and creator of songs. According to Stephen Tabor,' 'except for 'faun,' the poems were chosen by Olwyn Hughes,'[31] who must have known that she was producing a rather strange, even perverse homage to the Plath-Hughes partnership, its origin in sexual passion, and its end in fiery immolation. The last poem of the volume is in fact, 'Burning the Letters.'

The violence of Plath tearing a phone out of the wall and burning the contents of Hughes's study in early July might suggest that the Plath-Hughes marriage was moving rather quickly toward a crisis and dissolution, but the next two months are depicted by Plath's biographers as relatively calm and restrained. Of course, Aurelia's presence until August 4, 1962, and the desire of both Plath and Hughes to make her stay bearable, probably muted some of the discord. As described by Wagner-Martin, Plath also took advantage of her mother's presence to busy herself 'with activities directly related to her professional career' (209) as a writer – traveling to London to set up readings for the BBC, to arrange for the August broadcast of *Three Women*, to meet with a representative of the London Arts Council. Her Tablet Diary shows that she set up separate checking and savings accounts for herself, which may be read as self-protective measures, because lack of money would be one of her greatest anxieties, and her letters after Hughes leaves are peppered with extravagant (and probably false) accusations about his wild spending of their mutual earnings. After Aurelia Plath returned home to America, Plath also filled her days with visits to friends, new hobbies – horseback riding lessons and beekeeping – and caring for her children and her gardens. In the middle of August, Plath and Hughes dissembled the façade of a happy couple when they dined in London as guests of Olive Higgins Prouty, Plath's benefactress when she was a Smith scholarship student, and her financial savior when she attempted suicide in 1953 and needed intensive psychiatric care. This façade held in place long enough for a visit by Prouty on September 9 to Court Green to see the estate Plath had described to her so glowingly, and as Plath was to write to her at the end of September, a 'dream' that did not get very far (September 29, 1962, Lilly Library).

At the same time, Stevenson reports that 'by the time of Mrs Plath's departure Ted and Sylvia were considering a temporary separation in a civilized fashion' (252). To that end, Hughes accompanied Plath on a trip to Ireland (September 11–18) to assist her in finding a cottage for the winter (253). In the middle of this 'vacation,' which all of the biographers speculate Plath may have hoped would lead to a reconciliation with Hughes, he suddenly left her with their host, the poet Richard Murphy. It is not clear what provoked Hughes's sudden departure,[32] leaving Plath to 'enjoy' Ireland by herself, but what is certain is that Plath returned to Court Green with few illusions about the possibility of ignoring Hughes's frequent unexplained absences or of pretending to be in a happy marriage. After three months of hoping perhaps that 'it' would all go away, indeed, of playing the part counseled by all the popular advice columns of the day to wait patiently for the man to come to his senses and return home, Plath appears to have been ready for a confrontation and showdown. In language that echoes 'A Birthday Present,' Plath tells Aurelia that she has demanded 'the truth at last' from a leering Hughes. Tired of the bits and pieces she hears from the couple's friends, Plath wants to know the worst, but she describes a Hughes who is too cowardly to tell her everything. He cannot manage, it seems, to tell her all she wants to know (letter of October 9, 1962, Lilly Library). As early as August 27, Plath had written to Aurelia of her decision 'to try to get a legal separation from Ted. I do not believe in divorce and would never think of this, but I simply cannot go on living the degraded and agonized life I have been living, which has stopped my writing and just about ruined my sleep and my health' (*LH* 460). Anticipating the first poem she would write on September 26, 'For a Fatherless Son,' after a creative blockage lasting over a month, she tells Aurelia in the same letter that she will wait no longer for Hughes's 'chance' return, nor will she waste her best years on him. She and the children are better off without a father who 'is a liar and an adulterer and utterly selfish and irresponsible,' extravagantly throwing away their shared savings on selfish pleasures (Lilly Library). Yet she would not act on her feelings until September 25, finally seeing a solicitor in London about finalizing a separation agreement, possibly initiating divorce proceedings, and seeking an allowance from Hughes. When Hughes returned to Court Green at the end of September, Plath reportedly told him not to come back except to pack his things, and this is when Plath's poetry writing for the 'Other *Ariel*' truly begins.

'The little toy wife – / Erased, sigh, sigh'

One way of viewing Plath's decision to save all evidence of her composition and revision process is that it answers to an anguish repeatedly expressed – ironically in its most pronounced form – in several of the poems Hughes would choose to delete, to 'forget,' to consign to oblivion, at least temporarily, from the 'Other *Ariel*.' This is precisely what she fears and also believes – that she is being erased and forgotten by a husband who wears 'His high cold masks of amnesia' ('The Jailer,' *CP* 227), obliterated from consciousness by her 'Amnesiac' husband as surely as the Lyonnessians, whose

> . . . big God
> Had lazily closed one eye and let them slip
> Over the English cliff and under so much history!
> They did not see him smile,
> Turn, like an animal,

In his cage of ether, his cage of stars.
He'd had so many wars!
The white gape of his mind was the real Tabula Rasa.
('Lyonnesse,' *CP* 234)

As Sherlock Holmes, the speaker of 'The Detective' (*CP* 209),
defines the problem, 'It is a case of vaporization' so complete
that even he, the master detective, is stymied. All he can do is
tell Watson to 'Make notes,' as if the notes will make up for a
crime scene with no clues, no physical evidence. Everything,
it seems, has evaporated, and 'We walk on air, Watson.'

Writing is evidence, then, not only of the creative process but
also of her threatened existence and her suffering presence in
these poems, of her professed grievances and tortures. The
textual body comes to substitute for her actual body in
displaying her psychic wounds. As Rose theorizes this process in
the much earlier 'Poem for a Birthday,' Plath 'can be defined in
[Julia] Kristeva's terms as a writer of abjection, a writer
for whom the limits of the body and of symbolisation
are constantly worked over or put at risk,' and further, 'Plath
walks the edge, not only between the body and language but
also . . . the edge – occupied by body and language together –
between public and private space' (*Haunting* 37, 39–40).

Nowhere does this edge seem more collapsible than in 'The
Jailer.' The boundaries between textual bodies and physical
bodies here are so 'worked over' that even when the only
body 'put at risk' appears to be Plath's own, she ends the
poem by asking what her husband would do without her
body to consume and dismember, 'to eat' and 'to knife';

> What would the dark
> Do without fevers to eat?
> What would the light
> Do without eyes to knife, what would he
> Do, do, do without me?
> (*CP* 227)

Here she proposes a grim dependency of the torturer on the body he afflicts – 'Hung, starved, burned, hooked' (*CP* 227) – but earlier in the poem she is the part of his body that pleasures him, the 'Lever of his wet dreams' (*CP* 226). Similarly, despite the jailer's hidden crimes behind locked doors, Plath scoffs at his power: 'Is that all he can come up with, / The rattler of keys?' (*CP* 226).

Eventually, in fact, Plath's private abjection in 'The Jailer' would become a public scandal when feminist poet Robin Morgan identifies the jailer as Ted Hughes and charges him in 'Arraignment (I)' with torture and murder, in lines that reiterate Plath's accusations in 'The Jailer':

> I accuse
> Ted Hughes
> Of what the entire British and American
> literary and critical establishment
> has been at great lengths to deny
> (without ever saying it in so many words, of course):
> the murder of Sylvia Plath.
>
> Not that it isn't enough to condemn him
> of mind-rape and body-rape, infidelity,
> abduction and brainwashing of her
> children, plagiarism of her imagery,
> hiding of her most revealing indictments
> against her jailor
> (18)

The efforts of Random House to prevent publication of this inflammatory poem in Morgan's *Monster* only infuriated her and ensured that she would dramatize its suppression as a feminist issue. Asked by Random House lawyers to revise the poem, Morgan reluctantly did so, but published both versions in *Feminist Art Journal* with an attention-getting article about her 'political stand' (21), and continued to read both versions on public occasions.[33]

Overall, then, one might argue that Plath's persistent accumulation and careful hoarding of inscribed manuscript pages and typescripts prophetically counteracts the very threat defined in these poems of becoming 'no-one' and 'no body' ('The Detective'), or in writing terms, the persistent danger of empty pages, of textual lacunae or holes, for nothing is worse than a blank page, a 'Tabula Rasa' or 'beautiful blank,' in the case of the 'Amnesiac' husband:

> No use, no use, now, begging Recognize!
> There is nothing to do with such a beautiful blank but
>   smooth it.
> Name, house, car keys,
> The little toy wife—
> Erased, sigh, sigh.
> (CP 232–33)

Similarly, the 'The Jailer' tortures her by drugging her so that she loses consciousness for hours: 'What holes this papery day is already full of!' (CP 226). Here the day is itself like paper,[34] to be written on, not left with the 'little gimlets' her sadistic jailer makes, either by stippling her with an auger or by 'burning me with cigarettes, / Pretending I am a negress with pink paws' (CP 226).

The excised poems in which Plath seems most clearly to be ensuring that there will be a textual corpus delicti not so easily done away with as a 'little toy wife' include 'The Detective' (composed October I), 'The Courage of Shutting-Up' (composed October 2), 'A Secret' (composed October 10), 'The Jailer' (composed October 17), and 'Amnesiac' (composed October 21), which originally included 'Lyonnesse' as its second half. A literal translation of *corpus delicti* is 'the body of the offense,' and in law refers to 'the essential fact of the commission of a crime, as, in a case of murder, the finding of the body of the victim.' Together these poems have a mini-mystery plot revolving around finding evidence of a hidden domestic crime: a murder of some kind has been committed and, at least temporarily, successfully covered up; the victim has been silenced; but the secret of the crime is too titillating and too grotesque to remain undisclosed; the criminal is revealed as a sexual sadist, while the wife is his victim, imprisoned and ritualistically tortured and raped for his private pleasure. When he is done with her, he will forget: 'O sister, mother, wife, / Sweet Lethe is my life. / I am never, never, never coming home!' ('Amnesiac,' *CP* 233). As Plath finishes her composition of 'Amnesiac,' she also depletes the store of manuscript pages she has been recyling from an unpublished play by Hughes titled 'The Calm.' Hughes was at work on it during February 1961, when Plath miscarried, and as Plath describes it in a letter to Aurelia, it was intended as a 'dark opposite to Shakespeare's *Tempest*' (February 26, 1961, Lilly Library). As this description suggests, 'The Calm' might also be read as a 'dark' underside to poems that will eventually release Plath's muse, Ariel. Together, then, with portions of the typescript of *The Bell Jar* used for 'The Detective' and 'The Courage of Shutting-Up,' Hughes's manuscript for 'The Calm' is also part of Plath's corpus delicti for this group of poems.

'No-one is dead / There is no body in the house at all'

The speaker of 'The Detective,' written in anticipation perhaps of Hughes's arrival on October 4 to pack up his things, is a baffled Sherlock Holmes. He knows a woman has been murdered, but the murderer has either successfully hidden or destroyed her body. Plath's killer is slimy ('sluglike'), something of a coward, and willfully self-deceived. A bit like Macbeth ('Let the eye wink at the hand') or the murderer in Poe's story 'The Cask of Amontillado,' he is unwilling to face what his hands – his 'fingers' – have done:

> And the eyes of the killer moving sluglike and
> Unable to face the fingers, those egotists.
> The fingers were tamping a woman into a wall,
> A body into a pipe, and the smoke rising.
> (*CP* 208)

Reading metaphorically, we see that the woman has submitted to the pressure of being physically absorbed into the house's walls and furnishings: 'There is the smell of polish, there are plush carpets' (*CP* 209). Like the husband's pipe tobacco, a wife is one of his physical comforts and habits, but faceless, nameless, meant to be used and used up. The first title for the poem, 'The Millstones,' reflects Plath's growing sense of herself as a burdensome appendage to a husband who wants his freedom. In an October 9, 1962, letter to Aurelia, Plath describes a humilating confrontation with Hughes. He tells her that he can't wait to leave her; that he feels 'bored' and 'stifled' in a suffocating marriage that is depriving him of countless liaisons with women more beautiful than she – a 'hag' (Lilly Library).

Plath's insistence on the hyphenated 'no-one' in all of her manuscripts and typescripts for 'The Detective,' and the ambiguity of 'no body in the house at all,' hint at the self-erasure and self-abnegation of being the wife of a 'somebody,' a 'great man.' 'No-one' and 'nobody' do not define absence so much as an insignificant identity. He didn't need to kill the wife; she just gradually vaporized as an individual in marriage:

> The mouth first, its absence reported
> In the second year. It had been insatiable
> And in punishment was hung out like brown fruit
> To wrinkle and dry.
> (*CP* 209)

Her withering fate resembles that of another 'insatiable' literary heroine, Christina Rossetti's Laura in 'Goblin Market,' often read as a cautionary tale for women with ungovernable appetites. Laura's greedy desire and enjoyment of the goblins' fruit reflect her unwillingness to accept a feminine destiny. Only her sister Lizzie's steadfast denial of all desire and her sacrificial womanliness save Laura from shrivelling up altogether, and Laura is thereby restored to a womanly life of stay-at-home seclusion from worldly temptations. As Plath would describe this silencing reprimand in her *Journals*, it resembles Lizzie's self-denial, but is also tinged with malice directed at Hughes's presumed eminence over her: 'Write and work to please. No criticism or nagging. [Omission.] He is a genius. I his wife' (September 11, 1958, *J* 259), and 'Who else in the world could I live with and love? Nobody. I picked a hard way which has to be all self-mapped out and must *not* nag [omission] . . . (anything Ted doesn't like: this is nagging); he, of course, can nag me about light meals, straight-necks, writing exercises, from his superior seat' (September 14, 1958, *J* 258).

In 'The Detective,' more than an insatiable mouth is punished. As if the woman's absorption into the role of the silent woman – proverbially the best kind – were not enough, her breasts shrivel up next. If the mouth symbolizes here intellectual creativity, her breasts clearly represent her fertility as a woman, her ability to suckle her children, now 'vaporized,' too, for want of nurture: 'There was no absence of lips, there were two children, / But their bones showed, and the moon smiled' (*CP* 209). Plath's friend Elizabeth Sigmund reports that this was her complaint the night she flew out of the house after the phone incident: 'Then suddenly, late one evening, Sylvia arrived with Nick in his carry cot, and the change in her was appalling. She kept saying "My milk has dried up, I can't feed Nick. My milk has gone" ('Sylvia in Devon' 104). To her mother, Plath writes that Hughes desires only barren women like Olwyn and

Assia, that he fears her ability to create both as a woman producing babies and as an artist and novelist. She also hypothesizes that it is Hughes's fear that has made him vengefully isolate her in Devon, a provincial backwater where she has no opportunity to exercise her genius. This also explains why he prefers barren women, since they present no challenge to him (October 21, 1962, Lilly Library). Indeed, only a 'barren' wasteland remains for Holmes and Watson to survey and 'make notes.' After the mouth, the breasts, and finally 'the whole estate' vaporize. 'There is only the moon, embalmed in phosphorus' and 'a crow in a tree.' For Holmes, this might not be enough to solve the mystery, but for readers familiar with Plath's work, the moon is a presiding female deity who will ultimately oversee the 'perfected' and dead body of the woman in 'Edge,' and for readers who know Hughes's poetic investment in animals and folklore, the crow is his trickster figure – so clever in this instance that he has fooled Holmes and licked the platter clean of all clues.[35] In her first draft of 'The Detective,' Plath suggests that Hughes/crow may have outsmarted himself in getting rid of a woman who flattered him and sang his praises: 'Then there was no mouth at all / To polish crow's wing.'

For composition, Plath recycles leaves of typescript (on pink Smith memorandum paper) from *The Bell Jar* that show Esther Greenwood's growing cynicism toward men and romantic love. She chastises herself for stupidly needing male attention, either to 'materialize' for other women or because she is a fool for love and romance. The first episode revolves around the impact on her college dormitory friends of her receiving an invitation to the Yale Junior Prom: 'I found myself hugging the senior on watch. When she heard I was going to the Yale Junior Prom she treated me with amazement and respect. Oddly enough, things changed in the house after that. The seniors on my floor started speaking to me and every now and then one of them would answer the phone quite spontaneously and nobody made any more nasty loud remarks outside my door about people wasting their golden college days with their noses stuck in a book' (reverse, draft 1, 1). Without Buddy Willard's attentions, Esther would vaporize again for her fellow women students, just as the little wife of 'The Detective' disappears – dissolves into a 'no-one' and 'no body' – when the husband withdraws. Buddy Willard is also a complete disappointment as a romantic seducer. Instead of professing any affection for her after the prom, Buddy takes Esther to the chemistry lab – and he is a cheapskate:

> We walked very slowly the five miles back to the house where I was sleeping in the living room on a couch that was too short because it only cost fifty cents a night instead of two dollars like most of the other places with proper beds. I felt dull and flat and full of shattered visions.
>
> I had imagined Buddy would fall in love with me that weekend. (reverse draft 1, 1)

In New York City in the second episode, Esther is asked out by Constantin, a simultaneous interpreter at the UN, and immediately begins to fantasize romantically. She catches herself, however: 'There I went again, building up a glamorous picture of a man who would love me passionately the minute he met me and all out of a few prosey nothings' (reverse, draft 1, 2).

Plath's fears are present in these passages in a slightly different form. Without a husband, Plath worried that she might disappear, if not literally, then in terms of losing touch with herself as a poet and thinker, losing her place in London's literary life. She tells her mother that she must stay in England, because 'if I start running now, I will never stop. I shall hear of Ted all my life, of his success, his genius. . . . I must make a life all my own as fast as I can,' and a bit later, 'I want to have a flat in London, where the cultural life is what I am starved for' (*LH* 465, October 9, 1962). The last thing she wants is to be known as the forsaken little wife of the great man. She reports, discovering that Ted has spent the summer creating a 'secret London life,' and she accuses him again of sticking her into a 'sack' in Devon. She longs for the cultural vitality of London, a place where she can breathe again. She needs to assert her equal right to assume a place in London, not to retreat and hide, even though it is 'horribly humiliating' to be thrown away by her husband. Like Esther Greenwood about Buddy Willard, she feels 'dull and flat and full of shattered visions' about her marriage. Her sense of disillusionment and betrayal in a letter to Olive Higgins Prouty is profound – and melodramatic. She writes that Hughes sneers at her sentimental memories of their courtship, and now she grieves for a dead man, because the Ted Hughes she married is gone, replaced by a heartless villain (September 29, 1962, Lilly Library).

In 'The Courage of Shutting-Up,' this is, in fact, what the silenced and silent woman's eyes reflect: 'The face that lived in this mirror is the face of a dead man' (*CP* 210). Written the day after 'The Detective' on October 2, 'The Courage of Shutting-Up' transforms into an active virtue the passive victimization of having her mouth cut out and hung up to dry:

> The courage of the shut mouth, in spite of artillery!
> The line pink and quiet, a worm, basking.
> There are black disks behind it, the disks of outrage,
> And the courage of a sky, the lined brain of it.
> The disks revolve, they ask to be heard—
>
> Loaded, as they are, with accounts of bastardies.
> Bastardies, usages, desertions and doubleness,
> The needle journeying in its groove,
> Silver beast between two dark canyons . . .
> (*CP* 209–10)

Here the shut mouth is biding its time. Nothing has been lost or forgotten; all the husband's crimes – his 'Bastardies, usages, desertions and doubleness,' and in draft 1 (1) even the 'dates and times' when they were committed – have been recorded, 'loaded' on phonograph disks that 'ask to be heard.' Throughout, Plath creates multiple metaphorical contrivances for preserving evidentiary material. These phonograph disks are also 'the disks of the brain,' 'lined' like a ledger or a ruled piece of paper, and 'loaded' with accounts of outrage and villainy like Hamlet's tables; and the 'silver beast' of the phonograph needle is also the tattooist's needle, indelibly 'Tattooing over and over again the same blue grievances' (*CP* 210).

Plath stresses the compulsively redundant nature not only of the entry system, but also of the obsessive replaying and reiteration, as if a wrong done is never a one-time thing; it is felt by the victim as happening over and over, like a needle stuck in one groove, like the limited repertoire of the 'same blue' tattoo images. The act of suppression, although it may seem to be self-effacing, ultimately threatens explosive violence. Forced to hold in and hold back her anger through an act of self-silencing merely intensifies and accumulates the rage. Similarly, the 'underlying' narrative for the poem is about the relentless nature of painful memories. Plath chooses part of the birthing episode from *The Bell Jar* typescript, where Buddy Willard tells Esther about the drug administered to the woman in labor

that would make her forget she'd had any pain and that when she swore and groaned she really didn't know what she was doing becuase she was in a kind of twilight sleep.

I thought it sounded just like the sort of drug a man would invent. Here was a woman in terrible pain obviously feeling every bit of it or she wouldn't groan like that, and she would go straight home and start another baby because the drug would make her forget how bad

the pain had been when all the time, in some secret part
of her, that long, blind, doorless and windowless corridor
of pain was waiting to open up and shut her in again.
(reverse, draft 1, 2)

Perhaps it is this deferral of expression – whether self-
imposed or enforced as it is in this *Bell Jar* episode – that
creates such explosive potentiality.

Like the speaker in Emily Dickinson's 'My Life had stood –
a Loaded Gun,' the speaker in 'The Courage of Shutting-Up'
compares her concealed pain and anger to 'artillery' and,
later in the poem, 'the muzzles of cannon' (no. 754). Angry
speech could, if it would, kill. The tongue takes on many
lethal forms: first, it is an 'antique billhook,' a medieval
weapon that looks made for jabbing and then disemboweling
a foe; then it resembles classical monsters, although it is
hydra-tailed instead of -headed, and its tails are like razors
that scalp or flay – 'It has nine tails, it is dangerous. / And
the noise it flays from the air, once it gets going!' (*CP* 210).
Since, however, the 'courage' in this poem is self-imposed
silence,[36] a decision not to speak, the tongue

> . . . has been put by,
Hung up in the library with the engravings of Rangoon
And the fox heads, the otter heads, the heads of dead
rabbits.
It is a marvelous object—
(*CP* 210)

While not shriveled up and then vaporized, as in 'The Detective,'
the tongue is certainly not being used; hence its 'antique' status,
and the suggestion that it is gathering dust in a collection of
objets or stuffed trophies belonging to a male hunter.[37]

Although the woman has not vaporized in 'The Courage of
Shutting-Up,' her choice of silence over verbal confrontation
and attack leaves her nothing, it would seem, but stubborn

pride. Plath briefly introduces the eyes as a substitute for the tongue in offering testimony of a crime. Like mirrors that 'can kill and talk, they are terrible rooms / In which a torture goes on one can only watch' (*CP* 210). Since, however, the torture is over the loss of a man who, in some sense, has died, has ceased to exist – indeed, may never have existed as the man she loved and cared about – the eyes, too, have nothing to say, no one to kill:

> They may be white and shy, they are no stool pigeons,
> Their death rays folded like flags
> Of a country no longer heard of,
> An obstinate independency
> Insolvent among the mountains.
> (*CP* 210)

It is this final stanza that Plath appears to struggle with longest. How pathetic and forgotten and penniless should this Liechtenstein-like 'independency' be? In her first draft, it is 'waterless,' 'useless to get to,' and 'of the last century' (2), in addition to being 'no longer heard of' and 'insolvent.' 'Courage,' as it is defined here, is neither saying nor showing how hurt and humiliated one feels, how isolated and ignored, how apparently outmoded and dispensable.

'How did I get here? / Indeterminate criminal'

The week following composition of 'The Detective' on October 1, 1962, and 'The Courage of Shutting-Up' on October 2, Hughes returned to Court Green to collect his belongings, and while he was there Plath composed her bee sequence: 'The Bee Meeting' (October 3), 'The Arrival of the Bee Box' (October 4), 'Stings' (October 6), 'The Swarm' (October 7), and 'Wintering' (October 9). Hughes seems to have regarded these poems as neither violently transgressing intimate marital terrain nor attacking him personally, because he left them in *Ariel*,'[38] perhaps intuiting that they would be judged as among Plath's finest achievements. Because this sequence also forms the narrative denouement for the 'Other *Ariel*,' thus crystallizing Plath's overall design for the volume, I will reserve discussion of them for the next chapter.

Instead, let me turn to the three poems Hughes did sever from the body of the 'Other *Ariel*,' also written on parts of his textual body – the manuscript for 'The Calm,' that 'dark opposite' to *The Tempest*. Plath's appropriation of this manuscript may also be conceived as a dark opposition to her husband's writing in several ways. Not only does she write on his 'backside,' but she subverts 'the calm' of Hughes's ocean in the play, creating a swelling tempest of angry accusation on her own textual surface. Plath's muse in her birthday poem, '*Ariel*,' would be released only six days after Hughes's pages for 'The Calm' ran out. 'A Secret' written on the day after Hughes left on October 10, is the first of the excised poems drafted on 'The Calm,' followed by 'The Jailer,' composed on October 17, and 'Amnesiac,' composed on October 21, and including the half later published as 'Lyonnesse.' They are part of a series of eight poems drafted on Hughes's play, and, in Van Dyne's words, 'among them some of Plath's most devastating reappraisals of Hughes' (*RL* 9).[39]

As Plath describes the week of Hughes's stay, it is filled with angry confrontations: 'He laughs at me, insults me, says my luck is over. . . . Even my beloved bees set upon me today when I numbly knocked aside their sugar feeder & I am all over stings. Ted just gloats. Perhaps when he is gone the air will clear' (letter to Aurelia, October 9, 1962, *LH* 465). After he left, Plath may well have felt a deadly calm settling over her isolation, not unlike the atmosphere in Hughes's play. The dialogue on the reverse of Plath's first draft of 'A Secret' shows the characters' fear of being trapped forever on an isolated island, waiting for a wind to carry them home. An uncanny stillness like a vacuum governs the island, and one character tells a new arrival that calms can endure for months. The dialogue is punctuated by silences that enforce their fear. Like Shakesepare's marooned survivors in *The Tempest*, the characters of 'The Calm' find the island filled with inexplicable, perhaps supernatural phenomena – underground caves, giant crabs, a persistent moaning like a baby crying – but these mysteries are not so much magically produced as the symptoms of an absurd existential condition, altogether more like Beckett's *Waiting for Godot* or Sartre's *No Exit* than Shakespeare. Hence, the characters have no memory of how they landed on the island, and new arrivals are equally enigmatic. One character wonders if this is hell, or a classical underworld for the dead – especially since all of the characters are suffering from amnesia and there are frequent new arrivals. They hypothesize not only about where they are but also how they were 'translated' to the island. Bertha, for example, is putting a shilling in the gas meter in her cellar when suddenly, groping in the darkness, she runs into Fred. Fred, in turn, asks whether she dropped down a manhole or sneezed her way to the island ('Daddy,' draft 1, 2).40 Throughout 'The Calm,' Hughes's characters have no control over their fate. They vaguely understand their suffering as a mode of punishment, but like the speaker in 'The Jailer' who also asks, 'How did I get here?' they are 'indeterminate criminal[s]' (*CP* 227), perhaps victims like Plath's Lyonnessians of a watery god who has simply overlooked – literally – a whole civilization:

> There's where it sunk.
> The blue, green,
> Gray, indeterminate gilt
>
> Sea of his eyes washing over it
> And a round bubble
> Popping upward from the mouths of bells
>
> People and cows.
> (*CP* 234)41

Indeterminacy of crime, guilt ('gilt'), and punishment are primary in Hughes's play as well. Like the drugged and raped woman in 'The Jailer,' the husband in 'Amnesiac,' and the god in 'Lyonnesse,' Hughes's prisoners have lost their memories, their individual pasts, and now find themselves in a limbo of uncertain duration. Plath's imprisoned woman is missing 'Seven hours knocked out of my right mind' (which may refer to the seven *years* of her marriage), and declares, 'Something is gone' (*CP* 226), while Hughes's characters scramble to retrieve their lost identities. One character proposes that memory might save them from a state of oblivion that defines the existential 'calm' – the monotony of their condition. He proposes that they jog their memories, and then 'walk back along your memories to the mainland' ('Daddy,' reverse of draft 1, 2). Elsewhere, Plath too remembers an old 'self to recover, a queen,' and wonders, 'Is she dead, is she sleeping? / Where has she been . . . ?' ('Stings,' *CP* 215). Inspired perhaps by Hughes's characters, Plath conceives of survival as being restored to a former identity and finding a way to leave Court Green for the cultural 'mainland' of London.

Plath's yoking together of profound human negligence in the figure of a deserting husband with divine malice in a deus ex machina who lets the whole city of Lyonnesse sink under the sea in 'Amnesiac' may well be directly inspired by 'The Calm.' The opening line of Plath's first draft of 'Amnesiac: The Man with Amnesia' is 'No use whistling for Lyonnesse' (draft 1, 1), as if it were hopeless – don't even try, any optimism is like whistling for a long-gone dog. The 'wise' tone imitates Hughes's portrayal of Fred in 'The Calm.' Fred is convinced that they are all dead and gone, and squelches the naïve optimism of a fellow amnesiac, who believes he can prove his existence simply because he is, he exclaims, in possession of his briefcase. He excitedly points to his name under the flap as evidence of his identity: 'That's me there.' This new arrival feels supremely confident and smugly differentiates his own documented existence with the others who have no documents, no wallets or passports ('Lesbos,' reverse of draft I, 4, 5). Skeptical Fred, however, challenges all of them to prove they have places to go home to, when whole cities – like Plath's Lyonnesse – have disappeared. He challenges another character to prove that Stamford still exists, when he knows that it's at the bottom of the sea. The papers of the new arrival show that Manchester may have recently been above water, but since the ink has washed off a great deal, even Manchester may have 'dissolved.' For Fred the mainland is already a myth like Lyonnesse ('Daddy,' reverse of draft 1, 3).

Recognition is also a critical theme in both 'The Calm' and 'Amnesiac.' In the play, family ties are at least momentarily suspended by the amnesia imposed on all of Hughes's characters. When they do begin to remember their names and relationships, it turns out that they are all in the same family. In a darkly comic version of Shakespeare's joyous recognition scenes – climactic moments in all of Shakespeare's final romances, including *The Tempest* – the characters either are reluctant or refuse to embrace their nearest and dearest, and recognition does not lead to any uplift or enlightenment. When one character claims Bertha for his wife, she replies, 'Nonsense!' In the same scene, another woman defies her husband's recognition, telling him, 'I'm nobody's wife, excuse me' ('The Applicant,' reverse of draft 1, 1). Such a scene seems to be the source for Plath's opening line in 'Amnesiac,' 'No use, no use, now, begging Recognize!' (*CP* 232), and the husband who molts into a new life:

> Old happenings

> Peel from his skin.
> Down the drain with all of it!
> (*CP* 233)

Like Hughes's characters who hypothesize that they may have inadvertently dropped into the Land of the Dead, the husband in Plath's poem cheerfully proclaims, 'Sweet Lethe is my life' (*CP* 223), invoking the river of forgetfulness that carries its travelers into Hades.

The problem of recognition takes a different form in 'A Secret.' Hughes's characters grasp at evidence and documentary traces that will open up the riddle of their identities, while at least one of the two speakers in Plath's poem wants to halt the release of information: 'You are blue and huge, a traffic policeman, / Holding up one palm—' (*CP* 219). Later, this metaphor is fulfilled when the secret gets out like 'The cars in the Place de la Concorde— / Watch out!' (*CP* 220). The effort to police the discovery of a nasty secret fails completely, despite the blurry nature of the clues. At first the secret is barely discernible – like ink that has washed off – and then gradually it insists on disclosure, through a surreal series of metaphorical leaps:

> The secret is stamped on you,
> Faint, undulant watermark.
>
> Will it show in the black detector?
> Will it come out
> Wavery, indelible, true
> Through the African giraffe in its Edeny greenery,
>
> The Moroccan hippopotamus?
> (*CP* 219)

The secret is simultaneously hard to read and, as in other poems, repetitively inscribed by Plath to ensure its discovery. First, the secret is like a water line left after the tide retreats, or a watermark on paper, visible when held to the light – but often distinctive and telltale evidence. Then it is like the evidence of a lie detector test – the truth of a 'wavery' needle when a liar is graphed and betrays himself. Finally, maybe it can be seen behind the exotic animals figured in the nursery – emerging from the wallpaper,[42] or, as Marjorie Perloff reads them, from 'a child's picture book,' a 'baby's coverlet,' or 'the canopy of the crib.' For Perloff, the giveaway that it is a nursery is the 'purposely foolish rhyme' ('Two *Ariels* 322) – 'Edeny greenery.'

Later in the poem (*CP* 220) Plath divulges the 'secret' as 'an illegitimate baby,' a 'bastard' and 'dwarf baby' who forces recognition – a baby who refuses to remain hidden away. The plaintive sound of a baby crying – or what resembles a baby's cry – on the island in 'The Calm' and the knife wielded by one character to protect the food provisions are both incorporated directly in 'A Secret' as part of the bastard child's discovery. It insists on making itself known. Though it is hidden in a 'bureau drawer,' its 'breathing' is audible and 'it smells of salt cod.' Even worse, 'it wants to get out! / Look, look! It is wanting to crawl.' Ultimately, the decision is made to 'Do away with the bastard. // Do away with it altogether,' with a knife in the baby's back.

Whereas Perloff argues that the poem is about paternity and paternal recognition, specifically Hughes's supposed desire to disown his infant son Nicholas ('Two *Ariels*' 323), I would argue that this is less an issue than whether or not something vaguely obscene and deformed, a closely guarded family secret, with be revealed.[43] Plath lingers over its 'juicy' possibilities: 'A secret! A secret! How superior' (*CP* 219). Again, Plath is toying with scandal – opening up intimate marital spaces and exposing what happens between a husband and wife behind closed doors. The husband's eyes reflect 'nothing . . . but monkeys' (*CP* 219), suggesting bestial fantasies. And then there are the secret smells of spilled semen – 'salt cod' – in the lingerie drawer, an unmistakable odor that cannot be disguised with a mere 'sachet.'[44] Similarly, when the secret spills out, Plath multiplies her metaphors, from a genie in a bottle ('there goes the stopper') to a surge of traffic, to 'An exploded bottle of stout, / Slack foam in the lap' (*CP* 220), which also suspiciously resembles an ejaculation. Even though 'A Secret' was one of the poems Plath read for the BBC on October 30, 1962, it was not published until 1973 in *Pursuit*, that limited edition which extends poetically from her first love for Hughes to 'Burning the Letters.'

'I wish him dead or away. / That, it seems, is the impossibility'

Hughes's decision to excise 'The Jailer' and 'Purdah' from *Ariel* ironically tends to confirm his depiction by Plath in these two poems as obsessed with ownership, sexual privacy, and power. In response to Ronald Hayman's criticism of Hughes's frequent skirmishes with Plath's biographers, he responds, 'I hope each of us owns the facts of her or his own life. Otherwise you, reader, might suddenly find yourself reinvented by a Mr Hayman who had decided that he owns your facts and can do what he likes with them, and you could then, I assure you, spend years struggling in court with some stranger for not having restrained the new "owner."' Of course, Plath had long been relieved of such ownership – by Hughes himself, who literally owned the facts of her life – and by his self-protective behavior, 'in so far as the facts of Sylvia Plath's life are the facts of my life' (*The Independent*, April 20, 1989). For Hughes, the editorial decisions that appear to be completely personal and proprietary in motive reflect his disgust with those who would attempt to interpret 'my feelings and actions,' and a desire for truth, which has been distorted by the public's lust for smut and scandal: 'I cannot regard the kind of discussion to which our private life has been dragged as anything more than gossip' (*London Observer*, October 29, 1989). When Hughes chose to delete and defer publication of Plath's poems about him and their private life, the effect was to confirm their literal biographical truth, even tough they are *poems* – Plath's reinventions.

For Sylvia Plath, the October poems were also opposed to precisely such concealment and privacy. They were about exhumation – dragging her father from his grave, dredging up the past for inspection and exorcism – and about violating taboos against self-exhibition. Making her private life and feelings public is exactly what Plath dared to do. At the top of her manuscript for 'Purdah,' Plath has inscribed the dictionary definition and derivation from Hindu and Persian ('Hind. & Per.'): 'Purdah = veil. curtain or screen. India. to seclude women' (draft 1, 1). If 'The Jailer,' written twelve days earlier, is about the impossibility of being free from sexual enslavement and seclusion behind closed doors, 'Purdah,' composed on October 29, is Plath's effort to break free from sexual possession.[45] Although the woman is supposed to be owned by the man – 'I am his. / Even in his // Absence' (*CP* 243) – by the end of the poem, a lioness, the outraged mother of Iphigenia, Clytemnestra, is unloosed to confront the returning Agamemnon, a 'bridegroom' and 'Lord of the mirrors!' (*CP* 242):

> I shall unloose—
> From the small jeweled
> Doll he guards like a heart—
>
> The lioness,
> The shriek in the bath,
> The cloak of holes.
> (*CP* 244)

The mere wishing of the male possessor dead or away in 'The Jailer' has now materialized into active vengeance.

It is virtually impossible not to read Hughes's decision to purge the 'Other *Ariel*' of these poems as self-defensive.

Who wants to be seen as the husband of 'Lies and smiles' (*CP* 226), who wears an 'armor of fakery' (*CP* 227) in 'The Jailer'? Here, Hughes is depicted as unavailable, deceiving, and masked.[46] Or even worse in some ways is the vain 'Lord of the mirrors' (*CP* 242), whose boudoir reflects only his own existence and sexual potency, to which the silenced, purdahed woman is merely an accessory. Plath challenges two of Hughes's frequently stated values here: the refusal to be her husband's private property challenges Hughes's ownership of the facts of Plath's life, and by extension the facts of his own shared life with her; and the stripping away of the veil from her mouth is a violation of his marital privacy and the silence in which he would have preferred their relationship to be shrouded for thirty-five years.

'And suddenly / Everybody knew everything'

If the excised poems are, as I have argued, Plath's marital corpus delicti, the evidence for supposed crimes against her by Hughes, for him they are the utterances of 'Your Aztec, Black Forest / God of the euphemism Grief' (*BL* 191). Grief was her excuse to divulge everything about her life and a euphemism for an idol appeased only by bloody offerings. One of Hughes's major themes in *Birthday Letters* is that Plath's prolonged mourning for Otto Plath turned viciously and mistakenly into a demand for human sacrifice that eventually included him, their children, and her mother.[47] Long before she composed the *Ariel* poems, Hughes believes 'The Machine' of tragedy was already set in motion. In the poem by this name he describes the as yet 'unwritten poems' where she would attack 'Mummy-Daddy' as a 'juggernaut' grinding its wheels toward him and then mowing down both 'My children. And my life' (*BL* 25). Similarly, in 'The Blackbird,' an outright rebuttal of Plath's 'The Jailer,' he is not her sadistic torturer but a companion fellow sufferer in the jail she – not he – insisted on building to keep her murderer alive and close by:

> You were the jailer of your murderer—
>   Which imprisoned you.
> And since I was your nurse and protector
>   Your sentence was mine too.
> (*BL* 162)

As her loving guardian, he 'never gave a thought' to what would eventually be written on 'the pristine waiting page' – 'a prison report' in which Plath made him both her jailer and her murderer – giving up all culpability for her fate.

As Hughes envisions what happened, Plath never rose poetically to the challenge of addressing her loss, which might have performed the miracle of rebirth and resurrection they struggled as partners to achieve for her, as in 'Suttee.' Sacrifice was her alternative, an exchange of death for life, and specifically for artificial life 'In the bronze of immortal poesy' ('The Cast,' *BL* 179). Several poems in *Birthday Letters*, I believe, reprove Plath for achieving public fame and only fleeting freedom from her own pain at the cost of inflicting lasting wounds on others in her verse. Hence, in 'The Cast,' her own 'cry of deliverance / Materialised in [her father's] / Sacrificed silence,' and

> Healed you vanished
> From the monumental
> Immortal form
> Of your injury: your Daddy's
> Body full of your arrows.
> (179–80)

Similarly, in 'The God,' the poetic story she creates and embellishes in October is a gruesome offering to a god who is nothing more than her own 'panic of emptiness' (*BL* 188). In worship to this god, Plath made sure that 'Everybody knew everything' (190). At first her 'little god' is suckled with blood from her nipples, but as it grows, so does its appetite, only satiated with 'Two handfuls of blood' (189) from her and in it 'gobbets' of his flesh. Later it grows into a 'fiery idol' (189), with a furnace-like maw needing to be fed

> . . . with the myrrh of your mother
> The frankincense of your father
> And your own amber and the tongues
> Of fire told their tale.
> (190)[48]

All of these poems admonish Plath for her 'screams / Of the mourner,' 'A scream stuck in a groove – unstoppable' (*BL* 148). For Hughes, Plath's mourning verses are neither just nor cathartic; they provide no lasting relief from grief, but, as with the impact of her suicide on those she left, the guilt and sadness are everlasting. Her mourning, then, is fueled by rage – or, as in 'Blackbird,' 'You fed your prisoner's rage' (*BL* 162).

'The fingerprints inside what you had done'

Many of Hughes's *Birthday Letters* also converse bitterly with Plath's fears of being 'no-one' and 'nobody' in the deleted poems. The textual corpus at Smith, with its multitude of drafts and under-writings, offers multiple modes of evidentiary inscription to ensure full discovery and recovery of 'the body of the offense' against her. The excised poems are especially embedded with Plath's anxieties about being, metaphorically, a missing person once she loses her identity as the wife to poet Hughes. For Hughes, however, her anxiety, like her jealousy, was a projection of other insecurities and led to disclosures tainted by her fears. Like the 'panic of emptiness,' a writer's block out of which her grim and implicitly false tale (he describes it as 'A story of which I knew nothing') emerges in 'The God,' writing is itself the 'terror' in 'Apprehensions' (140). Hughes insists that, instead of her fear of erasure, of being silenced or forgotten, which writing of and on her body (as in tattooing, bodily torture) and his textual body was meant to counteract, writing was itself the progenitor of all her insecurities. Remembering her study, he tells her, 'This fear was the colour of your desk-top' and made a noise like a typewriter,' and its 'favourite place' was her Shaeffer pen:

> The swelling terror that would any moment
> Suddenly burst out and take from you
> Your husband, your children, your body, your life.
> You could see it, there, in your pen.
>
> Somebody took that too.
> (140)

As the final line reminds her, and us, she foolishly gave away, both literally and metaphorically, everything and everyone, including herself, in her jealous fear of having them taken – being dispossessed.

Furthermore, if there was any mystery of disappearance or loss of identity, for Hughes it lay in the ease with which Plath relinquished her agency and voice as a writer to perform for and to please – even pander to – others. In 'Blood and Innocence,' she willingly endures shock treatments because 'They demanded it. No problem' (168); then 'they' want her to come back from her suicide attempt so long as she doesn't mind a poetic reconstructive surgery that is monstrous: 'Yourself by Frankenstein, stiff-kneed, / Matricidal, mask in swollen plaster' (168).[49] Still 'they' want more – the corpse of her father – and she is eager to oblige: 'Why on earth didn't you say. / Daddy unearthed' (168) in order for her to 'howl' her childhood loss and then avenge it by killing him again and dancing on his grave. 'They' are never identified, but at times resemble the doctors who, in Hughes's view, mismanaged her electroshock therapy and then patched her back together with Freudian theory, who encouraged her to 'kill' her mother and father so that she might be 'born again.' At other times 'they' are Plath's audience, the 'peanut-crunching crowd' of 'Lady Lazarus' who are thrilled by the show she is willing to put on for the sake of 'some acknowledgement.' They are 'Grinning squabbling overjoyed' (169) at the carnage she performs, in complicity with readers who want something juicy, all the gruesome details. For Hughes, these are betrayals meant to make her somebody in the eyes of the world, and they backfire. At the end, she is alone in a 'gilded theater,' surrounded with 'The faces faces faces faces / Of Mummy Daddy Mummy Daddy' (169) – with accusing reflections of her guilt.

When Plath is not prostituting her talent and maligning her family for the sake of approval and fame, she is manipulated by forces outside her control. In both 'The Ventriloquist' and 'The Hands,' Hughes portrays Plath as, in some sense, 'being spoken' by another in a macabre horror story. Hence in 'The Ventriloquist' (181), her poetic persona is a dummy or 'doll' who steals her voice. 'With her scream a whip,' this doll shrieks slanderous accusations 'to the world': 'Daddy was no good'; her Mummy is a sea monster, 'The Kraken of the seas'; and Hughes 'was with a whore.' The doll finally kills Plath so that the only voice left belongs to it: an artificed dummy-self, a persona Plath conjured into life for specific occasions of invented hate speech, finally assumes Plath's whole identity to the world and for all time. All evidence of the real woman – presumably the woman he loved – is gone in this gothic senario, a casualty of Plath's investment in the doll, who is left eternally shrieking her demands for justice.

Finally, in 'The Hands' (184–85), Hughes claims that he does not hold Plath responsible for the poems or 'last-stand letters' she wrote that were clearly meant to hurt him: 'those words you struck me with / That moved so much faster than your mouth / And that still ring in my ears.' Plath was only the gloves worn by 'Two immense hands' controling events.[50] Because these hands 'dandled' her infancy and 'positioned' her in the crawl space where she first attempted suicide, they probably belong to Otto Plath, the Daddy she died to get back to, the father she elevated into a god worthy of her sacrifice. Unlike all the evidentiary material Plath leaves behind, the only clue that the entire tragedy is the father's handiwork – from her rage-filled poems, to her suicide, even to Hughes's numb 'doing' of what the hands 'needed done' after her death – are his 'fingerprints / Inside empty gloves, these, here, / From which the hands have vanished.' What is finally imprinted in Plath's best-known poem, then, are the indelible marks of the father's hands, reaching out beyond his own death to control his daughter. These fingerprints are also labyrinthine whorls in Hughes's myth-laden poems, leading his reader with Plath to the minotaur and the 'horned, bellowing / Grave of your risen father' (120).

'You never knew / How I listened to our absence'

While many of Hughes's *Birthday Letters* address Plath critically as a poet of sacrificial grief, an equal number are valuable for what they add to incidents described in her letters and journals. The *St. Botolph's Review* party where they first met, their courtship and marriage are all poetically memorialized in *Birthday Letters* and collaborate with Plath's own youthful romantic exhilaration in their marital narrative, what Hughes names 'Your story. My story' (9), in one poem. 'Chaucer,' for example, looks back nostalgically on an incident Plath relates to her mother in *Letters Home*. It is during the first year of her marriage to Hughes, when Plath is finishing her studies at Cambridge:

> Got up at 4:30 a.m. this day with Ted and went for a long walk to Granchester before settling down to writing. I never want to miss another sunrise. First, the luminous blue light, with big stars hanging; then pinkness, spreading, translucent, and the birds beginning to burble and twit from every bramble and bush; owls flying home. We saw over fifteen rabbits feeding. I felt a peace and joy, being all alone in the most beautiful world with animals and birds. . . . We began mooing at a pasture of cows, and they all looked up, and, as if hypnotized, began to follow us in a crowd of about twenty across the pasture to a wooden stile, staring, fascinated. I stood on the stile and, in a resonant voice, recited all I knew of Chaucer's *Canterbury Tales* for about twenty minutes. I never had such an intelligent, fascinated audience. You should have seen their expressions as they came flocking up around me. I'm sure they loved it! (April 8, 1957, *LH* 307)

Hughes recreates this episode as one of humorously mutual possession by a 'rapt' Plath and her 'enthralled' bovine audience. Everything conspires in the poem to magnify the joy of her high-spirited performance:

> > –you declaimed Chaucer
> To a field of cows. And the spring sky had done it
> With its flying laundry, and the new emerald
> Of the thorns, the hawthorn, the blackthorn,
> And one of those bumpers of champagne
> You snatched unpredictably from pure spirit.
> (51)

This may not be 'the true, the blushful Hippocrene' Keats invokes for inspiration in "Ode to a Nightingale,' but Plath is similarly depicted as a celebrant of poetry's powers, inspired by a 'pure spirit' native to her own, claiming kinship with Chaucer's Wife of Bath, a vital and earthy woman. What has often been regarded as Plath's cloying and habitual gushing to her mother in *Letters Home* – and therefore highly suspect as revelation of Plath's character – is transformed by Hughes into admiration for her hypnotic powers: the cows 'shoved and jostled shoulders, making a ring, / To gaze into your face, with occasional snorts' as if to applaud her performance (51). His memory lapses at the end of the poem, as the tone shifts from admiration to bafflement and description gives way to emotional over-fullness: 'What followed / Found my attention too full / And had to go back into oblivion (51–52). 'What followed' with the cows remains obscure and forgotten, but so does 'what followed' between him and Plath, even though it absorbed all of his attention. Does he draw the curtain on a scene of marital intimacy? Did they make love? The plenitude of his own admiration for her is apparent in the immortality of her recitation, 'already perpetual.'

Equally striking moments of narrative collaboration and conversation with Plath are Hughes's poem-letters informing her of what he did not tell her at the time, or reflecting on moments when he erred. Because Hughes is rueful, apologetic at these places, it is as if he were trying to 'meet your voice / With all its urgent future' (9), to tell her what might have been, what they would have eventually shared as marital troubles in a common past, not portents of disaster. In 'The Inscription,' for example, he realizes that 'he reeled when he should have grabbed' (173) when she came to visit him in Soho, mistakenly letting her go. A series of poems about their decision to buy Court Green and to embrace the virtues of country life in England are especially self-chastising and reveal that a major source of tension in their marriage was Plath's homesickness for America, her disgust with the ugliness of the English countryside. In 'Stubbing Wharfe,' 'Error,' and 'The Lodger,' Hughes portrays himself as foolhardy, overconfident that he could offer his American wife, a 'pioneer / In the wrong direction' (106), a paradisal garden, a miracle of quaint device:

> 'These side-valleys,' I whispered,
> 'Are full of the most fantastic houses,
> Elizabethan, marvelous, little kingdoms,
> Going for next to nothing. For instance
> Up there opposite – up that valley –'
> My certainty was visionary,
> Waiting there, on its walled terrace – an eyrie
> Over the crevasse of trees and water.
> You had no idea what I was talking about.
> (107)

Nor, as it turned out, did Hughes, as he describes 'The labyrinth / Of brambly burrow lanes' (123) that is their village in 'Error,' and even worse, the snoopy villagers with the stature of dwarves:

> Bundled women—
> Stump-warts, you called them—
> Sniffing at your strangeness in wet shops.
> Their eyes followed you everywhere, loamy badgers,
> Dug you out of your sleep and pawed at your dreams,
> Jabbered hedge-bank judgements, a dark-age dialect,
> Peered from every burrow-mouth.
> (123)

While Hughes may accuse Plath of betrayals in her poems, he is equally hard on himself for making her life miserable by bringing her to Devon. Plath is stripped of her 'American royalty, garment by garment' (122), and sentenced to a place of utter 'desolation,' as it is depicted by Hughes: overgrown by weeds, mired in mud, a constant rain dripping through their thatched roof. Because so much depended on 'A house of our own / Answering all your problems was the answer / To all my problems' (107), Hughes could not confide his own fears to Plath – hypochondriac fears that he would die of a heart attack in the effort to create a paradisal garden. In 'The Lodger' he admits telling her nothing of his sense of impending doom, of the diary he keeps to record his 'heart's errata' (125), and doing nothing in his new study but imagining 'all the ways a heart can kill its owner' (126). Afraid that he has no more music, no more poetry in him, he describes himself as 'already a discard' and 'already posthumous.' Finally, in 'Robbing Myself' (165–67), he describes his clandestine return to Devon after Plath and their children move to London – 'A ghostly trespasser' in 'The house made newly precious to me / By your last lonely weeks there, and your crying' (166). Twice Hughes calls the house a 'casket.' Despite its emptiness and silence, the 'safe casket' is strangely comforting as uncanny evidence for the woman he believes is his still. Plath's absence is like a jewel being worn for a while, not stolen; eventually it will be returned, 'Tight as a plush-lined casket / In a safe.' As he tells her at poem's end, '(I did not know) / I had already lost the treasure.'

'He slid into me'

Although virtually all of Hughes's *Birthday Letters* are embedded with signs and portents of eventual disaster taken from everywhere – from classical myth to astrology to gypsies and Ouija boards – I would like to examine two 'letters' that specifically address the psychoanalytic narrative which Plath constructed while in therapy and imposed on her marriage to Hughes. For Hughes, I would argue, the Freudian story was catastrophic. With its fatal insistence on the daughter's incestuous desire for the dead father, this fiction menaced their marriage and instilled Plath's poetic symbolism with a morbid paternal influence. As he describes himself in a poem published in another volume, *Howls and Whispers*, he is 'Electra's husband,' and 'Gossip has it / He's a befogged buffoon' who 'can't make out / What's eating his wife' ('The Hidden Orestes').[51] Furthermore, he claims ignorance and innocence of the role she cast him in, portraying himself as an unknowing and unwilling actor in a psycho-drama that took shape for Plath in 1958–59, the year they spent in Boston attempting to earn their livelihood solely by writing. Both 'Black Coat' (*BL* 102–3) and 'The Rag Rug' (BL 135–37) return to this year and are about 'what went wrong' – in 'Black Coat,' how Hughes became the villain in Plath's psychobiography, his identity confused with Otto Plath's ('He slid into me' [103]), and in 'The Rag Rug,' how they came to lose 'our Eden' (137), largely because of the 'tapeworm of the psyche' (135) she pulled out of herself in psychoanalysis. These are also 'letters' to his wife which respond specifically to poems and journal entries by Plath, once again extending the marital dialogue.

Plath's year in Boston was devoted in part to psychoanalytic therapy with Ruth Beuscher, the psychiatrist she came to know and trust during her first breakdown and suicide attempt in 1953, and the *Journals* from this period are filled with self-interrogations that implicate Hughes as a scapegoat for unresolved feelings toward Otto Plath:

I identify him with my father at certain times, and these times take on great importance: e.g., that one fight at the end of the school year when I found him not-there on the special day and with another woman. I had a furious access of rage. He knew how I love him and felt, and yet wasn't there. Isn't this an image of what I feel my father did me me? I think it may be. The reason I haven't discussed it with Ted is that *the situation hasn't*

come up again and it is not a characteristic of his: I would
feel wronged in my trust on him. It was an incident only
that drew forth echoes, not the complete withdrawal of
my father, who deserted me forever. . . . Ted, insofar as
he is a male presence, is a substitute for my father: *but in
no other way.* Images of his faithlessness with women
echo my fear of my father's relation with my mother
and Lady Death. (J 278–79; my italics)

Plath seems fully aware here of how she is 'exploiting' Hughes
to work through feelings about her father – that the rage she
felt toward her husband was misdirected and meant for her
dead father. Awareness, however, did not prevent 'the furious
access of rage,' and, once made, the transference between Otto
Plath and Hughes, on the basis of a shared 'faithlessness with
women,' presages the disastrous rage of 1962, well grounded
in Hughes's real, not imagined, infidelity.

In 'Black Coat,' Hughes claims ignorance of the
transference Plath imposed, compared by Hughes to sniper
fire or the snapshots of paparazzi for the tabloid press.[52]
Oblivious to his wife's 'projection' (103) of the father's
identity onto him, he was only engaging in a simpler kind of
'therapy' of his own when she caught him in her 'sights.' In
silent communion with the sea, he has no words:

> My shoe-sole shapes
> My only sign.
> My minimal but satisfying discussion
> With the sea.
> (102)

Hughes extols the scene as one where writing and the
meanings created by writing are 'minimal,' even absent, he
and the sea together are 'one big tabula rasa,' and his
footprints, easily washed away, are his 'only sign' of presence.
Even as Hughes is claiming the virtues of erasure in this

confrontation with the sea – that is, the proverbial sense of human diminishment before a mighty natural force – Plath's gaze insists on appropriating his image for her own, perhaps unconscious, meanings, and she inscribes his tabula rasa with paternal signification:

> How that double image—
> Your eye's inbuilt double exposure,
> Which was the projection
> Of your two-way heart's diplopic error—
> The body of the ghost and me the blurred see-through
> Came into single focus,
> Sharp-edged, stark as a target
> Set up like a decoy
> Against that freezing sea
> From which your dead father had just crawled.
> (103)

The 'sharp edges' which signify the distinctness of being 'simply myself' in the first part of the poem serve only to make him a good 'target' and 'decoy' for embodying Plath's dead father at the poem's end. Hughes implies that from this moment on, he will be as much the ghost of her dead father as her living husband.

'Black Coat' is in dialogue with Plath's poem 'Man in Black,' but also with her journals for the spring of 1959, where she describes the poem's genesis, if not its inspiration, in an emotionally cathartic visit to Winthrop and her father's grave: 'My temptation to dig him up. To prove he existed and really was dead. How far gone would he be? No trees, no peace, his headstone jammed up against the body on the other side. Left shortly. It is good to have the place in mind' (Monday, March 9, *J* 298). The visit, because it is therapeutically 'fruitful,' indirectly releases Plath from creative blockage to write 'Man in Black,' a poem she describes as 'the only "love" poem in my book, and the 'book poem' which I wrote only a little over a month ago on one of my fruitful visits to Winthrop. Must do justice to my father's grave.' Initially, the link between her father's grave and 'Man in Black' is coincidental, but then a few lines later she realizes a stronger bond between her 'love' poem and her dead father: 'The "dead black" in my poem may be a transference from the visit to my father's grave' (Thursday, April 23, *J* 300). What Plath does here is to dress Hughes in her father's coat. In 'Man in Black,' Hughes's image in the 'black coat' ('Black Coat,' *BL* 102) against the ocean and shore is what pulls the poem formally together:

> And you, across those white
>
> Stones, strode out in your dead
> Black coat, black shoes, and your
> Black hair till there you stood,
> Fixed vortex on the far
> Tip, riveting stones, air,
> All of it, together.
> (*CP* 119–20)

What Plath means by 'love' here is more aesthetic than romantic. The figure in black is a centering axle, a violent, 'riveting' source of centripetal energy, and virtually identical with writing, with the bold stroke of black on white paper.

Hughes contradicts this moment of intense focus in his own poem, claiming he was only a 'blurred see-through' for bringing 'the body of the ghost' (*BL* 103) into view. His insistence, too, on Plath's 'two-way heart' and her 'double image,' her 'double exposure' and 'diplopic error,' refutes the persistent charges in her poems that Hughes is a master of smiling pretense, charming duplicity, and dishonesty. In her projections on the world, she is the source of the doubleness she perceives, not he. Hughes also moves beyond the original transference of 1959 to its eventual climax in the marital disputes of 1962 when he alludes to Plath's unfinished and unpublished second novel *Double Exposure*, the one that Hughes tells us 'disappeared somewhere around 1970' (*JP* 1). As Plath describes it to Olive Higgins Prouty, its title will be 'Double-take,' about taking a second look and finding a hidden meaning. She also tells Prouty it is 'semi-autobiographical' and follows a wife's terrible awakening to her husband's infidelities, made worse by virtue of her original idolization of him. She thought he was 'perfect,' but now sees him as a 'deserter and philanderer' (letter of November 20, 1962, Lilly Library). He is the victim of Plath's need for 'deeper, double' meanings, not their source. In its photographic imagery, Hughes's 'Black Coat' also returns to the moment of jealous rage that ended Plath's year of teaching at Smith:

> Ted was coming up the road from Paradise Pond, where girls take their boys to neck on weekends. He was walking with a broad, intense smile, eyes into the uplifted doe-eyes of a strange girl with brownish hair, a large lipstick grin, and bare thick legs in khaki Bermuda shorts. I saw this in several sharp flashes, like blows. I could not tell the color of the girl's eyes, but Ted could, and his smile, though open and engaging as the girl's was, took on an ugliness in context. His stance next to Van Voris [a lecherous professor at Smith] clicked into place, his smile became too white-hot, became fatuous, admiration-seeking. (Monday, May 19, 1958, *J* 232)

With a sudden 'click' or 'several sharp flashes,' like the 'shots' of a 'paparazzo sniper,' Hughes is caught in a pose of all too familiar male vanity, eagerly solicitous of female adoration – at least from Plath's perspective. He loses his identity in what Plath regards as a tiresome tradition in academia, at least at Smith: she has just described Van Voris in a booth with an admiring young woman student, eagerly 'sniffing, inhaling the daisies in his own field' as he impresses her with his knowledge of Restoration drama (*J* 230), and then remembers, 'I could see Al Fisher [one of Plath's favorite teachers when she attended Smith], sitting in the same seat [as Van Voris], and me opposite, that official sexual rapport. Al Fisher and his dynasties of students: students made mistresses. Students make wives' (Monday, May 19, 1958, *J* 231). What Hughes depicts, then, in 'Black Coat,' is his victimization by Plath's psychological need to transform all of her mentors into faithless father figures, and thereby targets and decoys for her rage.

Hughes's other version of 'what went wrong' between them, 'The Rag Rug,' burrows from fairy tale in its figuration but is firmly based on an actual rug Plath started braiding while they were in Boston. The rug eventually comes to embody their alienation. It is a monstrous and poisonous serpent, a 'mamba' that destroys their prelapsarian innocence.[53] Coiled between them on the floor, the rag rug 'found its tongue, its fang, its meaning' and 'survived our Eden' (*BL* 137). Hughes returns to that year in Boston, a year when he and Plath were also trying to conceive a child, and conflates this time with their move to Devon. In her *Journals*, Plath explicitly associates the rag rug with her desires for a baby and a conventional feminine role:

Amazingly happy afternoon with Shirley [a woman friend and young mother] yesterday. Took subway out. Smoky day, smoke white against snow-filled sky, smoke gray-black against pale twilight sky coming back. Brought my bundle of woolens and began to make the braided rug: immense pleasure cutting the good thick stuggs, wrestling with the material and getting a braid begun. Talked easily about babies, fertility, amazingly frank and pleasant. Have always wanted to 'make something' by hand, where other women sew and knit and embroider, and this I feel is my thing. John sat in his high chair, Shirley fed and bathed and bedded him, very easily. He was loving to me, hugging me and rubbing his forehead against mine. Felt part of young womanhood. (Wednesday, January 28, 1959, *J* 293)

Plath alludes here to her problems with fertility. She is having difficulty conceiving and fears she will be deprived of this womanly experience:

I will enter in to the horrible clinical cycle of diagramming intercourse, rushing to be analyzed when I've had a period, when I've had intercourse. Getting injections of this and that, hormones, thyroid, becoming something other than myself, becoming synthetic. My body a test tube. 'People who haven't conceived in six months have a problem, dearie,' the doctor said. And, taking out the little stick with cotton on the end from my cervix, held it up to his assistant nurse: 'Black as black.' If I had ovulated it would be green. . . . Suddenly the deep foundations of my being are gnawn. I have come, with great pain and effort, to the point where my desires and emotions and thoughts center around what the normal woman's center around, and what do I find? Barrenness. (Saturday, June 20, 1959, *J* 310)

In contrast, a 'rug-braided mood' is 'very sleepy, as after a good love-making' (*J* 307).

As these associations between womanliness, babies, and feminine creativity are played out in Hughes's poem, however, they are lethal to the intimacy between husband and wife. Plath's need to feel grounded, womanly, 'normal,' is acknowledged in Hughes's 'You needed an earth' (*BL* 135), but her need for a child, to give birth, is quickly burdened with other intentions relating to her psychoanalytic therapy. She needed 'To pull something out of yourself – / Some tapeworm of the psyche' (135). He watches her slice her old clothes and plait them

> Into a rope. You massaged them
> Into the new life of a motley viper
> That writhed out of the grave
> Of your wardrobe. Like the buried wrapping
> Of old mummy non-selves.
> (135)

Here the rug-braiding symbolizes Plath's need for psychological catharsis – purging a tapeworm gnawing at her from within – and creating a 'new life,' but a 'new life' that is far from benign: 'a motley viper / That writhed.' The 'old mummy non-selves' may also refer to Plath's efforts to break free from maternal influence while in therapy. Her therapist helps to relieve her of the guilt she feels in her hostility toward Aurelia:

> Ever since Wednesday I have been feeling like a 'new person.' Like a shot of brandy went home, a sniff of cocaine, hit me where I live and I am alive and so-there. Better than shock treatment: 'I give you permission to hate your mother.'
>   . . . So I feel terrific. In a smarmy matriarchy of togetherness it is hard to get a sanction to hate one's mother especially a sanction one believes in. I believe in R. B. [Ruth Beuscher] because she is a clever woman who knows her business & I admire her. She is for me 'a permissive mother figure.' I can tell her anything, and she won't turn a hair or scold or withhold her listening, which is a pleasant substitute for love. (Friday, December 12, 1958, *J* 265–66)

Innocent of the eventual outcome of her rug-braiding, Hughes casts himself as fostering this 'new life' because 'It claimed you / Creating the serpent that coiled / Into a carpet' (135), and

> Whenever you worked at your carpet I felt happy.
> Then I could read Conrad's novels to you.
> Then I could cradle your freed mind in my voice,
> Chapter by chapter, sentence by sentence,
> Word by word: 'Heart of Darkness,'
> 'The Secret Sharer.'
> (135–36)

As the word 'cradle' suggests, Hughes thinks of himself as mothering her 'freed mind,' and the 'heaped coils' are like a new umbilical cord being plaited between them.[54] The allusions to Conrad, however, imply a destructive core to this womb-like intimacy in 'that crimson room of our cardiac days' (135), but only later in the poem does he question his naïveté about their closeness:

> Was I the child or the mother? Did you braid it,
> That umbilicus between us,
> To free yourself from my contraction or was it
> Pushing me out and away?
> (136)

The sense throughout 'The Rug Rag' is that Plath creates something that destroys the marriage from within. She 'Unearthed something deeper than our verses' (136) that pulls her away from him like the other half of a 'broken magnet' (136), and the rug, when finished, is imbued with 'A drooled curse / From some old bitter woman's rusty mouth' (136) that ensures the final alteration in their relationship:

> Its gentle tap, when you trod on it for finality,
> Would alter your blood. When I stepped over it
> Would alter my nerves and brain.
> (137)

It is hard not to read these lines as encoded with his avoidance, his desire to step 'over' the permanence of their marriage vows. For Plath this was 'a hearth rug,' a symbol of 'finality' and the product of a womanly kind of activity. Despite Hughes's profusion of fairy-tale and serpent images and the depiction of rug-making as a metaphor for her psychoanalytic therapy—

> Your diary confided to whomever
> What furies you bled into that rug.
> As if you had dug and dragged it, like your own entrails,
> Out through your navel.
> (136)

the rug also seems to embody Plath's simple desire to give birth, to be a mother. The snake's final appearance in Hughes's poem is from the well in their house, and it is, in fact, a birth of sorts: 'A golden serpent, thick as a child's body / Eased from the open well' (137). Whether intended or not, then, Hughes confirms Plath's sense that children are what finally pulled them apart, that, as she wrote to Aurelia, he preferred barren women to her and feared being trapped in marriage and domesticity (October 21, 1962, Lilly Library). She describes her desire for a baby in her *Journals*:

> And for a woman to be deprived of the Great experience her body is formed to partake of, to nourish, is a great and wasting Death. After all, a man need physically do no more than have the usual intercourse to become a father. A woman has 9 months of becoming something other than herself, of separating from this otherness, of feeding it and being a source of milk and honey to it. To be deprived of this is a death indeed. And to consummate love by bearing the child of the loved one is far profounder than any orgasm or intellectual rapport. (Sunday, May 21, 1962, *J* 308)

Private Property

As Hughes depicts Plath's rug-braiding, it is an act of 'becoming something other than herself,' but primarily other to him. His baffled query about this umbilicus – does it free her or push 'me out and away'?— reflects, perhaps, an intuition that having children would create a rift in their extraordinary intimacy, profoundly separating them both sexually and in their 'intellectual rapport.'

THREE

A Late Winter Miracle

Will the hive survive, will the gladiolas
Succeed in banking their fires
To enter another year?
What will they taste of, the Christmas roses?
The bees are flying. They taste the spring.

Sylvia Plath, 'Wintering'

Christmas Rose. A late winter miracle, *Helleborus niger*
blooms as early as February, undaunted even by a crust
of snow. Hard to find in nurseries due to its reputation
for fussiness (undeserved except when carelessly
transplanted), this evergreen perennial produces divided
leaves and cup-shaped, nodding white flowers.

Smith & Hawken catalog, 1995

Viewed from a biographical perspective, the narrative of
Plath's 'Other *Ariel*' begins with the conception and birth
of her daughter Frieda on April 1, 1960, and ends with the
anticipated blooming of Christmas roses in February 1963,
when Plath hoped for a late winter miracle: she would be
successfully transplanted from her home in the country and
settled with daughter Frieda and son Nicholas in a London
flat. She would 'taste the spring' of a new life without Ted
Hughes. As she writes to her friend Marcia Plumer – 'Dearest

Marty' – on February 4, 1963, she was hurled out of the 'cow-like bliss' of nursing the infant Nicholas by Hughes's desertion. Refusing to remain stuck in Devon, she 'fought' her way back to London, faced the gossipmongers and the humiliation, and now she can move on, 'making a life of my own' (Smith College Library, Mortimer Rare Book Room). 'A life of my own' suggests a prior dispossession of self in marriage to Hughes. She writes to Aurelia, 'It [her marriage] is *over*. My life can begin' (October 12, 1962, *LH* 466), and this new beginning is completely dependent on 'a poem a day,' on the freedom 'to write myself out of this hole' (*LH* 466) of obscurity her life seemed to be in Devon.

This was by no means the first time Plath conceived of herself as creating a new life. Virtually every major crisis or new joy signaled a birth into a new state of being and a sense of authoring a new person or persona.[1] Presaging her choice of 'Morning Song' as the first poem in the 'Other *Ariel*,' Plath wrote her mother on March 12, 1962, only a few months previously, 'I have queerest feeling of having been reborn with Frieda – it's as if my real, rich, happy life only started just about then' (*LH* 450).[2] Her opening line in 'Morning Song' commemorates both Frieda's and *Ariel*'s genesis as an act of love: 'Love set you going like a fat gold watch' (*CP* 156). This 'real, rich, happy life' invested in the conception and birth of Frieda is very early derailed if not doomed in Plath's 'Other *Ariel*,' as the second poem, 'The Couriers,' arrives with news that her marriage is not what it seems, that this is fool's gold: 'A ring of gold with the sun in it? / Lies. Lies and a Grief' (*CP* 247). Plath's next two poems, 'The Rabbit Catcher' and 'Thalidomide,' are excised by Hughes, hence diverting Plath's reader from the indictment of her propitious beginning in 'Thalidomide,' a poem intended, it would seem, to cancel 'Morning Song' with a second conception and birth. A deformed baby takes shape with only a 'half-brain' and 'dark / amputations' for limbs that 'crawl and appall' – 'knuckles at shoulder-blades' (*CP* 252). Not love but the 'White spirit / Of indifference!' (*CP* 252) is what set this thalidomide baby going in its mother's womb.

In *Ariel*, Hughes replaces these two poems with 'Sheep in Fog,' described by him as a 'small cool poem [that] is the epitaph and funeral cortege of the whole extraordinary adventure dramatized in the poems of *Ariel* – the endeavour that, as far as she was concerned, failed' (*WP* 207). Hughes also thereby effectively detours Plath's narrative for the 'Other *Ariel*,' away from his role in it and the exploration of a marriage gone awry, and toward the fatal destination Plath added to 'Sheep in Fog' on January 28, 1963: 'a heaven / Starless and fatherless, a dark water' (*CP* 262). Hughes has a very specific psychological 'adventure' in mind here, and this guides him to a reshaping of Plath's narrative such that the lineaments of Otto Plath take precedence over his own image in the 'Other *Ariel*.' Throughout *Birthday Letters* as well, it is clear that Hughes believes he was 'a whole myth too late to replace' the father ('A Picture of Otto,' *BL* 103) in Plath's affections. His poem 'Fairy Tale' makes her the unfaithful one, 'As if you died each night to be with him' (*BL* 159), and in 'Being Christlike,' he tells her,

> You wanted
> To be with your father
> In wherever he was. And your body
> Barred your passage.
> (BL 153)

Her own 'flesh and blood' and that of her family are only burdens keeping her from her father's grave. In his version of their marriage, Hughes never had a chance. Even before they married, he was only 'being auditioned / For the male lead in your drama' ('Visit,' *BL* 7), and, as we have seen, in 'Black Coat' he unknowingly takes on Daddy's role. He is victimized by her 'two-way heart's diplopic error' and reduced to the 'blurred see-through' for Otto Plath (*BL* 103).

A Late Winter Miracle

Although Plath did not include 'Sheep in Fog' in the 'Other *Ariel*,' Hughes feels justified in doing so because it highlights his view of what Plath's 'endeavour' was in the *Ariel* poems: to find 'a door / Opening downwards into your Daddy's grave' ('The Table,' BL 138) and to join him there in death. Notice in the following passage that Hughes includes only the first version of 'Sheep in Fog' as part of Plath's original inspiration for the *Ariel* poems, but he also does not wish to examine this first version of *Ariel* - the 'Other *Ariel*' - too closely:

Because we have all the manuscripts, all dated, of all her late poems, we can trace the course of the two amazing surges of inspiration that produced them – two waves of excitement like two successive waves on a graph. The first of these surges produced three poems in July of 1962, one in August, then twenty-seven between the end of Spetember and the end of October, ten in November, two on the first day of December, ending abruptly with a final poem. 'Sheep in Fog,' on 2 December.

She collected most of these, with a few others from just before, and called the volume *Ariel*. Without going into detailed analysis, it is possible to point out that the *Ariel* poems document Plath's struggle to deal with a double situation - when her sudden separation from her husband coincided with a crisis in her traumatic feelings about her father's death which had occurred when she was eight years old (and which had been complicated by her all but successful attempt to follow him in a suicidal act in 1953). Against these very strong, negative feelings, and others associated with them, her battle to create a new life, with her children and with what she regarded as her new, reborn self, supplies the extraordinary positive resolution of the poems that she wrote up to 2 December 1962. (*WP* 191)

Here the 'crisis' revolves around her dead father more than it does her separation from Hughes. Hughes goes on to interpret the revision of 'Sheep in Fog' as a bridge of sorts between 'two amazing surges of inspiration.' Of this poem, begun on December 2 but not completed by Plath until a second surge of inspiration two months later, Hughes argues that 'we can't help seeing, I think, how with this poem, quite suddenly the *Ariel* inspiration has changed. The astonishing, sustained, soaring defiance of the previous eight weeks has suddenly failed. Or rather has reversed. Or rather, maybe, has revealed what was always there. It is still inspiration' (*WP* 198). Lurking behind the dramatized 'battle to create a new life' in the *Ariel* poems, Hughes sees 'what was always there' – 'a heaven / Starless and fatherless, a dark water' (*CP* 262).

In some ways this is a vindication for what Hughes did to the 'Other *Ariel*.' Far from producing a mutilation or dismemberment of her text for *Ariel*, he helped to reveal its dominant psychodrama. In *Birthday Letters*, its January 29, 1998, publication date coinciding with the thirty-fifth anniversary of this reversal and revelation. Hughes expands on which he means by 'what was always there.' His 'Suttee' describes their joint endeavor to bring about a birthday of Plath's 'new reborn self':

> In the myth of your first death our deity
> Was yourself resurrected.
> Yourself reborn. The holy one.
> (*BL* 147)

Instead of a 'new babe of light,' though, only 'the old / Babe of dark flames and screams' (*BL* 149) is delivered. Just as a Hindu widow is sacrificed on the burning pyre of her dead husband, so Plath's new self is still incestuously wed to her dead father, to a mourning that insists on her own fiery immolation:

> And you had been delivered of yourself
> In flames. Our newborn
> Was your own self in flames.
> (*BL* 148)

Meant to save her, the *Ariel* poems are finally a suicidal medium in which both she and Hughes are suffocated, as if Plath spoke in tongues of flame 'That sucked the oxygen out of both of us' (*BL* 149).

Since Plath's 'battle to create a new life' and 'a new reborn self' failed miserably, Hughes retrospectively excuses his alteration of Plath's design, especially its ending with the bee poems, which he implies, 'without going into detailed analysis,' provide a 'positive resolution' not borne out by her suicide in February 1963. Though Hughes does not excise the bee poems, he follows them in *Ariel* with a series leading inexorably from her shock treatments and attempted suicide in 1953 ('The Hanging Man') to the 'perfected' woman of 'Edge' (*CP* 272) and the 'Words dry and riderless' of 'Words' (*CP* 270). Together these two poems constitute a farewell to life and to writing. 'The Hanging Man,' composed in June 1960, is assuredly too early to belong to what Hughes calls the 'Ariel inspiration,' but one that he presses on the reader as delineating the original trauma and source of Plath's final despair. 'Words,' composed on February 1, 1963, and 'Edge,' composed on February 5, 1963, also her last poem, together form a tragic denouement.

Alternatively, the 'positive resolution' for the 'Other *Ariel*' depends especially on 'Wintering,' the last of the bee poems and Plath's conclusion for her version of *Ariel*. Its closing line ostensibly celebrates rebirth, seasonal renewal, and the resumption of the beehives's honey-making activity in the spring: 'The bees are flying. They taste the spring' (*CP* 219). This optimistic frame is endorsed, but with varying degrees of fervor, by several Plath critics. As we have seen, Marjorie Perloff is the most convinced of a poetic narrative affirming triumph over adversity. As she describes the overarching movement of the 'Other *Ariel*' from 'Morning Song' to 'Wintering,' it begins with birthing children and ends with birthing poems and a poetic self ('Two *Ariels*' 318). Most other feminist critics, including myself, have seen the bee sequence as more ambiguous in its triumph than Perloff. Susan Van Dyne, for example, fears that the final line of 'Wintering' is forced: Plath 'wills herself to assert a compelling prophecy' (*RL* 115). She continues, however, to endorse a reading of 'the entire bee sequence as Plath's struggle to bring forth an articulate, intelligible self from the potential death box of the hive,' and claims that 'Wintering' points, 'at least figuratively, toward survival' (*RL* 104, 101). Finally, Mary Lynn Broe, who includes the early 'Beekeeper's Daughter' among the bee poems, discerns 'a curve of maturation in their dramatic movement from youthful naïveté and disillusionment ('Beekeeper's Daughter') to vigorous explanation of contradictions inherent in power ('Arrival of the Bee Box,' 'The Bee Meeting,' and 'Stings') and finally to a grasp of a new mode of power ('Wintering,' 'The Swarm')' (*PP* 144).[3] This 'new mode of power,' as Broe describes it, however, resembles the 'courage' in 'The Courage of Shutting-Up' in that it is predominantly passive, even inert – so that it is, at least to this reader, barely recognizable as power. Hence, the strategy of the speaker in 'The Bee Meeting,' according to Broe, 'is to diminish herself in an act of mental powerlessness, willing her own inertia'; the queen bee throughout is powerful less for her activity than her evasive strategies; and '"Wintering" praises the workers for their minimal survival' (146, 148, 152).

Overall, then, and despite frequent critical comparisons of Plath's queen bee in 'Stings' to the fierce 'lioness' figure in 'Ariel' and 'Purdah,' and to the sarcastically assertive female figures in 'Lady Lazarus' and 'Fever 103°,' the bee sequence seems very tentative in its embrace of power – or, for that matter, in its grasp of a strong female identity. Mere survival seems hardly cause for celebration. My own earlier assessment of the bee poems in *Plath's Incarnations*, before I learned that they were intended to conclude the 'Other *Ariel*,' was that they allegorized many of Plath's deepest fears about her femininity: 'In beekeeping . . . it is almost impossible to determine who rules whom, who owns whom. Do the queen and keeper rule, or are they 'lot-drawn scapegoats' for the hive?' (*PI* 179). The workers who run the hive are social insects, combining 'individual mindlessness with overall design and intelligence'; and because they have no personality, but are 'the collective mind of the hive,' I argued that they allegorize Plath's fears that she would lose 'her individuality' and become a 'honey-drudger,' another 'unmiraculous housewife,' if she were to become similarly 'hived' in caring only for her home and children (178, 184). Finally, then, I claimed that 'the bee colony offers a double image of femininity – the queen creator-destroyer [also scapegoat and murderess on behalf of the hive's fertility] and dust-eating worker – adequate to Plath's conflicted feelings toward her womanhood and her own creative powers as an artist' (186).

In what follows, I return to the issue of allegory and suggest layers of meaning that might account for the uneasiness many feminist critics have expressed about the ambiguous nature of feminine power as it is represented in the bee poems. Perhaps the desire to celebrate – unambiguously – what Perloff describes as Plath's 'rebirth as an isolate self, a rebirth that produces the honey of poetry' ('Two *Ariels*'), has masked not only the problems allegory poses for a reader, but also the enigma of Plath's choice of allegory when she composed these poems.

'Possession. / It is they who own me'

Feminist critics are not alone in their sense of Plath's triumph in completing the 'Other *Ariel*.' In a 1982 essay

Hughes, too, describes Plath as emerging victorious from the battle with her psychological demons when she finished the 'Other *Ariel*' in November 1962: 'And she had overcome, by a stunning display of power, the bogies of her life. Yet her attitude to the poems was detached. 'They saved me,' she said, and spoke of them as an episode that was past. And indeed it was blazingly clear that she had come through, in Lawrence's sense, and that she was triumphant. The impression of growth and new large strength in her personality was striking. The book lay completed, the poems carefully ordered' (*WP* 189). When we look to the bee poems, 'carefully ordered' to complete the 'Other *Ariel*,' do they support this sense of closure to an 'episode that was past'? Does the volume end on a note of 'blazingly clear' triumph and 'new large strength'?

Knowing as I do now that she intended the bee sequence to conclude the 'Other *Ariel*,' I am struck not by the resounding finality of the poems but by their inconclusiveness, indeed, by their lack of clearly delineated authority and authorship. From the very outset, in 'The Bee Meeting,' the speaker is bewildered and fearful of what the rituals of beekeeping mean. The poem is virtually a series of questions with no adequate answers, and the poem ends menacingly with the speaker asking, 'Whose is that long white box in the grove, what have they accomplished, why am I cold' (*CP* 212). Has she been coffined or confined, made a scapegoat to the hive? Is she, delirious, hallucinating her identification with the queen? She is uncomfortable with the power of owning a hive and with the otherness of bees in 'The Arrival of the Bee Box': 'I am not a Caesar, / I have simply ordered a box of maniacs' (*CP* 213). Similarly, in 'Stings' she wonders, 'What am I buying, wormy mahogany?' and 'Will they hate me . . . ?' (*CP* 214). In 'The Swarm,' the collective mind of the bees as they swarm is 'So dumb it thinks bullets are thunder' (*CP* 216), and as easily manipulated as human masses are by a charismatic ruler like Napoleon: 'The dumb, banded bodies / Walking the plank draped with Mother France's upholstery' (*CP* 127) are willing sacrifices. Finally, in 'Wintering,' far from assuming control of the bees and the hive's honey-making potential, the speaker admits, 'It is they who own me' (*CP* 218).

There is, in addition, Plath's choice of extended allegory in representing her own concerns through the life cycle of the bees and the rituals of beekeeping. Authorship and authority are thereby distributed – located at times in the human beekeeper, but also in the royal activities of the queen, at others in the industrious female workers, at still others in the virginal princesses who are a menace to the queen bee's throne, and finally in the collective mind of the hive. Indeed, this distribution of sites of power and activity might be construed as resistance to the singularity of authorial intention – what Perloff calls 'the isolate self' ('Two *Ariels*' 318). As a narrative mode, does allegory thereby invest authority in industrious and ingenious readers? If so, there is a complementarity between the workings of the beehive, which depends on the subjugation of its individual members – even the queen – to a collective intentionality and the collaborative honey-drudging that goes into interpreting allegory, where a single reader or reading is inadequate to the text.

There is something contradictory, too, about the placement of the bee poems - if closure, resolution, or being saved from 'the bogies of her life' is Plath's motive. By no means do they provide the 'astonishing, sustained, soaring defiance' Hughes credits to the first wave of *Ariel* inspiration. Plath might have chosen different poems to end the 'Other *Ariel*' – poems such as 'Lady Lazarus,' 'Purdah,' 'Fever 103°,' 'Daddy,' or even 'Ariel,' the poem written on her birthday. Despite some allegorical 'veiling' of identities and actions in Electra complexes, Holocaust imagery, or analogies to Oriental social customs, these are poems that directly address her rage and desire for vengeance against husband and father, poems that release an often uncontrollable energy and transformative power. And finally, they are dazzling and confident performances showcasing Plath's wickedly sardonic wit. Former selves melt, unloose, unpeel, or dissolve like 'old whore petticoats' ('Fever 103°,' *CP* 232), giving way to the 'White / Godiva' (*CP* 239) of 'Ariel,' the 'lioness' (*CP* 244) of 'Purdah,' the 'acetylene / Virgin' (*CP* 232) of 'Fever 103°,' and the man-eater of 'Lady Lazarus.' These are preeminently poems of self-authorization.

In the bee poems, as we shall see, rage and vengeance-seeking are muted. In contrast to Plath's powerful self-representations in other poems, the bee sequence expresses her fear that a new self might not emerge from what she described to her brother Warren and his new wife, Maggie, as 'the most incredible hell' she had endured 'for six months' (October 12, 1962, *LH* 467). Even more, she dreads the winter about to close in on her and what it will mean if she cannot find a way to leave Court Green:

> I am and have been an intelligent woman, and this year of country life has been, for me, a cultural death. No plays, films, art shows, books, people! . . . Now I am stuck; but not for long. I plan to go to Ireland to a lovely cottage by the sea from December to February to recover my health and my heart, then return here for spring and summer. . . . The loneliness here now is appalling. Then I shall fight for a London flat . . . I shall be able to do free-lance broadcasting, reviewing, and have a circle of intellectual friends in London. I loved living there and never wanted to leave. (*LH* 467)

And a bit later, in the same letter to Warren and Maggie: 'Tell me you'll consider taking . . . me to Austria with you, even if you don't, so I'll have that to look forward to. I've had nothing to look forward to for so long! The half year ahead seems like a lifetime, and the half behind an endless hell' (*LH* 468). Over and over again, Plath expresses her need to be in London – indeed, to 'have a salon in London,' to have a 'bloody holiday' from 'this cow life,' to surround herself 'with intelligent, good people' and live the life of a 'famous poetess here – mentioned this week in *The Listener* as one of the half-dozen women who will last – including Marianne Moore and the Bröntes!' (letter to Aurelia, October 12, 1962, *LH* 466–67). In this context, the bee poems represent something less promising than the hope for a miraculous rebirth. Indeed, they embody the mind-numbing menace of a life in the country, a potentially deadly winter of female hibernation that Plath feared she would not survive.

'How very much I do need a spring tonic'

The bee poems were composed from October 3 to October 9, 1962, while Hughes was packing up his belongings and preparing to leave Court Green. They were originally grouped under a generic title, first 'The Beekeeper' (draft 1 of 'The Bee Meeting,' 1), then 'The Beekeeper's Daybook' (draft 2 of 'The Bee Meeting,' 1),[4] and their titles numbered to indicate their place in a sequence:

1. 'The Bee Meeting' (October 3, 1962), originally titled 'The Meeting'
2. 'The Arrival of the Bee Box' (October 4, 1962)
3. 'Stings' (October 6, 1962)
4. 'The Swarm' (October 7, 1962)
5. 'Wintering' (October 9, 1962)

They are all composed in five-line stanzas and are roughly the same length. They have the quality of episodes in a narrative beginning in about mid-June, when the beekeeper anticipates the hive's swarming, and extending to mid-February of the following year, when a few warm days may well seduce bees to emerge from their clustering ball in the hive, and also when the queen begins to increase her egg-laying activity to ensure a substantial number of workers for the spring.

We may never know any details about what happened between Plath and Hughes during the week when these poems were composed. After Hughes's departure, Plath's letters to Aurelia, to her brother Warren, and to her friends must not be read as necessarily dedicated to giving them an objective account of her situation, but must be considered as at least partially designed to elicit sympathy and to mobilize support, because, as she writes Warren, 'It is hurtful to be ditched' (October 12, 1962, *LH* 467). The journal from this period was either lost or destroyed, the biographers have no insights to offer about this particular week, and there are only blanks and some missing pages in her Tablet Diary. I speculate that this period must have been marked by a highly volatile, potentially confrontational atmosphere, and this sense of unpredictability and danger is represented in the unknowable otherness of bees, the persistent threat of their dangerous stings for the inexperienced beekeeper. In the letter written to her mother on the same day she composed 'Wintering,' October 9, Plath ends a list of domestic woes – 'Everything is breaking' – with 'Even my beloved bees set upon me today when I numbly knocked aside their sugar feeder, and I am all over stings' (*LH* 465). The dramatization of open conflict between a woman and male antagonists must wait, however, for poems written later in October.

A primary question for me, as I have indicated, is why did Plath choose allegory as her mode of expression? Given the week of composition, are there potential answers to be found in the specific timing of that choice? Allegory might be construed as an indirect poetic strategy that disguises rather than discovers her fears and masks rather than expresses her anger – even to herself. The author is also, in some sense, dissembled and dis-assembled among several sites of activity – by the beekeeper and community of beekeepers, by the queen, by the workers, and by the social unit of the hive as a thinking be(e)ing. Of course, the bee poems immediately follow 'The Detective' (October 1) and 'The Courage of Shutting-Up' (October 2), both poems about a woman who has disappeared as a unified presence, who is at least complicit in her own silencing, and who extols the virtue of restraint in keeping her mouth shut, when she could, if she gave her tongue freedom, be brutally cutting. Furthermore, the revisions in some of the bee poems suggest that Plath was trying to free herself from expressions of jealousy and a desire for vengeance – to rise above the role of ditched wife and assume higher ground. As Van Dyne describes the evolution of 'Stings,' particularly: 'The earlier versions show the speaker engaged in a definition of herself that is primarily vengeful. She is the wrong wife and deserted mother whose verbal assault disfigures, emasculates, and finally destroys a male opponent. During the process of revision, Plath redirects her energy toward imagining an autonomous creative self in the queen' (*Stings* 7). Similarly, as I noted about the final version of 'Stings,' 'the speaker refuses an identity as a vengeance-seeking housewife; for unlike the female workers, who must die by stinging the man [in the poem] to death, she, the queen, will not commit suicide for the sake of revenge. Instead, the discovery of the man's infedelity releases both the speaker and the queen from being honey-drudgers for the hive' (*PI* 184). In her letters as well, Plath at times takes a 'noble' stand toward Hughes: 'The one thing I retain is love for and admiration of [Ted's] writing. I know he is a genius, and for a genius there are no bonds and no bounds.' She believes – probably rightly – that she played a major role in advancing his career as a writer, typing his manuscripts and sending them out to American journals, serving in Hughes's early years as his agent: 'I feel I did discover him, worked to free him for writing for six years' (letter to Warren and Maggie, October 12, 1962, *LH* 467). The typescripts of Hughes's published work she recycled for her own composition represented, after all, her secretarial work on his behalf.

Perhaps allegory offered her a certain freedom from what it is clear she regarded as the too literal horror of her situation. The previous winter in Court Green – her first – was very harsh, but at least there was the pride in new ownership, the sharing of spartan conditions with a beloved husband and toddler, and the anticipated birth of baby Nicholas in January:

> The cold is bitter. Even my midwife said it was too Spartan for a new baby and to warm things up. The halls are hopeless, of course, but the Pifcos [four electric heaters] do a wonderful job in closed-off rooms. The cold seems to keep us healthy – not one of us has been taken with a cold yet (knock on wood). We look fat as bears with all our sweaters, but I find this nippy air very bracing and so does Frieda. Her fat cheeks bloom, even though her breath comes out in little puffs. Much healthier than the overheating we had in America. (letter to Aurelia, December 7, 1961, *LH* 439)

By February she is 'so longing for spring' and an escape from 'this six months' cooping-up of damp and rain and blackness we get here – like the six months Persephone had to spend with Pluto' (letter to Aurelia, February 7, 1962, *LH* 446). Even in March, Plath's spirits are depressed by 'grey tombstone skies, sleet, a mean wind set perpetually in the east' (letter to Ann and Leo Goodman, March 28, 1962, Smith College Library, Mortimer Rare Book Room). Contemplating the plight and courage of bees in 'Wintering' – 'This is the time of hanging on for the bees' (*CP* 218) – may have been a strategy of containment for Plath, keeping her own fears as secured as the bees in 'The Arrival of the Bee Box': 'How can I let them out?' (*CP* 213).

'What to do with your hate for . . . all mother figures?'

The cycle of life in the beehive, run as it is by a queen and female workers, also converged with other stories Plath told about herself. In her *Journals* and in *The Bell Jar*, Plath brutally satirized the lives of women apart from men. When she returned to psychotherapy in 1958, she worked through many of her hostilities toward an upbringing without a father or father figure – without the presence of Otto Plath and 'the love of a steady blood-related man after the age of eight' (*J* 266). Instead, she was reared in a 'smarmy matriarchy of togetherness' (*J* 265):

> The little white house on the corner with a family full of women. So many women, the house stank of them. The grandfather lived and worked in the country club, but the grandmother stayed home and cooked like a grandmother should. The father dead and rotten in the grave he barely paid for, and the mother working for bread like no poor woman should have to and being a good mother on top of it. . . . A stink of women: Lysol, cologne, rose water and glycerine, cocoa butter on the nipples so they won't crack, lipstick red on all three mouths. (*J* 267)

Defying this all-female social order and its devotion to good housekeeping and feminine hygiene, Plath describes herself – in a manner dripping with sarcasm – as seeking passion instead of security in her mate and ultimately marrying the 'wrong' sort of man. She 'turned down the nicest boys whom *she* [Aurelia] would have married like a shot' (*J* 268) and ignored her mother's good advice: 'Get a nice little, safe little, sweet little loving little imitation man who'll give you babies and bread and a secure roof and a green lawn and money

money money every month. Compromise. A smart girl can't have everything she wants. Take second best. Take anything nice you think you can manage and sweetly master. Don't let him get mad or die or go to Paris with his sexy secretary. Be sure he's nice nice nice' (*J* 267).

In October 1962, though, Plath suddenly finds herself enacting the fate of the poor little wife in all too familiar cautionary tales she had imbibed from her mother, who 'gave her daughter books by noble women called *The Case for Chastity*' and was warned: 'Men, nasty lousy men. They took all they could get and then had temper tantrums or died or went to Spain like Mrs So-and-so's husband with his lusty lips' (*J* 268, 267). Plath may well have felt that she was turning into a cliché. In September 1962, the local midwife Winifred Davies writes to Aurelia about Plath's marital problems, hinting that Plath has failed to master the feminine wiles necessary for managing her husband; it sounds as though she has become too dominant, threatening the husband's 'right to wear the pants in the family,' and as though Hughes has the proverbial 'seven-year itch.' Plath wants to domesticate a reluctant Hughes and performs all the 'practical side of the partnership,' and as Davies puts it, 'no man really likes that.' As for Hughes, he wants freedom to party and to travel (letter of September 22, 1962, Lilly Library).

There were, additionally, inescapable analogies between Plath's situation and her mother's when Otto Plath died, leaving Aurelia with two children dependent on her, just as Frieda and Nicholas were on Plath. She complains to Mrs Prouty that Ted has ordered her to buy her clothing in a thrift shop – 'the British equivalent of Filene's basement' (December 15, 1962, Lilly Library). Plath's repeatedly expressed fears that Hughes would not provide any financial support, that she would be forced to scrimp and save and deprive herself while Hughes enjoyed the high life in London and presumably ignored his children,[5] echo her mean-spirited description of Aurelia's impoverishment after Otto Plath died:

Life was hell. She had to work. Work, and be a mother, too, a man and a woman in one sweet ulcerous ball. She pinched. Scraped. Wore the same old coat. But the children had new school clothes and shoes that fit. Piano lessons, viola lessons, French horn lessons. They went to Scouts. They went to summer camp and learned to sail. One of them went to private school on scholarship and got good marks. In all honesty and with her whole unhappy heart she worked to give those two innocent little children the world of joy she'd never had. She'd had a lousy world. But they went to college, the best in the nation, on scholarship and work and part of her money, and didn't have to study nasty business subjects. One day they would marry for love and have plenty of money and everything would be honey sweet. They wouldn't have to support her in her old age. (J 266)

Far from being 'honey sweet,' Plath's domestic situation is more like the hive she worries about in 'Stings':

> Brood cells gray as the fossils of shells
> Terrify me, they seem so old.
> What am I buying, wormy mahogany?
> (CP 214)

All of Plath's extraordinary efforts to make a home of Court Green, 'Thinking "Sweetness, sweetness"' (CP 214), may be allegorized here. She described Court Green as 'a person; it responds to the slightest touch and looks wonderful immediately' (letter to Aurelia, September 4, 1961, LH 427); but this ancient thatch-roofed manor house needed a good deal more than a 'touch' of work to make it habitable, much less homey. Virtually all of Plath's letters in the fall of 1961 mention new purchases or projects for the house and hopeless efforts to warm up a place with no central heating. According to Anne Stevenson, even with four space heaters and a coal stove, the temperature did not get above fifty degrees in the winter (*BF* 230), and Plath suffered from chilblains (letter to Ann and Leo Goodman, March 28, 1962, Smith College Library, Mortimer Rare Book Room). As she tells her brother Warren and his wife, 'Winter can't at the North Pole be worse than here!' (letter dated October 25, 1962, *LH* 476).

While the newly bought hive in 'Stings' resembles 'wormy mahogany' to the apprentice beekeeper, many of the floors in Court Green were in fact infested with deathwatch beetles and needed either expensive treatment of replacement by Plath and Hughes, both novices at owning a home. Like the speaker in 'Stings,' who enamels her hive with 'excessive love,' Plath lavished her artistic efforts on Court Green's furnishings, painting and enameling furniture and doorways, sewing curtains, choosing red for everything.[6] As Hughes describes her in 'Totem,' she 'painted little hearts on everything' (*BL* 163) – mirror frames, cradles, thresholds. She may well have wondered, barely a year later, whether the 'excessive love' invested in her own hive/home had produced the 'honeysweet' returns due a queen/mother: 'Is there any queen at all in it?' (*CP* 214). Alternatively, had marriage, motherhood, and housekeeping robbed Plath of her royalty? 'If there is [a queen],

> . . . she is old,
> her wings torn shawls, her long body
> Rubbed of its plush –
> Poor and bare and unqueenly and even shameful.
> I stand in a column
>
> Of winged, unmiraculous women,
> Honey-drudgers.
> I am no drudge
> Though for years I have eaten dust
> And dried plates with my dense hair.

And seen my strangeness evaporate,
Blue dew from dangerous skin.
(*CP* 214)

The poverty of her dress – 'torn' and 'rubbed . . . bare' –
recalls her mother's old coat, but also expresses Plath's sense
of having sacrificed too much in the way of female finery
and vanity for the sake of frugality. Hence, one of the first
things she does with Christmas money from Mrs Prouty is to
treat herself to glamorous, even vampy new clothes, to
restore her 'strangeness' and re-cover her 'dangerous skin':
'Got a Florence-Italy blue and white velvet overblouse, a deep
brown velvet Italian shirt, black fake-fur toreador pants, a
straight black velvet skirt and metallic blue-and-black French
top. . . . I haven't had a new wardrobe for over seven years,
and it's done wonders for my morale' (letter to Aurelia,
December 21, 1962, *LH* 491).[7] There is a strong
undercurrent of pathos to Stevenson's account of Plath's
final days, when she carried these new clothes with her to
stay with friends, even while 'drugged and ill . . . still anxious
to be ready for some possible social occasion. Her cocktail
outfit, coming and going in her suitcase . . . , is as poignant
in retrospect as Ophelia's flowers' (*BF* 294).

Read as an allegory on her likeness to her mother and
grandmother or as a protest against any siimilarities to the
deserted and widowed wives in their stories – 'a column' of
'unmiraculous women' and 'honey-drudgers' – 'Stings'
proposes the awakening and flight of a queenly self different
from these lesser females:

Now she is flying
More terrible than she ever was, red
Scar in the sky, red comet
Over the engine that killed her –
The mausoleum, the wax house.
(*CP* 215)

Since the queen emerges alone from the hive only for the nuptial flight, this moment of self-recovery is also a reclamation of her vitality as a sexual being. Unlike the sterile female workers, the honey-drudgers, Plath is a fertile queen. Her first efforts to draft the penultimate stanza stress this restored sexual impulse, and further, her own desertion of the children in order to fulfill another 'bride-flight':

> [I] have a self to recover, a queen,
> That dreams of a second bride-flight
> Her wings of clear glass,
> Her banded body
> More terrible than it ever was.
> Deserting the nurseries, the workers,
> The years. A glitter of dew
> On blades she will not return to.
> (draft 1, 3)

Here, instead of the male leaving the hive behind, which would be closer to the truth of Hughes's departure, it is the queen who does not return, who 'dreams' of a second sexual consummation.[8] More than a dramatic reversal of her current situation, this also constitutes an optimistic revision of her mother's fate. After losing Otto Plath, Aurelia gave up men altogether, or as Plath describes this decision, 'My mother had sacrificed her life for me. A sacrifice I didn't want. . . . I made her sign a promise she'd never marry. When [I was nine.] Too bad she didn't break it' (J 268). Furthermore, the queen bee's blazoned fertility, though presented as wounded and portending disaster – a 'red scar' and 'red comet' – differentiates with Plath from the 'barren' women, in her eyes, who surround Hughes. Assia Wevill is vilified as having 'had so many abortions, she can't have children' (letter to Aurelia, September 23, 1962, Lilly Library), and she is 'beautiful & barren and hates all I have created here' (letter to Olive Higgins Prouty, September 29, 1962, Lilly Library). Even

Hughes confirms Plath's horror of and fascination with Assia Wevill's supposedly barren womanhood: 'Who was this Lilith of abortions / Touching the hair of your children / With tiger-painted nails?' (*BL* 157).

Finally, it is clear that Plath solicited support and solace from a host of women during this period. She once again sought counsel from her psychiatrist Ruth Beuscher, who recommended she file for divorce immediately. In addition to her correspondence with her mother, Mrs Prouty, her Aunt Dot, and married women friends, often painting a melodramatic picture of embattled womanhood, entries in the Tablet Diary for the month of October and part of November show a steady stream of women visitors, many of them arriving to tend Plath's needs. Her midwife Winifred Davies looks in on her from time to time at the behest of Aurelia, and there are days when Plath schedules visits from her cleaning woman and someone to cut and curl her own and Frieda's hair. She also hires an au pair to watch the children and cook meals while she retreats to her study. Given the amount of help and attention Plath seeks and receives from women, it would not be an exaggeration to compare her role to that of a queen bee, cared for at all times by a host of worker females.[9]

'What a man wants is a mate and what a woman wants is infinite security'

Plath recycles typescript pages from chapters 4, 5, and 6 of *The Bell Jar* for composition of the bee poems. As Van Dyne remarks, 'It seems too neat to be coincidence that Plath began composing these poems that respond so immediately to the breakup of her marriage at the point in the novel that marks Esther Greenwood's discovery of Buddy Willard's sexual infidelity' (*RL* 102). While the choice of these chapters as an underlying narrative may be seen, then, as intending an analogy between Plath and Esther, Hughes and Buddy, there are also ways in which Plath is writing in opposition to *The Bell Jar*. Just as Hughes's manuscript for 'The Calm' is a counterpoint to the tempest on the surface created by the *Ariel* poet, so these chapters from *The Bell Jar* are a bleak narrative about Plath's past in tension with the unfolding story of the bee sequence. While Esther heads inexorably toward breakdown, depression, and attempted suicide in these early episodes of the novel, Plath is writing poems in an effort to save herself from a compulsion to repeat this pattern.

But why a narrative about honeybees and beekeeping? As we shall see, at the most general level, the elaborately designed beehive provides the poet with virtually timeless strategies for survival and endless allegorical possibilities for poetic manipulation of narrative. As one modern beekeeping handbook points out, reminding the reader of honeybees' mellifluous/melliferous ancient heritage in the poetry of book 4 of *The Georgics*, 'The bees Virgil tended in his garden were probably similar to those of his contemporary descendants' (Taylor 3). The female-dominated beehive also provides an alternative to the human communities of women in *The Bell Jar*, all of them disadvantaged by comparison to men as Plath depicts America in the 1950s. In fact, these chapters from *The Bell Jar* focus specifically on the sexual double standard imposed on young men and women and its negative impact on Esther. At least one of the factors contributing to Esther's eventual mental breakdown is the sense Plath gives us that bright young women like her heroine will eventually be forced to give up their aspirations when they marry. Buddy disparages Esther's writing ambitions by telling her that a poem is 'A piece of dust' (45), and her mother 'was always on me to learn shorthand after college, so I'd have a practical skill as well as a college degree' (32), knowing as she does what kind of work is available to women, even those with a good education. Like Aurelia Plath, Esther's widowed mother 'had taught shorthand and typing to support us ever since my father died' (32).

In these episodes underlying the bee poems, Esther is preoccupied with Buddy Willard, specifically outraged at him for being a hypocrite, for 'pretending all this time to be so innocent' (56) about sex. It turns out that despite Mrs Willard's fanaticism 'about virginity for men and women both' (58), and despite being in a dating relationship with Esther, Buddy enjoys and doesn't mind confessing to premarital sex with a 'tatty waitress' – and not just once, but 'a couple of times a week' for a whole summer. Esther tells us: 'Back at college I started asking a senior here and a senior there what they would do if a boy they knew suddenly told them he'd slept thirty times with some slutty waitress one summer, smack in the middle of knowing them. But these seniors said most boys were like that and you couldn't honestly accuse them of anything until you were at least pinned or engaged to be married.' (57). Esther would like to 'even things up' (57) by sleeping with someone, too, but Plath makes it clear that sex outside marriage is far riskier for a young woman. Esther is constantly being reminded of the limitations on her sexuality as a young woman and being assailed with pithy proverbs about sex roles, like the one from Buddy's mother – 'What a man wants is a mate and what a woman wants is infinite security' – a fount of verities about sexual difference, most of which sustain the notion of masculinity as active and aggressive and femininity as passive and inert. Mrs Willard's version of 'Men are hunters and women, gatherers' is 'What a man is is an arrow into the future and what a woman is is the place the arrow shoots off from' (58), which goes directly against Esther's desires: 'The last thing I wanted was infinite security and to be the place an arrow shoots off from. I wanted change and excitement and to shoot off in all directions myself, like the coloured arrows from a Fourth of July rocket' (68). Esther is also bombarded with popular cultural messages, warning her as her mother does about remaining pure for marriage. The movie she attends in chapter 4 is just such a cautionary tale, 'a football romance . . . in Technicolor': 'Finally I could see the nice girl was going to end up with the nice football hero and the sexy girl was going to end up with nobody, because the man named Gil had only wanted a mistress and not a wife all along and was now packing off to Europe on a single ticket' (34). Finally, in chapter 6, Esther sees a baby being born, but instead of this affirming her powers as a woman, she sees that birth is controlled by male doctors. She is warned by Buddy's friend Will, 'a third-year man' (52) in medical school, 'You oughtn't to see this . . . You'll never want to have a baby if you do. They oughtn't to let women watch. It'll be the end of the human race' (52–53).

'The almost perfect but pitiless society of our lives'

The bee poems composed on top of these pages from *The Bell Jar* explore a sexual and social order both parallel to and different from the human one depicted in the novel. Sexual roles in the beehive are opposite to those described by Mrs Willard as 'natural' to men and women. The females are active, while the drones are relatively passive, lazing about the hive and eating the honey created by the workers. Contemporary beekeepers characterize drones as 'freeloaders.' A bit like men behaving badly, they have favoured hangouts within the hive and are known to venture out in groups once a day in the hope of 'getting lucky' and running into a queen. Equally colorful is the nineteenth-century beekeeper Maurice Maeterlinck's portrayal of these courtly lovers: 'Each day, from noon till three, when the sun shines resplendent, this plumed horde sallies forth in search of the bride, who is indeed more royal, more difficult of conquest, than the most inaccessible princess of fairy legend' (297). The drones are, at best, only potential sexual consorts for the queen, who is the apiary's essential inhabitant; without her, quite simply, the hive dies. It is the sterile female worker bees who perform the myriad tasks of the hive: the nurses who tend the nymphs and larvae, controlling the birthing process and feeding royal jelly to transform some developing eggs into potential queens; the ladies of honour who wait on the queen; the housekeeper bees who fan their wings to air, refresh, and heat the hive; the comb builders and cleaners; the gatekeepers – Maeterlinck calls them 'Amazons' – who guard the hive's entrance; and the foragers for nectar and pollen who feed the hive and add to its wealth (42–44). These perpetually chaste female workers might live longer than four or five weeks, but because of 'the fatal ecstasy of work' that possesses all of them, their bodies are quickly worn smooth – 'polished, thinner, and almost bald' – and their wings tattered, because 'hard work uses and tears' (68,87). The expendable male drones, who do nothing productive for the hive, who are 'forever drunk on honey' while waiting around for 'one act of love' (298), are also completely at the mercy of the workers. As Plath describes their fate in a discarded line from 'The Bee Meeting,' they are accessories to the queen: 'The drones are <merely> <only> her instruments, it is death in cold weather' (draft 1, 2). According to Maeterlinck, 'after the queen's impregnation, when flowers begin to close sooner, and open later, the spirit one morning will coldly decree the simultaneous and general massacre of every male' by dismemberment (42). Then, 'before the bewildered parasites are able to realise that the happy laws of the city have crumbled, dragging down in most inconceivable fashion their own plentiful destiny, each one is assailed by three or four envoys of justice; and these vigorously proceed to cut off his wings, saw through the petiole that connects the abdomen with the thorax, amputate the feverish antennae, and seek an opening between the rings of his cuirass through which to pass their sword' (352). If they escape dismemberment, they are unceremoniously booted out of the hive to die alone. This topsy-turvy version of femininity and masculinity may be seen as in dialogue with *The Bell Jar*'s underlying allegory and narrative – indeed in argument with its depiction of seemingly intractable norms for submissive female behaviour toward the superior male.

Since Plath had recently become a beekeeper, her investment in what beekeepers refer to as the mind of the hive was literal as well as metaphorical. As we shall see, the metaphorical dependence of these poems on factual knowledge as well as poetry and folklore about honeybees and the rituals of beekeeping may help to explain why Plath wrote them when she did, and, further, may provide some tentative ideas about why she placed them at the end of the 'Other *Ariel*.' Indeed, the allegorical richness of the poems emerges from analogies and tensions between beekeeping lore and the ways we have seen her depict her situation in Court Green in the fall of 1962. These analogies probably supersede the frequently cited importance of her father's profession as an entomologist and his expertise on bumblebees as providing the impetus for writing about bees.

Bumblebees are, in fact, very different from honeybees,[10] so Otto Plath's *Bumblebees and Their Ways* tells us little about the life cycle of the honeybees Plath came to own in June 1962:

Today, guess what, we became *beekeepers*! We went to the local meeting last week (attended by the rector, the midwife, and assorted beekeeping people from neighbouring villages) to watch a Mr Pollard make three hives out of one (by transferring his queen cells) under the supervision of the official Government beeman. We all wore masks and it was thrilling. . . . Mr Pollard let us have an old hive for nothing which we painted white and green, and today he brought over the swarm of docile Italian hybrid bees we ordered and installed them.

We placed the hive in a sheltered out-of-the-way spot in the orchard – the bees were furious from being in a box. Ted had only put a handkerchief over his head where the hat should go in the bee-mask, and the bees crawled into his hair, and he flew off with half-a-dozen stings. I didn't get stung at all, and when I went back to the hive later, I was delighted to see bees entering with pollen sacs full and leaving with them empty – at least I *think* that's what they were doing. I feel very ignorant, but shall try to read up and learn all I can. (letter to Aurelia, June 15, 1962, *LH* 457)

The first three poems in the bee sequence refer to the events Plath describes here. 'The Bee Meeting' is an initiation into the rituals of beekeeping that reminds readers of 'The Lottery' more often than Plath's jolly description here of a community gathering might suggest. 'The Arrival of the Bee Box' transforms her 'docile Italian Hybrid bees' into a 'Roman mob' (*CP* 213), and 'Stings,' while recalling the attack on Hughes as a 'great scapegoat' (*CP* 215), is more worried about the value and potential productivity of her hive, which depend on the elusive queen: 'Is there any queen at all in it?' (*CP* 214), she asks. The bee sequence begins, then, with a palpable lack of ease in the speaker, a sense of extreme anxiety, fearful anticipation, even paranoia about this 'almost perfect but pitiless society' (Maeterlinck 32) of the beehive. Perhaps if we see beekeeping as an allegorical quest, as promising treasure at journey's end, as dangerous but ultimately worth the initiation and ordeals she must endure, then this alternating fearfulness about an alien culture and attraction to its potential richness – both literally, in terms of the honey, and in terms of poetic meaning – signify an openness to the future.

This would, of course, go against the *Ariel* poet firmly etched in literary history by Robert Lowell's foreword in 1966: 'This poetry and life are not a career: they tell that life, even when disciplined, is simply not worth it' (*Ariel* viii-ix). Even more, this sense of experiment and open-endedness would contradict the automatic writing described by Hughes and inspired by Plath's belief that 'God is speaking through me' ('The God,' *BL* 191):

> In your sleep, glassy-eyed,
> You heard its instructions. When you woke
> Your hands moved. You watched them in dismay[.]
> (*BL* 189)

Finally, it would go against the poetic inspiration described by Judith Kroll as already knowing what happens next and conveying 'the sense that the future is foreclosed' (3). Despite the ostensible automatism of the hive, 'It is to the future . . . that the bees subordinate all things' (Maeterlinck 110), and for Plath, at least in October 1962, the future was still ripe with possibilities. Despite her fears, she could also be hopeful:

> I must be one of the most creative people in the world. I *must* keep a live-in girl so I can get myself back to the live, lively, always learning and developing peson I was! I want to study, learn history, politics, languages, travel. I want to be the most loving and fascinating mother in the world. London, a flat, is my aim, and I shall, in spite of all the obstacles that rear, have that; and Frieda and Nick shall have the intelligences of the day as their visitors, and I the Salon that I will deserve. I am *glad* this happened and happened *now*. I shall be a rich, active woman. (letter to Aurelia, October 23, 1962, *LH* 475)

'I could not run without having to run forever'

In many ways, the first of the bee poems, 'The Bee Meeting,' is the most enigmatic of the sequence, because the speaker is still an outsider to the mysteries of beekeeping. Midway through the sequence as a whole, she will confidently declare, 'I am in control' ('Stings,' *CP* 214), and revel in the wealth she will acquire when her hive begins its production:

Here is my honey-machine,
It will work without thinking,
Opening, in spring, like an industrious virgin[.]
(*CP* 214–15)

In 'The Bee Meeting,' however, she is completely controlled by the bee-keeping community, and has not yet gained possession of the 'white hive,' a female being that looks to her enviably self-sufficient: 'snug as a virgin, / Sealing off her brood cells, her honey, and quietly humming' (*CP* 212).[11] What most worries the speaker – and a reader – is that in order to gain access to this chaste virgin and her honey hoard, she must submit to a ritual devised by her neighbors, but the speaker's unanswered questions:

Is it some operation that is taking place?
It is the surgeon my neighbors are waiting for,
This apparition in a green helmet,
Shining gloves and white suit.
Is it the butcher, the grocer, the postman, someone I know?
(*CP* 211)

The homely, the familiar, the ordinary figures of village life all appear ominous and threatening, because she does not know her part in this rite and has little sense of its meaning or outcome. Not dressed protectively for venturing forth into a circle of hives, she asks, 'I am nude as a chicken neck, does nobody love me?' (*CP* 211).[12] Her neighbors, by contrast, are all wearing disguises that both protect them and mask their everyday identities. The sense throughout the poem is one of deception, of the poor speaker, a mere girl in the final stanza, being duped. In the first draft, even the smoke used to calm the bees is described as 'the smoke of lies' (2), surrounding the speaker in an atmosphere in which nothing looks normal or quite right. The poem ends by suggesting that she has become a sacrificial victim of some kind, but neither she, nor a reader, is certain why or to what:

> I am exhausted, I am exhausted –
> Pillar of white in a blackout of knives.
> I am the magician's girl who does not flinch.
> The villagers are untying their disguises, they are shaking
>   hands.
> Whose is that long white box in the grove, what have they
>   accomplished, why am I cold.
> (*CP* 212)

The long white box is, ultimately, the encased hive, but the speaker suddenly finds herself inside, as if she is now a member of the bee colony. The box also reminds her of the role played by the female assistant in magic performances. Placed in a box, she does not move while the magician inserts knife after knife. To flinch would show fear and undermine the performance. Even more, any movement throwing off the magician's careful insertion of knives might also lead to her death. In the first draft, her sacrificial death seems even more definite in the final line where the 'long white box' is unambiguously a casket: 'Whose is that coffin, so white & silent, what have they accomplished, why am I cold!' (draft 1, p 3).

What kind of beekeeping 'operation' is this and what is its purpose? We are told, 'The villagers open the chambers, they are hunting the queen' (*CP* 212), which implies either that they want to make sure of her presence and condition, or that they plan to move her. She foils the villagers, however, cleverly hiding and forcing them to adopt another strategy: 'The villagers are moving the virgins, there will be no killing,' and the old queen thereby escapes 'a duel' with these young virgins and will 'live another year' (*CP* 212). The purpose of moving the virgin princesses, while they are still confined by 'a curtain of wax' in cells that do, in fact, resemble anomalous 'fingerjoints' protruding from the otherwise uniform hexagonal cells that house the ordinary larvae, is not only to save the old queen but also, probably, to control swarming and to start new hives.[13] Unlike her explanatory letter to her mother, the poem obscures, indeed shrouds, this beekeeping ritual in the veil of allegory.

The impact of this mystification is to create and support multiple ambiguities about the speaker's identity and fate at the poem's conclusion. If she is a 'Pillar of white in a blackout of knives,' does this mean she is assassinated by stinging bees – insufficiently protected by the 'smock,' 'black veil,' and 'white straw Italian hat' provided by her neighbors to make her one of them? Or is she the 'old queen,' prevented from swarming and so forced to remain confined in her 'long white box' when she might prefer flight and a move of the hive to a new place?[14] Although Plath will imagine a second bride flight for the old queen bee in 'Stings,' this is entirely poetic license. After the initial mating with drones, the 'nuptial flight' as it is termed by beekeepers, the queen 'will never again leave the hive, unless to accompany a swarm (Maeterlinck 320). Or, finally, is she one of the transplanted virgins, moved into another box to reign over a new hive? A new queen is in fact introduced into an alien hive by means of a small wire cage with a wall on one side, protecting her from her own panicky movements (like flinching?) that might provoke an attack by a colony of workers unfamiliar with her smell. Like the speaker in the poem, who hopes the bees 'will not smell my fear, my fear, my fear' (*CP* 211), the virgin queen might betray herself as a foreigner. The beekeeper hopes that the workers will accept and adopt her after a few days and chew through the wall of sugar or candied paper to release her into the hive. There is, however, the possibility of rejection and that she will be 'balled' by the hive, literally suffocated in what Plath may be referring to as a 'blackout of knives.'[15]

Kroll, Broe, and Van Dyne all read Plath's fate as being bound to that of the ageing queen bee. For Kroll, the queen bee is 'a totem of the protagonist' (138); Broe argues that the 'controlling force of the poem is the shrewd queen bee, powerful in her very evasiveness' (*PP* 148); and Van Dyne, while noting that the queen must live in nearly 'perpetual confinement' and 'the end of her story is her biological exhaustion and inevitable replacement by young virgins,' also insists on Plath's 'imaginative alliance with the aging queen' (*RL* 103). Such a reading dramatizes Plath's preeminence and prcedence as the wife and mother over the rival who would challenge her rule – duel her to the death if need be.[16] Simultaneously, however, this reading ignores Plath's distinction from her rival, her sense of being fecund, and in this superior to the women who surround Hughes, repeatedly described as 'barren.' It also ignores Plath's sense of being an American foreigner in Court Green, in England, and how this might have increased dramatically her sense of vulnerability. When she asks, 'does nobody love me?' it is as much an appeal as a question, an expression of her desire for the community's support now that she is alone in alien territory. She arrives defenseless: 'In my sleeveless summery dress I have no protection,' and at this point she is inducted into the community by the 'secretary of the bees' (*CP* 211), who dresses her in appropriate attire.

Plath's allegory does not, I believe, confirm her specific role in the beekeeping ritual, only that it must be endured. Hence her sense of paralysis: 'I cannot run, I am rooted' (*CP* 211); and pertinent to Plath's current situation: 'I could not run without having to run forever' (*CP* 212). Though she has plans to 'make steps *out*, like Cornwall, like Ireland' (*LH* 469) – or, eventually, like London – Plath insists repeatedly to Aurelia that running back to America would be a defeat: 'Home is impossible,' 'it would be psychologically the worst thing to see you now or to go home,' 'I must not go back to the womb or retreat,' and 'I cannot come home' (October 16, 1962, *LH* 468–69). Whatever happens, it – and the 'it' remains unclear to her – must be faced in England. Flight is not an option. 'The Bee Meeting' mimics this situation in important ways. The speaker is constantly battling her anxiety over what will happen next, but she also 'cannot run' or retreat to safe noninvolvement. She reluctantly joins the other 'knights in visors' (*CP* 211) in quest of opening the wealth of the hive, as in a fairy tale, 'snug as a virgin' and awaiting, it would seem, their possession – and this despite her ignorance about the ceremony. Only the outcome will determine her role in relation to the hive – as its keeper or its queen; as the 'old, old, old' queen who seems reluctant but 'must live another year,' or one of the 'new virgins' destined to 'the bride flight, / The upflight of the murderess into a heaven that loves her' (*CP* 212), and the establishment of a new hive.

The veil of allegory in 'The Bee Meeting' creates indeterminates, then, that governs identity, fate, and meaning in the sequence as a whole. Although 'The mind of the hive thinks this is the end of everything' (*CP* 212), stupidly believing, as bees do, that 'their home may be on fire' (Aebi and Aebi 59) when the beekeeper uses a smoker on the hive, this is only a diversion to prevent the bees from stinging the human intruder. Similarly, this seeming catastrophe in 'The Bee Meeting' does not signal either the speaker's death or the end of the hive, but is instead an initiation into beekeeping and the life of bees in the poems that follow. Simultaneously, as we shall see, Plath apprentices herself to a literary tradition and history that has often identified the poet as a bee or beekeeper, the bee's activity as akin to the creative labor of the poet, and the honey produced as song.

'For he on honeydew hath fed, /
And drunk the milk of paradise'

Initiation into beekeeping may be understood allegorically as
an apprenticeship to writing poetry. Both the wealth of the
beehive in its honey and the endless labor of the workers in
creating this golden hoard offer Plath a rich store of
metaphorical possibility. Plath could not have been unaware
of the poetry, both homely and high, and all of it allegorical,
that surrounds bees and honey. Borrowing the honeybee as
her metaphor, Emily Dickinson celebrates 'moments of
Escape' for the soul,

> When bursting all the doors –
> She dances like a Bomb, abroad,
> And swings upon the Hours,
> As do the Bee – delirious borne –
> Long dungeoned from his Rose –
> (no. 512)

Feminist critics Sandra Gilbert and Susan Gubar argue that
the reclusive Dickinson did indeed venture 'abroad' through
her poetry, in a delirium no less intent on sweet reward than
the honeybee's. Similarly, the Greek poet Pindar describes his
crafting of songs of praise as 'flitting' from flower to flower
like the honeybee (Pythian 10.53–54).[17] According to the
classical scholar Deborah Steiner, Pindar was reputed to have
been 'anointed on the lips with honey' as an infant, 'a
presage of sweetness that would come from his mouth' (45).
  Pindar is important as well for establishing honey as the
gift of the Muses (Olympian 7.7). The Muses would,
reciprocally, accept *melikrata*, thankful offerings of honey
from poets (Steiner 45), and in one passage (Olympian
10.98), Pindar 'imagines his song in the form of showers of
honey as the poet delivers what he himself has taken in from

his divine sources' (Steiner 46). Perhaps the best evidence that Plath had these classical associations in mind is in a book she used at the Smith College Library at the end of her teaching year there. In a journal entry dated August 27, 1957, she describes her fascination with *Possession Demoniacal and Other among Primitive Races, in Antiquity, the Middle Ages, and Modern Times*[18] The author, T.K. Oesterreich, quotes Plato in the *Ion*, and an underlined and asterisked portion of the citation reads:

> For the souls of the poets, as poets tell us, have this peculiar ministration in the world. They tell us that their souls, flying like bees from flower to flower, and wandering over the gardens and the meadows, with the honey-flowing fountains of the Muses, return to us laden with the sweetness of melody; and arrayed as they are in the plumes of rapid imagination, they speak truth. For a poet is indeed a thing ethereally light, winged and sacred, nor can he compose anything worth calling poetry until he becomes inspired, and, as it were, mad, or whilst any reason remains to him. (347)

This poetic identity as being 'ethereally light, winged and sacred' converges with Plath's appropriation of Shakespeare's *Ariel*, but Plato also offers a more fierce portrayal of the poet as completely possessed by 'the God' Bacchus, deprived of 'every particle of reason and understanding, the better to adapt them to [the] employment as his ministers and interpreters,' and further, the inspired poet is like 'the Bacchantes, who, when possessed by the god, draw honey and milk from the rivers, in which, when they come to their senses, they find nothing but simple water from the rivers' (Oesterreich 347). Honey is food for poetic frenzy and ecstasy – a divine seizure like that of Coleridge's bard in 'Kubla Khan,' who 'hath fed' on 'honeydew.' As Hughes describes Plath in 'The God,' she too claimed possession of this kind:

Then you wrote in a fury, weeping,
Your joy a trance-dancer
In the smoke in the flames.
'God is speaking through me,' you told me.
(*BL* 191)

Neither the Greeks nor Romans knew how bees create honey. According to the classical scholar Deborah Boedeker, citing the Greek Hesiod's *Theogony* and Roman Pliny's *Natural History*, they believed that 'honey originates in a kind of 'dew' collected by bees' (47). The poetic impact of this confusion is evident in Coleridge's 'honeydew,' derived perhaps from Pliny, who, in a famous passage, describes the descent of honey-dew before dawn, 'pure and liquid and genuine' in its 'heavenly nature,' and tells how the bees sip this elixir from 'foliage and pastures' (Rackham 1967.450–53). Virgil also praises 'the heavenly gift of honey from the air' and takes it as his 'theme' in book 4 of the *Georgics* (124), a text that poses as a handbook to beekeeping, but is in fact didactic in quite other ways, establishing allegorical links between the beehive and poiesis.

Honey for Virgil is simultaneously his inspiration and his song.[19] At the end of the *Georgics*, the poet describes himself as being nourished by 'sweet Parthenope' and composing the *Georgics*, 'enjoying there / The studies of inglorious ease' (11.564–65, 143) and dallying in pastoral verse in the same kind of landscape he has recommended for bees. While this may seem a self-disparaging commentary on his 'slender' or 'slight' labor as a poet (*in tenui labor*), it links him with the bee, who also labors *in slendor*. The bee's domain, though humble, is 'a world in miniature':

> Little the scale
> To work on, yet not little is the glory
> If unpropitious spirits do not cramp
> A poet and Apollo hears his prayer.
> (11.4–7, 124)

A Late Winter Miracle

For Roman poets, then, as for the Greek Pindar, the bee in its labors, is a poet of sorts. Horace came to be known as 'the Bee of Matina,' a mountainous spot near his birthplace in Apulia, for his liquid and bee-like humming verses, as in the following passage from *Odes* 4.2: 'I, in the way and mode of a bee of Matina [*Matinae / more modoque*], plucking the pleasing thyme with the greatest labor about the grove and the banks of moist Tiber, [I] small, fashion songs full of work.' This representation of poets and orators as honey-tongued bees, and the metaphorical exchange between the work of honeybees and poets, is a tradition of long standing, then, from Pindar to Virgil to Dickinson.[20]

On a less exalted level, the honeybee's labours inspire the housewife's homilies about busyness, memorialized in samplers and commonplace books:

> Th' Industrious bee extracts from ev'ry flow'r
> Its fragrant sweets, and mild balsamic pow'r.
> Learn thence, with greatest care & nicest skill
> To take the good, and to reject the ill:
> By her example taught, enrich thy mind,
> Improve kind nature's gifts, by sense refin'd;
> Be thou the honey-comb – in whom may dwell
> Each mental sweet, nor leave one vacant cell.
> (embroidery by Sarah Ann Hitch, 1790, quoted in Style 6)

The leap here from honey to 'mental' sweets says much about the ease with which the honeybee could serve didactic ends. From Isaac Watt's reliance on the 'little busy bee' to convey his warnings *Against Idleness and Mischief* (Style 28) to Tickner Edwards's admiration for its 'definite plan of life' (*The Bee-master of Warrilow*, 1920, cited in Style 42), the honeybee was an especially appealing allegorical example of the value of hard work and good husbandry. This tradition extends once again back to the epic poet Virgil in his pastoral mode, who devotes book 4 of *The Georgics* not only to telling the story of Aristaeus, the mythical patron of bees, but also to providing humble commandments on the rituals of beekeeping: 'Let no yew / Be found too near the hive. Let no red crab / Be roasted on your hearth' (11.46–48, 125). As these superstitious warnings suggest, he holds honeybees in high esteem and treats them with reverence for their power to bring wealth and good luck to their human keeper.

From the honeybee, then, there are ancient lessons to be learned about diligence and healing power, about self-improvement and frugality, all of which may have appealed to Plath's sense in these final months of being 'like a very efficient tool or weapon' (letter to Marcia Brown, January 2, 1963, Smith College Library, Mortimer Rare Book Room) in her handling of a writing career, single motherhood, and caretaking of Court Green. She is especially proud of the yield of crops from her country estate and tells her friend that she has harvested seventy apple trees, strung all of her onions, dug up and scrubbed all of the potatoes, and extracted and bottled her honey. She is 'flattened' by her labors, but revels in being an 'all-round desperado.' Similarly, to Olive Higgins Prouty she boasts of her housewifely resourcefulness, her 'practicality' and 'business sense.' She has taken on the burden of managing everything – 'taxes, insurance, repairs' – even lugging 'great buckets of coal' to keep a stove going constantly, something she says Ted could not do. She has become 'hard-headed,' toughened mentally under the duress of being a single mother, and has discovered how capable she is (letter of November 20, 1962, Smith College Library, Mortimer Rare Book Room). Indeed, it would be a mistake to disregard Plath's pride in her competence. In 'Letter in November,' she is like a guard dog, jealously patrolling her estate:

> This is my property.
> Two times a day
> I pace it, sniffing
> (*CP* 253)

and joyously taking account of her harvest:

> The apples are golden,
> Imagine it –
> My seventy trees
> Holding their gold-ruddy balls[.]
> (*CP* 253)

In a seemingly Virgilian mood, Plath told her interviewer after a BBC reading in October 1962, 'I like my little *Lares* and *Penates*,' the Roman household gods who ruled over the hearth and heart of the house, and further, that she much preferred the company of her friends with practical knowledge over her fellow poets: 'But I must say what I admire most is the person who masters an area of practical experience, and can teach me something. I mean, my local midwife taught me how to keep bees. Well, she can't understand anything I write. And I find myself liking her, may I say, more than most poets. . . . As a poet, one lives a bit on air. I always like someone who can teach me something practical' (171). Like Virgil's 'song of the husbandry of crops and beasts' (*Georgics* 4.1, 558, 143), Plath's bee poems also have a humble dimension, reflecting her veneration for householding virtues – 'something practical.'[21]

Combining these metaphorical associations with both hard work and poetic magic, with both drudgery and honey-sweet song, is the relationship between Shakespeare's Prospero and Ariel, a more direct inspiration for Plath. Throughout *The Tempest*, Prospero commands the energies of Ariel to assist in his illusions.[22] Ariel sings as he helps Prospero to 'discase' himself from a magician's robes and to dress as a man:

> Where the bee sucks, there suck I,
> In a cowslip's bell I lie;
> There I couch when owls do cry.

> On the bat's back I do fly
> After summer merrily.
> Merrily, merrily shall I live now,
> Under the blossom that hangs on the bough.
> (*The Tempest* 5.188–94)

Ariel's song is framed by the twice-reiterated promise of Prospero to his 'dainty Ariel' that 'Thou shalt ere long be free' and 'yet thou shalt have freedom' (5.1.87,96). Ariel's honeybee-like industriousness – Prospero calls him 'my diligence' (5.1.240) – as a slave in Prospero's service is here associated with his gift for song, and together these win his emancipation.[23]

Apis mellifera / apis mellifica: Bearer or producer of sweets

The allegory in 'The Arrival of the Bee Box,' the second poem of the bee sequence, is embedded, I believe, in the luxuriant associative structure surrounding bees and honey. If we read the speaker in 'The Arrival of the Bee Box' as the poet being presented with a potent source of both honey-sweetness and melodic song (Greek and Latin poets were fond of punning on *melos*, 'melody,' and *mellifera*, 'bearer of sweets'), then Plath seems to be confronting the problem of poetic identity and the burden of authorship and control. To what degree does she own the hive and its honey, and to what degree is she owned by it? To what extent is this gift of poetic production also a curse? The speaker's relationship to her bees also mimics Prospero's to Ariel and Caliban, except that unlike Prospero, she is an unwilling master to the bees' slavery, ambivalent toward exploiting the quite evident power trapped in the box for her own advantage. Of course, Plath's bees seem more threatening than industrious. Unlike Ariel, but much like Prospero's other slave, Caliban, they have no mellifluous songs to offer their owner, but only 'noise' – 'The unintelligible syllables' of 'a Roman mob' (*CP* 213) – or, in Caliban's case, verbal abuse: 'You taught me language, and my profit on't / Is, I know how to curse' (1.2.363–64). Prospero is willing to exercise his power, and regularly punishes Caliban for being a laggard in doing his work: 'thou shalt be pinch'd / As thick as honeycomb, each pinch more stinging / Than bees that made 'em' (1.2.328–30).

Despite the obvious differences between Prospero and Plath's speaker, their predicament is analogous. They are both burdened with responsibilities they would prefer to cast off – as Prospero is permitted to do at play's end, when he 'abjures' his 'so potent art' (5.1.50–51) and returns to assume his throne as Duke of Milan. He overcomes his desire for vengeance against his brother and the others who conspired to deprive him of his dukedom, and with a magic akin to Shakespeare's own poetic artifice, contrives a 'brave new world' (5.1.184) and happy ending commensurate to his daughter Miranda's innocence and wonder. His work done, Prospero gives Ariel one more 'charge' – 'calm seas, auspicious gales' to bring everyone home to Milan – and then keeps his promise to set Ariel free: 'Then to the elements / Be free, and fare thou well!' (5.1.317–18). It is not clear, however, what his plans are for Caliban, who seems incapable of imagining his own freedom. When Caliban rebels against Prospero, he simply chooses another master in the drunken sailor Stephano, far inferior to Prospero. Similar to the speaker in Plath's poem, who reluctantly acknowledges, whether she likes it or not, 'I am the owner' (*CP* 213), Prospero has to take responsibility for Caliban:

> Two of these fellows you
> Must know and own, this thing of darkness I
> Acknowledge mine.
> (5.1.274–76)

Plath's speaker explains, with some amazement at her entrepreneurial stupidity: 'I have simply ordered a box of maniacs' (*CP* 213). Like Prospero, who finds Caliban intractable and unteachable in learning language, who 'wouldst gabble like / A thing most brutish' (1.2.356–57), the question for Plath's speaker is, how will she ever extract honey – allegorically, poetry, and meaning – from this 'din' (*CP* 212) of angry bees?

> How can I let them out?
> It is the noise that appalls me most of all,
> The unintelligible syllables.
> It is like a Roman mob,
> Small, taken one by one, but my god, together!
> (*CP* 213)

The choice of 'appalls' supports the allegory here since it means, literally, to make white – like a blank page that will remain so if she can make no sense out of this noise.[24] The individual bees are syllables that refuse to become words or sentences, to assume meaning. When they come together, they are an unintelligible mob, not a hardworking, honey-producing hive, nor are they, in terms of allegory, capable of either understanding the poet's bidding or producing poetic utterance. In contrast, when Prospero says, 'then exactly do / All points of my command,' the supremely literate Ariel responds, 'To th' syllable' (1.2.500–502).

What compounds these difficulties with literacy is that Plath's speaker also does not seem to know whether she has ordered Italian bees, famed for their gentleness and ample honey production, or the Africanized bee, 'which was let out of its Pandora's box in Brazil in 1957' and is characterized as 'a sort of Jaws of modern apiculture' for its aggressive nature (Style 50). In one stanza the speaker characterizes her bee box as a 'thing of darkness,' an African slave ship:

A Late Winter Miracle

> It is dark, dark,
> With the swarmy feeling of African hands
> Minute and shrunk for export,
> Black on black, angrily clambering.
> (*CP* 213)

Once again the 'black on black' suggests a mob of disconnected syllables, an ink-blotted inscription that garbles language. In the first draft Plath precedes this line with the crossed-out 'Crawling, waiting for a white' (1), as if the 'African hands' are seeking a white enemy to grasp, but also, allegorically, as words looking for a white page to attach with their (s)crawl. This final line recalls the 'words' like crawling hands in Plath's drafts for 'Burning the Letters,' also 'clambering' over one another to escape the fire. In the next two stanzas, however, the speaker identifies her bees as Italian in origin – as a 'Roman mob,' and then, 'I lay my ear to furious Latin. / I am not a Caesar' (*CP* 213). Finally the bees are understood by the speaker as having a language – Latin – but it is foreign to her. Even worse, she fears they are plotting her assassination, just as Julius Caesar was killed by a political conspiracy – or as Prospero was overthrown by his brother.

Once again, if we look to *The Tempest* for guidance in reading this allegory, we find an analogous conflict surrounding the uses of magic for Prospero, and Caliban and Ariel as representing his choices. Caliban's spiteful and vengeful nature, immune to Prospero's 'nurture' (4.1.189), has its origin in his mother's the witch Sycorax. Banished from 'Argier' in Africa 'For mischiefs manifold, and sorceries terrible / To enter human hearing' (1.2.264–65), she was a practitioner of the art of black magic on the island before Prospero and Miranda were marooned there. Prospero explicitly connects Sycorax's magic with what is, if not illiterate or unintelligible, unspeakable. With Caliban, characterized as 'being capable of all ill' (1.2.354), Sycorax represents one possibility open to Prospero of using his magic, his art, to satisfy his anger and punish both the brother who usurped his throne and those who conspired with him to kill Porspero. Prospero's other option – and the one he takes – is to subdue his enemies by making them penitent. Ariel, though not human, encourages Prospero to temper the exercise of his power with tenderness:

> Your charm so strongly works 'em
> That if you now beheld them, your affections
> Would become tender.
> (5.1.17–19)

Prospero assures Ariel that

> Though with their high wrongs I am strook to th' quick,
> Yet, with nobler reason, 'gainst my fury
> Do I take part. The rarer action is
> In virtue than in vengeance.
> (5.1.25–28)

For Plath as well, especially at this moment in her life, the choice is between an art that seeks vengeance and an art that, if not capable of forgiveness for what she believes are 'high wrongs' committed against her, will at least choose virtuous 'rare action.' Briefly, Plath's speaker imagines a Sycorax-like move against her beees: 'They can die, I need feed them nothing, I am the owner' (*CP* 213). Then, in a Prospero-like gesture, she decides, 'Tomorrow I will be sweet God, I will set them free' (*CP* 213). The choice, too, is between two languages – Caliban's curses and Ariel's dulcet lyrics. She decides to release her bees to their Ariel-like task of collecting nectar from 'the laburnum, its blond colonnades, / And the petticoats of the cherry' (*CP* 213) as a prelude to her release in the next poem, 'Stings,' as a queen bee.

'The sad thing is that the power for destruction is real and universal'

Like all allegories, the bee poems have several levels, and it would be a mistake to ignore their political and historical dimensions. Hence, the Prospero-like decision to set the bees free needs to be seen as more than poetic justice, but also as an endorsement of the right to self-government. Indeed, for the bees to be productive on behalf of the beekeeper, and for the queen bee in 'Stings' to be fecund, the beekeeper must relinquish absolute control over the hive. Before looking at 'Stings,' regarded by many critics as the centerpiece of the bee sequence, I would like to turn to 'The Swarm' and its relationship to 'The Ariel of the Bee Box' on the basis of their shared concern with the exercise of political power over the bees and with the hive as a social and political entity. Whereas in both 'Stings' and 'Wintering,' Plath seems almost exclusively interested in the hive as a poetic organism and with her poetic identity in relation to the hive as a 'honey-machine' (*CP* 206), these other two bee poems cast beekeeping as an art of political maneuvering. In 'Stings' and 'Wintering,' she derives personal power and healing balm from beekeeping through a dramatization of herself in intimate exchange with the feminine symbolism inherent in honeybees. By intimate exchange, I mean that she is the poetic artificer of this symbolism and also permits her identity to be constructed by it. She is both owner of and owned by the hive, and while never fully at ease with this inseparable condition, she still appears to find support in 'telling the bees' her inner state.[25] Her discomfort with this relationship of identity and sameness – with being, as she says, 'Like the pack, the pack, like everybody' (*CP* 216) – is explored as a political anxiety in 'The Arrival of the Bee Box' and 'The Swarm.'

In contrast, then, to the feminine and personal dimension

of 'Stings' and 'Wintering,' both 'The Arrival of the Bee Box' and 'The Swarm' interrogate power relationships with the hive that seem primarily masculine and public, and historically recognizable. In 'The Arrival of the Bee Box,' as we have seen, there is an extended analogy between honeybees and a Roman mob, and the speaker is worried about her godlike power, alternately depicted as akin to slave owning and being a Caesar to unwilling citizens. 'The Swarm,' in turn, depends on a metaphorical likeness between Napoleon's Grand Army and the swarming activity of honeybees in spring. There is also an analogy, I would argue, between the dramatic situation in 'The Swarm,' which opens with a sense of random and unexplained violence – 'Somebody is shooting at something in our town' (*CP* 215) – and Plath's distress over news from America: 'the public announcements of Americans arming against each other – the citizens of Nevada announcing they will turn out bombed and ill people from Los Angeles into the desert (all this official), and ministers and priests preaching that it is all right to shoot neighbors who try to come into one's bomb shelters.' In this letter she is also 'depressed . . . about the terrifying marriage of big business and the military in America' (letter to Aurelia Plath, December 7, 1961, *LH* 438, 437), and this finds expression in her depiction of the beekeeper in 'The Swarm' as both a military figure and 'a man of business, intensely practical' (*CP* 217).

Finally, whereas 'Stings' and 'Wintering' worry privately over the recovery of a royal identity as queen – 'Is she dead, is she sleeping? / Where has she been' (*CP* 215) – and whether the hive's 'Maids and the long royal lady' (*CP* 218) will 'Succeed in banking their fires / To enter another year' (*CP* 219), the anxieties in both 'The Arrival of the Bee Box' and 'The Swarm' are directed at the bees as a violent populace. The question of how to pacify or to govern them is primary. While the decision of the speaker as beekeeper in 'The Arrival of the Bee Box' appears finally to be toleration, in the ruling style of a Prospero, the representation of the beekeeper in 'The Swarm' is of a greedy military man – a little Caesar like Napoleon – who wants complete control, even at the cost of many lives.

Political readings of the allegory in 'The Arrival of the Bee Box' circulate around the speaker's ambivalence toward being in a position of coercive power over a hive. Hence, Rose Kamel interprets the stanza about the African bees as concerned with 'exploited blacks in the Third World,'[26] and goes on to scold Plath's speaker for her unwillingness to assume responsibility for their release: 'As a kind of Pandora she toys with the notion of unleashing their violence on the world. . . . Their release, however, would not ensure her safety, for their political instability has a long history' (310), alluded to in the reminder of Julius Caesar's assassination of the menacing 'Roman mob' of the next stanza. Barbara Hardy is likewise concerned with the poem's instability in terms of closure, ending as it does with the observation, 'The box is only temporary' (*CP* 213). For Hardy, Plath 'puts the beekeeper into an unstable allegorical God-position' (73) – unstable principally because the speaker is too fearful, too much a victim to play God. Both of these readings look forward to feminist readings of the speaker as a woman, and therefore reluctant to assume the masculine roles of master or God.

Building on Hardy's observations, Mary Lynn Broe, for example, designates this 'God-position' as 'authoritarian ownership,' and because Plath's speaker ultimately rejects this position and ownership – here and in the bee sequence as a whole – Broe argues that 'Plath has discovered that the power of inertia is, paradoxically, one of the greatest literary possibilities for contemporary women' (*PP* 149, 155). Finally, Van Dyne further indicates the authoritarian mastery in the poem as 'experimenting with fathering' even while the poem allegorizes a woman's 'frightening, uneasy intuitions of a poetic pregnancy' that threatens to take control over her body (*RL* 107, 106). Indeed, Van Dyne interprets the poem overall as exploring, through beekeeping, feelings mothers are normally taught to deny and powers mothers do indeed have over their children but are socially encouraged to suppress: 'As she reenacts pregnancy in the poem, the speaker pretends the mother-child bond can be claimed or severed at will and that dependencies can be controlled,' and further, 'In toying with the freedom that male authority might bring to the task of mothering in 'Bee Box,' the poet's tone teeters between horrified fascination and feigned indifference as she tries . . . impermissible options' (*RL* 151).

As this review of the critics suggests, Plath has been regarded as incipiently feminist in her attitudes toward political power in the bee sequence. Carole Ferrier's argument in 'The Beekeeper's Apprentice,' for example, is that there is 'an attempt first to consciously realize and then to eliminate or exorcise the destructive or repressive aspects of dominating maculinity' in Plath's later poems. Ferrier goes on to specify both the beekeeper and Napoleon in 'The Swarm' as projections of patriarchy and patriarchal power, as father figures who stand in the way of 'revolutionary social change' (204). My own earlier assessment of the 'mind of the hive' in Plath's bee sequence was that, in addition to providing possibilities for Plath to explore the social role(s) of women, this 'mind' embodied an existential terror for her. The beehive's 'combination of individual mindlessness with overall design and intelligence' spoke to her sense that evil in the world could be explained only by a 'master mindlessness' at work: 'Is it coincidence or design that governs the 'gross eating game,' the 'one death with many sticks'? Is there a divine intelligence in the order of the universe, or just a *tabula rasa?*' In answer to these questions, 'the "black, intractable mind" of the beehive, with its efficient order of queen, workers, and drones, and the rituals of beekeeping, provide Plath with an objective correlative for this terror, on both a personal and historical level' (*PI* 178, 177).

In 'The Swarm,' as with 'The Arrival of the Bee Box,' I

now believe that other influences may be more important than Plath's incipient feminism. Without repudiating or denying the critique of patriarchy as one element in the multilayered allegory of the bee poems, I would like to move the discussion in a different, less overtly feminist direction in terms of how Plath unites the personal and political in 'The Swarm.' Plath's private drama and Napoleonic history also coalesce in ways far more peculiar and complex than my own previous account of the mind of the hive would suggest. Indeed, the poem's many eccentricities may have prevented it from being accepted for publication before Plath's death, and persuaded her to pull it as an entry from her final typescript for the 'Other *Ariel*.' The reading of 'The Swarm' that follows relies once again on *The Tempest* as one context, on the collective wisdom of beekeepers on swarming behavior, and on Plath's sense of the allegorical richness of bees as a poetic medium for her to yoke together very disparate motives, and to satisfy simultaneously very different ends.

'A new destiny is being prepared'

Swarming is probably the least understood phenomenon connected with honeybees. Maurice Maeterlinck professes to feel something like religious awe at 'the genius of the race' (44) when, at the height of its prosperity, a colony of bees will leave its thriving polis: 'Never is the hive more beautiful than on the eve of its heroic renouncement, in its unrivalled hour of fullest abundance and joy; serene for all its apparent excitement and feverishness.' Unlike human history, which, to Maeterlinck's nineteenth-century imagination, follows a pattern of decline and fall in cities, states, and entire civilizations, the honeybee colony swarms as a 'great immolation to the exacting gods of the race.' Thus, 'they will not leave at a moment of despair; or desert, with sudden and wild resolve, a home laid waste by famine, disease, or war.

No, the exile has long been planned, and the favourable hour patiently awaited. Were the hive poor, had it suffered from pillage or storm, had misfortune befallen the royal family, the bees would not forsake it. They leave it only when it has attained the apogee of its prosperity' (46–47). The sense of noble resolve and sacrifice is especially apparent for Maeterlinck in the behaviour of the queen, who initiates swarming in response to the hive's zeitgeist:

> Restlessness seizes the people, and the old queen begins to stir. She feels that a new destiny is being prepared. She has religiously fulfilled her duty as a good creatress; and from this duty done there result only tribulations and sorrow. An invincible power menaces her tranquillity; she will soon be forced to quit this city of hers, where she reigned. But this city is her work, it is she, herself. She is not its queen in the sense in which men use the word. She issues no orders; she obeys, as meekly as the humblest of her subjects, the masked power, sovereignty wise, that . . . we will term the 'spirit of the hive.' But she is the unique organ of love; she is the mother of the city. She founded it amid uncertainty and poverty. She has peopled it with her own substance; and all who move within its walls . . . all those have issued from her flanks. (39)

Maeterlinck admires what is known as the 'prime swarm' with the old queen, usually in late May or June, to distinguish it from other and later types of swarming, and to stress the behaviour whereby a colony reproduces itself through migration and temporary depopulation of the old hive.[27] One of the symptoms of swarming is, in fact, the formation of queen cells with rival virgins (Root 605), one of which will take over the old hive after the old queen leaves. One could argue that the old queen is forced to migrate in order to avoid confrontation with a younger rival and perhaps to save herself, although Maeterlinck prefers to praise both her and her companions for their valor, not their discretion: 'Let us, yet once again, admire the courage with which they begin life anew in the desert whereupon they have fallen. They have forgotten the splendour and wealth of their native city, where existence had been so admirably organised and certain, where the essence of every flower reminiscent of sunshine had enabled them to smile at the menace of winter' (131–132).

There are some obvious analogies between the migration of the queen bee in the 'prime swarm' and Plath's courageous efforts 'to begin life anew' away from the 'splendour and wealth' of the home she had created for herself in Court Green. The danger of a young rival, the sense of self-investment in her home, of being disrupted from an 'organised and certain' existence just when the 'menace of winter' looms – Maeterlinck unknowingly seems to capture the drama of Plath's situation. Yet this is not the way swarming is motivated in Plath's poem, nor does the beekeeper, the Napoleon figure of 'The Swarm,' appear to understand the bees except as a potential source of wealth – 'O ton of honey!' (*CP* 217) – or, alternately, a menace: 'Pom! Pom! "They would have killed *me*"' (*CP* 217).

As Plath depicts the swarming bees in her poem, they are far removed from the nobility Maeterlinck gives them. Plath's swarm does not seem to have a queen leading it, but instead is a mass-motivated mob:

> So dumb it thinks bullets are thunder.
>
> It thinks they are the voice of God
> Condoning the beak, the claw, the grin of the dog
> Yellow-haunched, a pack-dog,
> Grinning over its bone of ivory
> Like the pack, the pack, like everybody.
> (*CP* 216)

Maeterlinck's 'genius of the race' is here reduced to a pack mentality, and the governing law is Darwinian – nature red in tooth and claw. Because of their stupidity, the bees are easily manipulated by the beekeeper, who shoots them down from their perch in a tree.[28] According to beekeeping experts, this is an unnecessarily violent and extreme tactic that also is unlikely to succeed: 'If the bees cluster on a limb of a tree or bush where they can be conveniently reached, one of the simplest ways of hiving them is to cut off the limb above the clustered bees and carry it to the hive. Care must be taken in cutting off the limb not to jar it or the bees may drop off, take wing, and cluster elsewhere' (Root 608). Plath's bees, though, 'have got so far. Seventy feet high!' (*CP* 216), making capture difficult. Even at this unmanageable height, the recommendation is to use a ladder to reach them; better still, the competent beekeeper thinks ahead and clips the wings of the queen in advance of swarming so that she will fly neither too high nor too far and thereby escape capture (Root 609, 607). Finally, Plath's beekeeper appears to justify his shooting on the basis of the swarm's 'Stings big as drawing pins!' (*CP* 217). Swarming bees, however, only look threatening: 'A flying hedgehog, all prickles' (*CP* 216). In reality, they do not sting. Because they are so heavily laden with a store of honey for their migration, they cannot bend their bodies into stinging position.[29] But Plath also appears to be sarcastic in her exclamatory 'drawing pins,' which are, after all, mere thumbtacks.

The satiric tone of 'The Swarm' suggests that Plath was fully aware of the beekeeper's ignorance and hubris, which takes the form of Napoleonic delusions of grandeur. Of course, Napoleon himself might be said to have suffered from such delusions. Plath's speaker taunts him in her first draft, 'You fatten. You're forty' (2), and cuts him down to size with a line alluding to his short stature and the burden of his exile carried like a deformity: 'The hump of Elba on your short back' (*CP* 216). Napoleon's territorial ambitions to annex 'Russia, Poland and Germany!' are mocked by diminution through a sustained comparison with the beekeeper's military pursuit of the swarming bees into

> The mild hills, the same old magenta
> Fields shrunk to a penny
> Spun into a river, the river crossed.
> (CP 216)

The reader is forced continually into a Swiftian game of ascertaining scale and translating sizes into values – of alternating between a perception of human ambition and greed as reflecting a puny, Lilliputian human nature, or as gargantuan, excessive, reflecting an overweening pride in self. Are Napoleon and his history no larger than the efforts of a beekeeper to capture his swarm of bees? Or, alternatively, is the beekeeper so self-important that he sees himself as an emperor of sorts over his bees? In four lines Plath juxtaposes for our consideration and comparison the beekeeper's capture of the swarm, Napoleon's exile on Elba, and the self-glorification of military men:

> The swarm is knocked into a cocked straw hat.
> Elba, Elba, bleb on the sea!
> The white busts of marshals, admirals, generals
> Worming themselves into niches.
> (CP 217)

After all the unnecessary shooting, the beekeeper performs a simple task, Napoleon is finally emperor of a mere 'bleb,' and military leaders are immortalized in monumental statuary, lest we forget their exploits in war. In draft 1 these leaders 'Are carving themselves into niches' (2), which doesn't sound quite so insidious or ignoble as Plath's final choice of 'worming.' In a didactic gesture I read as mocking and insincere, the speaker follows this satiric grouping with 'How instructive this is!' (CP 217)

In terms of instruction, what might be said of the beekeeper, Napoleon, and military men is that they all abuse their power over the bees – allegorically, the beings they attempt to lead and to rule. This is instruction of a negative kind, that is, how not to govern. Napoleon and his 'marshals, admirals, genrals' treat the French soldiers/bees as pawns in a game of empire:

> Shh! These are chess people you play with,
> Still figures of ivory.
> The mud squirms with throats,
> Stepping stones for French bootsoles.
> The gilt and pink domes of Russia melt and float off
>
> In the furnace of greed. Clouds, clouds.
> (*CP* 216)

The debacle of Napoleon's Russian campaign and the muddy defeat at Waterloo are condensed here into a satire on Napoleon's insatiable ambition. The lives lost in battle are treated as no more than 'stepping stones' for his own advancement, wickedly pictured as a lurid fantasy of 'gilt and pink domes.' The wealth of czarist Russia eludes Napoleon, first like a cloud that dematerializes. Then Moscow burns, as if it is only fuel for imperial greed. Perhaps, too, Plath is assuming a Prospero-like disdain for this greed: he likewise views the 'cloud-capp'd towers' and 'gorgeous palaces' of earthly power as an 'insubstantial pageant' that will finally melt 'into air, into thin air' (4.1.149–54).

In advance of this ostensibly strange yoking of Napoleon with beekeeping, Plath was aware of his appropriation of bee symbolism to express his imperial power. The emblem of golden bees was 'chosen to replace the fleur-de-lis of the Bourbons. It appears to have been the cypher of one of the ancient kings of France. Embroidered on dresses, sewn onto mantles, woven into carpets, worked into hangings, mounted onto coats of arms, swarming across every available surface in palace, cathedral and processional way, were thousands upon thousands of glittering golden bees' (Aronson 69). Given the years Napoleon spent in Egypt, bees must have been especially appealing to him for their appearance in tombs as hieroglyphs representing the royalty of the pharaohs (Style 12). Ultimately, this manipulation of honeybees, whether their wealth is conceived of literally as in the beekeeper's seizure of their honey or symbolically as Napoleon's ubiquitous embellishment of 'Mother France's upholstery' with golden bees, is viewed as self-aggrandizing puffery. The poem's final two lines bring the two metaphorical registers together as signifying the beekeeper/Napoleon's smug triumph: 'Napoleon is pleased, he is pleased with everything. / O Europe! O ton of honey!' (*CP* 217).

'It was mine art / . . . that made gape / The pine, and let thee out'

As might be expected, there is also a personal level to this satiric allegory. Plath reviewed *Josephine*, a biography of Napoleon's wife, in April 1962, emphasizing, in Linda Wagner's view, 'Josephine's devotion to her husband, even as he plans to divorce her and force her to Navarre.' and her nobility and fidelity, even while Napoleon engaged in many affairs ('Plath on Napoleon' 6). The beekeeper/Napoleon identity, in Van Dyne's view, is a 'surrogate for the absent Hughes' (Stings 10), and as evidence she cites Elizabeth Sigmund's memoir. Plath, Sigmund reports, told her, 'Ted lies to me, he lies all the time, he had become a little man' (104). Van Dyne also suggests that the Russian allusions – the poem's 'emotional landscape' – may well be inspired by Assia Wevill's ancestry (*Stings* 10); Assia is described later by Hughes in 'Dreamers' as 'A German / Russian Israeli' with 'Her father / Doctor to the Bolshoi Ballet' (*BL* 158). Van Dyne specifies Plath's overall 'goals' in the poem as, first, to create an opportunity for the 'venting of dangerous emotions' towards Hughes and Assia Wevill, and second, to find 'a historical analogue for her own case' (*Stings* 10).

My own sense of this personal level of symbolic meaning is that it also has poetic dimensions. One may read Napoleon's plunder of Europe's wealth and the beekeeper's greedy desire for the hive's honey as expressions, once again, of Plath's complaint that Hughes was expending large sums of money from their shared bank account. This money, as Plath repeated reminds a reader of her letters, was earned principally by their writing, and therefore also represents their achievement as artists. If beekeeper/Napoleon is a surrogate for Hughes as a poet as well as husband, then the abuse of the swarming bees and theft of their honey, together with Napoleon's looting of Europe and ultimate defeat and exile, are simultaneously indictments of him as an artist. Napoleon's self-embellishment with the royal insignia of golden bees may well symbolize Plath's derision of Hughes's inflated artistic ego. Even more, such display constitutes a usurpation of what rightfully belongs to her adornment as the daughter of Otto Plath – a royal descent already claimed earlier, in 'The Beekeeper's Daughter':

> Father, bridegroom, in this Easter egg
> Under the coronal of sugar roses
>
> The queen bee marries the winter of your year.
> (*CP* 118)

What leads me especially to this reading, however, is the beekeeper's ineptitude in 'The Swarm.'

Whereas the father in 'The Beekeeper's Daughter' is a 'maestro of the bees,' tending to the fertility of 'the many-breasted hives' (*CP* 118), the beekeeper of 'The Swarm'

184

appears to have greedily botched his work. He may have successfully hived the swarm, but the bees are described as 'banded' as if in bondage, and

> Walking the plank draped with <wifely> Mother France's
>   upholstery,
> Into a new <coffin> mausoleum <with a new number,>
> An ivory palace, a crotch pine.
> (draft 1, 2)

The beekeeper is a pirate here, and the booty is the bees' honey, while his captives are all choosing to die rather than join his ranks. As Plath says in the final stanza, 'It seems the bees have a notion of honor' (*CP* 217). Behaving honorably, they are willing to die for their hive – and for their queen, for Mother France. In terms of the art of beekeeping, the beekeeper's incompetence in shooting wildly at the swarm has probably cost him the queen necessary for the hive's survival. These bees, the imagery suggests, are dying – hived in a 'coffin' or 'mausoleum' – and therefore unlikely to produce any more honey for him. Like Napoleon and the beekeeper, the poet Hughes has, by violence, exhausted the source of his wealth. He has paid an exorbitant price for a minor victory. Finally, if the bees are being forced to enter a 'crotch pine,' then Hughes, like the witch Sycorax, has temporarily imprisoned – also in a pine – the poetic muse Ariel. Only a Prospero-like art will recover a queen and release Ariel and the bees from their imprisonment.

'A queen \<she has been\> boxed \<a long time\> too long'

Although Van Dyne does not compare Plath to Prospero in her interpretation of 'Stings,' she argues persuasively that the poem's extensive revisions reflect a desire to transform vengeful energy directed at Hughes toward what Prospero might deem the virtuous and rare task of 'resuscitating the queen' (*RL* 108) and thereby quelling a usurpation of her throne. The first drafts to 'Stings' date back to early August and vividly describe the bees stinging a beekeeper assumed to be a representation of Hughes:

> Their death-pegs stud your gloves, it is no use running.
> The black veil molds to your lips:
> They think they must kiss you, they think death is worth it.
> (draft 1, 2)

The queen bee does not figure at all in this first narrative, nor is the trespasser identified clearly in the male antagonist who plays an important role in the final poem.[30] Instead, the poem circles around the 'suicidal' energies of the worker bees, who are driven ('they must kiss you') to 'assail' the human intruder, even though a sting means certain death, since a worker bee disembowels herself with the embedding of her stinger.[31] The speaker is in no way intimately identified with the bees or their fate in this early version. Indeed, she seems to be shaking her head in disapproval at times at the bees' irrational behaviour. They are like a routed army – 'After, they stagger and weave, under no banner' (drafts 1–4) – and because the hive is without human sentiment, their deaths are \<Ignominious!\>:

> \<They have no heart for martyrs.\>
> \<They must die by themselves.\>
> \<They are no more use.\>
> (draft 1, 2)

In draft 4 she exlaims, 'They are fools!' and all drafts conclude with the line 'Gelded and wingless. Not heroes. Not heroes.' This final line rather oddly masculinizes the injury done to the female worker bees, who are 'gelded,' commonly connoting castration of a male creature, by virtue of losing their stings. The mortally wounded workers are also treated rather like the stingless drones when they are dismembered and the hive's 'housewives' <will not have> are clearing them <on> from their <white> doorsill.' In the 'Stings' written in October, this element of male injury, loss, and death will be incorporated into the representation of what implicitly must be the queen bee's second nuptial flight and her mating with the hapless drones, who also believe 'death is worth it.'

Indeed, the only line she salvages from the earlier 'Stings' for the October version is 'They thought death was worth it' (CP 215). The revision to past tense indicates that she has already moved beyond the motivation of impotent workers. In the new poem, this line functions as a point of distinction for the speaker, who refuses identification with the vengeful and suicidal workers and shifts her attention completely away from their attack on a male onlooker: 'but I / Have a self to recover, a queen' (CP 215). This new version of the poem, with its investment in the queen, may also be read allegorically as seeking the revival and release of the Ariel persona as a queenly self – an imprisoned artist figure and muse. As we shall see, the prison is not a tree in this instance but domestic incarceration and an identity as an industrious housewife, as one of 'These women who only scurry, / Whose news is the open cherry, the open clover' (CP 214).

When the poem begins, beekeeping is represented as entirely a domestic economy, a transaction between a bee seller and the sentimental housewife, who fondly describes her hive as 'a teacup, / White with pink flowers on it' (CP 214). In lady poet diction, like the inserts in women's magazines, she coos over her 'neat and sweet' gloves and

portrays the bee seller's and her own wrists as 'brave lilies.'
Like a bride who is setting up her house for the first time, she
has somewhat foolishly, 'With excessive love . . . enameled [the
hive] / Thinking "Sweetness, sweetness"' (*CP* 214). Although
she seems quite pleased with the hive's honey sealed in 'Eight
combs of yellow cups,' the 'Brood cells gray as the fossils of
shells / Terrify me, they seem so old' (*CP* 214).

These details betray a speaker who is naïve about the
meaning of the hive and blind to its sexual energies. Plath
must have known that it is precisely the presence of brood
cells which assures a new beekeeper that the hive contains a
queen (Root 105), while her speaker, squeamish about their
appearance, worries, 'Is there any queen at all in it?' (*CP*
213). Midway through the poem, this naïve speaker also
describes her hive as

> . . . my honey-machine,
> It will work without thinking,
> Opening, in spring, like an industrious virgin
>
> To scour the creaming crests
> As the moon, for its ivory powders, scours the sea.
> (*CP* 214–15)

Personified as an 'industrious virgin,' the hive has purity,
but at the expense of thought. There is also something
odd about the repeated 'scour' and 'scours' to describe the
labor of bees. Instead of collecting nectar, dew, or pollen,
instead of being fertilizing propagators of flowers and
fruit, these bees are cleansers. Despite the loveliness of
'creaming crests' and 'ivory powders,' there is something
sterile about these 'honey-drudgers' (*CP* 214), and, even
more important, little recognition by this innocent speaker of
honey-making as poiesis.

'How long she has been unheard of!'

The climactic release of the queen bee at the end of 'Stings' – her singular appearance in the bee poems – depends, first, on the speaker's rejection of this naïve and 'unmiraculous' identity for the hive, for herself, and for its honey-making activity, and second, on a self-awakening to the 'terrible' power of the queen. Initially, the speaker is unsure whether there is a queen, but 'If there is, she is old' (CP 214). In terms of beekeeping, an old queen's emergence defies all the rules. After the initial bride flight and mating with drones, the queen is 'possessed of a dual sex, having within her an inexhaustible male, [and] she begins her veritable life; she will never again leave the hive, unless to accompany a swarm; and her fecundity will cease only at the approach of death' (Maeterlinck 320). Before mating with the drones, a queen bee is capable of laying eggs, but ironically they all hatch as drones: 'Through a curious inversion, it is she who furnishes the male principle, and the drone who provides the female' (Materlinck 319). What must have been especially appealing to Plath is the queen's possession of a male principle even before the bride flight, and then the fertile sufficiency of the queen after her nuptials, for then, 'in the obscurity of her body [is] accomplish[ed] the mysterious union of the male and female element, whence the worker-bees are born' (Maeterlinck 319). From the queen's body, then, all of the hive's activity is born, and all of its wealth derived.

Like the worker bees when they sting, the drone is disemboweled in the act of mating, and the queen 'descends from the azure heights and returns to the hive, trailing behind her, like an oriflamme, the unfolded entrails of her lover' (Maeterlinck 316). In 'Stings,' Plath's image of the queen as a 'red comet' (CP 215) simulates this moment of triumph and disaster for the drone, now but a comet's tail, or a banner in her wake, heralding her queenly victory. The queen internalizes the drone's sexuality that is necessary both to complete her own and for the full exercise of her creative power, but once this is accomplished, the male is 'a great scapegoat' to the hive: 'He was sweet, / The sweat of his efforts a rain / Tugging the world to fruit' (*CP* 215). Here Plath replaces the 'ivory powders' and scouring agency with the male's sweetness and sweat, suggesting a world dewed in honey. His 'efforts' resemble the 'tugging' labor of childbirth, and his sweat is like breaking waters. In an earlier draft, his sweat/rain falls 'On the world that grew under his belly' (draft 1, 3), recalling a pregnant woman.

The nuptial flight happens only once normally, after a virginal queen emerges from her wax-covered 'cradle' and either defeats the old queen, if she is still in the hive, or 'massacres' all of her 'rival queens' (Maeterlinck 317). Plath knows that she is imposing her own desire on the 'normal' bee narrative, poetically transgressing a biological destiny. She discards lines in an earlier draft that 'explain' the impossibility of a second bride flight:

> . . . I
> Have a <soul> self to recover, a queen
> Climbing into a bride-flight
> In a glitter of years like dew diamonds.
> The new queen sings over the old queen.
> I am unstung.
> Now we are one.
> A queen <she has been> boxed <a long time> too long.
> (draft 1, 2)

In this earlier version, the new queen appears to be born out of the body of the old – as if released from 'the engine that killed her – / The mausoleum, the wax house' (*CP* 215) that is the hive as domestic carceral. They 'are one' and the same being; there is no battle, since the speaker, who identifies with the queen, is miraculously, 'unstung,' and the release and marriage are crowned with 'dew diamonds.' The new queen is also drenched in these 'dew diamonds,' as if anointed with a royal unguent like the ancient honey-dew, a gift of the Muses to the poet that even here produces song in the new queen. In the final version of 'Stings' as well, dew remains important as a royal distinction, as what separates her from the worker bees:

> I am no drudge
> Though for years I have eaten dust
> And dried plates with my dense hair.
>
> And seen my strangeness evaporate,
> Blue dew from dangerous skin.
> (*CP* 214)

Other poems by Plath also seem pertinent here in linking the presence of dew with an election by the Muse of poetry. Rebirth in 'Getting There' is figured as 'a minute at the end of it / A minute, a dewdrop' (*CP* 248), and in a rite that borrows language from beekeeping, the speaker, like a queen bee over her cells or 'cradles,' releases the souls of others through the medium of dew:

> I shall bury the wounded like pupas,
> I shall count and bury the dead.
> Let their souls writhe in a dew,
> Incense in my track.
> The carriages rock, they are cradles.
> (*CP* 249)

Written on her birthday, 'Ariel' defines the speaker as 'The dew that flies / Suicidal' (*CP* 240), and even in 'Death & Co.,' 'The frost makes a flower / The dew makes a star' (*CP* 255). In the aftermath of a killing frost, the dew on the dead flower still 'makes,' as in 'crafts' or 'artifices' a star. In the earlier 'Stings,' these lethal senses of dew are absent, as Plath celebrates the nuptials of the queen bee.

'Telling the Bees'

In terms of beekeeping lore, perhaps the best explanation for why Plath chose these bee poems to end the 'Other *Ariel*' is the widespread folk custom of 'telling the bees.' In her 1939 memoirs of life in Oxfordshire, *Lark Rise*, Flora Thompson describes an incident when a beekeeper died and the bees were told, 'Bees, bees, your master's dead, an' now you must work for your missis' (87).[32] According to beekeeper Sue Style, in Ted Hughes's native Yorkshire this custom of 'telling the bees' is still widely practiced: 'When the beekeeper died, the bees had to be told of his death otherwise they too would die. Less commonly other family events of note were also told to the bees, indicating the special place of honour they held in the family' (18). A Yorkshire proverb counsels:

> Marriage, birth or burying,
> News across the seas,
> All your sad or merrying
> You must tell the bees.
> (18)

Plath may have been aware of this British custom, and in placing her bee poems at the end of the 'Other *Ariel*,' she gives them the privileged burden of knowing all the 'sad or merrying' she has experienced and recorded in this poetic narrative.

Like so many contemporary beekeeping superstitions, 'telling the bees' has an ancient analogue in Pindar's Pythian odes and the Homeric Hymn to Hermes. Pindar calls the oracle at Delphi the 'Melissa Delphidos,' or the Delphic Bee, with whom suppliants consulted or received prophecies (Pythian 4.60).[33] Susan Scheinberg describes the bee maidens of Delphi in the Hymn to Hermes as 'honey-maddened' prophetesses who look and behave like bees. They tell the truth after eating honey and the honeycomb, but 'deprived of honey,' may well mislead their petitioners: 'As an outward sign of their mental state, they fly 'now here, now there' when truthful, but they 'swarm in and out together' when they lie' (11). Knowingly or not, the poet of the Hymn ascribes veracity to the maidens when they imitate nectar-sipping bees, and deception to them when they imitate bees' winter clustering. In tracing the origins of the bee maidens, Scheinberg also notes that the poet's association of bees with divination and chaste maidenhood was not eccentric: 'Bees were associated with Demeter's cult: the first priestess of Demeter at Corinth, according to legend, was an old woman named Melissa (Servius on *Aeneid* I.430); the initiates in the Eleusinian mysteries and the participants in the Thesmophoria are called "bees"' (fn. 80, 20). This latter connection may have been important to Plath, who borrowed fron the Demeter-Persephone myth for her early poem 'Two Sisters of Persephone,' and devoted one elaborate pen and ink drawing to a portrayal of Ceres.[34]

Whether or not Plath knew about either the folk tradition of 'telling the bees' or, as I have argued, the ancient alliance of bees with oracles and poets, her final bee poem, 'Wintering,' seeks both prophecy and intimate communion with the hive. The connections between honey and both poetry and soothsaying, between the mind of the hive and the poet's interior creative life, all seem to be completely in place in this final poem of the 'Other *Ariel*.' Together with knowledge about the winter behavior of the bees, these folk and literary traditions also provide a rich allegorical context for understanding Plath's finale for the 'Other *Ariel*.'

The timing of Hughes's departure in early October from Court Green and the enforced leavetaking of the drones is a parallel that could not have escaped Plath. Drones are commonly expelled from the hive in late September or early October, when flowers begin to grow scarce and the honey-making activity of the hive slows down. Indeed, 'There is no way in which one can tell so well that the yield of honey has

ceased as by the behaviour of the bees toward their drones'
(Root 221). It is almost as if the workers are distracted by
their constant summer labor from noticing the lazy drones,
and then suddenly become intolerant and irritated by their
presence when the harvesting of nectar and pollen ceases.
The worker bees begin to prod the drones, threatening to
sting them, and the guards, sometimes referred to by
beekeepers as Amazons, refuse the drones reentry after their
habitual afternoon flight.[35] What I have already described as
the massacre of the males is not far away. In her first draft
for 'Wintering,' Plath's speaker explains why the males are
expendable in winter:

> The bees are all women,
> Maids and the long royal lady.
> They have got rid of the men,
> The men have only their sex & they eat too much honey.
> <They will make men again>
> <Anyway,> Winter is for women[.]
> (draft 1, 2)

Domestic economy dictates eviction, and 'anyway,' drones
will once again be created for the spring, when they are
needed.

The simultaneous departure of the drones and the ensuing
halt to honey-making also cause Plath some allegorical
difficulty: if honey-making is also poiesis and both song and
prophecy are honey-induced, then won't the creative process,
like the bees, also cease its labor with the onset of winter? At
the beginning of the poem, the speaker is very briefly
complacent about this cessation and content with what is a
rather slight harvest:

> This is the easy time, there is nothing doing.
> I have whirled the midwife's extractor,
> I have my honey,

A Late Winter Miracle

> Six jars of it,
> Six cat's eyes in the wine cellar[.]
> (*CP* 217)

In her first draft, these jars are also 'Six corn nubs' and 'six gold teeth' (1), extending the metaphors of extraction and treasure, but also stressing the minuscule size of what her summer has produced. The insistence on 'six' may refer to the number of poems written over the summer, as a poetic harvest of sorts, or to the first six years of her marriage.[36] Either or both may explain the sudden shift in mood in the second stanza, from placid to disparaging and then to anxious. These jars are sitting next to clutter that has been forgotten, used up – 'the last tenant's rancid jam' and empty bottles of 'Sir so-and-so's gin' – and stored in a 'room I could never breathe in. / The black bunched in there like a bat' (*CP* 218). Suddenly the 'easy time' of winter begins to look like a gothic prison, and the speaker, not unlike the heroine of gothic novels, has a sense of being inhabited by the house's past, ghosted and dispossessed of her selfhood by

> . . . appalling objects –
> Black asininity. Decay.
> Possession.
> It is they who own me.
> (*CP* 218)

In the first draft, it is clear that the junk, the objects in the wine cellar, are what own her. They are 'Appalling for their cheapness, their decay! / Their possession!' (1). In the final poem, however, 'they' quickly slides metaphorically into the bees, the room into the hive's interior, and the speaker is possessed not by objects but by the consciousness of this female society in its winter hibernation.

'<What sort of spring?>'

In her life as in her poetry, Plath looked for signs and portents. Her discovery of the flat in London, 'with its blue plaque announcing that Yates had lived there,' seemed to her a summons from the dead poet: 'Back in Devon, jubilant, full of plans, she consulted Yeats's Collected Plays, hoping for a message from the great poet. Sure enough, when she opened the book at random her finger fell on the passage 'Get wine and food to give you strength and courage, and I will get the house ready' in *The Unicorn from the Stars*' (BF 275).

If Plath is seeking mantic power in 'Wintering' by giving herself over to 'possession' by the hive, then the ending of the poem may be read like other oracles, as a seductive riddle, easy at first glance, but meant to foil the supplicant trying to unveil the mystery of her fate. As Scheinberg notes, 'Even the oracle of Apollo withholds the truth at times, though accepting all offerings. The revelation of accurate prophecies is thus a matter of discretion for the gods' (11). Plath's first draft of 'Wintering' ends with a frantic series of questions and a final prayer which leave the petitioner in a state of uncertainty, dependent utterly on the 'discretion' of the gods:

> Snow water? Corpses? <Thin, sweet – A sweet spring.
>   Spring?> Spring?
> <Impossible spring?>
> <What sort of spring?>
> <O God, let them taste the spring.>
> (2)

As another winter in Devon approached, Plath struggled to discern a miracle of survival for herself through the medium of the bees. Nowhere is her fear of the months to come expressed more viscerally than on the reverse side of her draft of 'Wintering,' where the typescript for *The Bell Jar* reads, 'I could feel the winter shaking my bones and banging my teeth together, and the big white hotel towel I dragged down with me lay under my head numb as a snowdrift' (draft 1, 2).[37]

During the winter months, honeybees do not, strictly speaking, hibernate. Despite their cessation of honey-making, they are far from being in a deep sleep or dormant. Their behavior is described as 'clustering' (Root 620–24), or as Plath describes them, 'Now they ball in a mass' (*CP* 218). There is continual movement of bees from the surface of this cluster or ball to the center, where there is optimal warmth. It is a system of heat exchange, and in many ways the ball behaves as a single organism, circulating warmth throughout the hive's body. In a discarded stanza Plath shows her expertise on bees' winter activity:

> <Now they are clustering.
> Banded body to banded body.
> Warmth is life,
> It is how they <<you> tell themselves <<yourself>> from the dead.
> It is cold. <<Now>> they will <<not>> risk nothing.>
> (draft 1, 2)

Here, too, the bees – 'they' – commune with 'themselves' and are virtually interchangeable with the poem's speaker, 'you,' communing with 'yourself.' Later these lines will evolve into Plath's description of the hive as a 'Black / Mind against all that white' (*CP* 218), suggesting a unity of thought and purpose. Past readings of this mind and Plath's communion or identification with it have been predominantly negative, as in Van Dyne's summary: 'In her body's imitation of the bees' minimal survival, the poet is nearly immobilized, her consciousness on the verge of extinction' (*RL* 114).

Yet this consciousness is also obstinately resistant to extinction, to the menacing whiteness of the snow, and further, this mind of the hive is also related to her poetic muse Ariel. An earlier draft of this stanza reads, 'Black mind against all that white – / The Ariel kisses, the scissory facets. <snow, snow, the smiling killer!>' (2). This is consistent with the identification of beekeeping, honey-making, and the mind of the hive with poetic melody – honey – and the diligent bee, Plath's Ariel persona, in the other bee poems. In winter clustering, the bees are in a continual state of touching one another; hence the description of this 'black mind' as brooding on itself through its 'kisses.' In draft 2 the 'scissory facets' are 'Six-sided kisses' (1), which may refer to the honeycomb's hexagonal structure, from which the bees sip – kiss – honey, or to the multifaceted eyes of bees. There is a suggestion, too, that this complex facetedness is 'scissory' and visionary weaponry, able to cut and to see through the blinding whiteness.

Allegorically, the blackness of the mind opposed to the obliterating whiteness of winter snow is, as in 'The Arrival of the Bee Box,' black ink against blank white paper, the writing process as an act of both survival and purgation during the winter months. The hive expresses itself through a cleansing process in final stanzas of the poem which rids the hive of drones but also, 'on warm days,' ritualistically removes the dead. Visually, Plath asks us to imagine a hive cleaning that spatters the snow with bee corpses, or, metaphorically, with whatever is dead inside the poet, served up on snow compared to the finest bone china from Meissen – that 'spreads itself out, a mile-long body of Meissen' (*CP* 218). Even more important in terms of this black against white visual imagery is the flight of bees in Plath's concluding stanza:

> Will the hive survive, will the gladiolas
> Succeed in banking their fires
> To enter another year?
> What will they taste of, the Christmas roses?
> The bees are flying, they taste the spring.
> (*CP* 219)

A Late Winter Miracle

The time of year is February, with the blooming of the evergreen Christmas rose, *Helleborus niger*, a 'late winter miracle' that is 'undaunted even by a crust of snow.' February is also when the queen bee begins laying eggs again, in preparation for early spring flowers, and when bees are seduced out of the hive's protection by a winter thaw. A flight at this time of year is obviously premature, but German beekeepers also celebrate this moment of awakening in the hive: 'Great store is set by this delicately termed *Reinigungsflug* ('cleansing flight'), one of the earliest signs of life from the hive' (Style 55). Beekeeper William Longgood is less delicate in his description of the cleansing process: 'Soon the pristine snow is soiled with brown splotches of excreta around the hive. Other bees, already relieved and returned to quarters, are busy with housekeeping chores, dragging out corpses to drop them over the edge of the landing board, sweeping aside wax cappings, and restoring order' (226). This snow is spattered with evidence of the hive's need to purge dead matter.

If we also understand Plath's allegorical intention as the desire to purge dead matter, her choice of the Christmas rose is especially pertinent. The root of this plant is a powerful cathartic, and administered carelessly, as its Latin name suggests, may poison rather than cure the patient. Additionally, as a medicinal purgative, *Helleborus niger* was used not only for stomach ailments but also for mental disease, to exorcise or purge the mind of painful delusions and hallucinations. Because of its dangerous potential to cause seizures, however, this purgative was used rarely and sparingly. (*OED*, s.v. 'hellebore'). As with the flight of bees on deceptively warm winter days, the Christmas rose is, in terms of its prophetic meanings, both promising and menacing, both a curative medicine and a deadly poison. A cleansing flight might easily lead to death for the bees, just as anything more than a 'taste' of the Christmas rose would be a tragic catharsis.

In 'Wintering,' the affirmative line 'The bees are flying. They taste the spring' (*CP* 219) is a prophecy in response to the suppliant's questions about survival, and must be read like all oracles with great caution, as a riddle, with two equally plausible answers. Plath struggled with this final stanza, multiplying her questions before arriving at her final line.

Snow water? Corpses? A glass wing? A gold bee, flying?
A bee's on the wing.
The first glass
A gold
Resurrected,
Bee songs?
Is a bee flying?
(draft 3, 2)

'Snow water' and 'corpses' are familiar images to the beekeeper, who knows how easily bees drown in water, but also allude to the 'refined snow' fed to the bees in winter – the sugar syrup 'Tate and Lyle they live on, instead of flowers' (*CP* 218).[38] In these fumbling lines, too, she returns to the solitary bee, perhaps the queen again, since 'glass,' 'gold,' and 'resurrected' allude to her appearance in 'Stings.' 'Bee songs' tends to affirm the melodious joy of a spring rebirth for the poet-as-bee, as does the line 'A bee's on the wing.' Ultimately, Plath pursues none of these more certain revelations, and prefers 'the hive' and 'they' and an answer that is inconclusive. Plath did not know what flight to London would bring, nor could she guess how prophetic 'Wintering' would be.

'Nun-like / You nursed what was left of your Daddy'

On February 5, 1963, six days before her suicide, Plath began composition of the deadly poem 'Edge' on the reverse side of a typescript for 'Wintering' (typed copy 2, revised). As if inspired by the image of her bees against the backdrop of winter snow, 'Filing like soldiers / To the syrup tin' (*CP* 218), she initially titles this new poem 'Nuns in Snow' ('Edge,' draft 1, discarded title), and borrows the image of a white body – 'a mile-long body of Meissen' – for the dead body of a woman, now resting in a garden tableau. Hardened in rigor mortis, she resembles a piece of Greek statuary, and – nunlike – her body is chastely closed to the sexual seductions of the garden that 'Stiffens and odors bleed / From the sweet, deep throats of the night flower' (*CP* 273). Plath eventually discards this title with its Christian associations, but it evokes, once again, a legend about the worker bee as a figure of female chastity: 'The worker bee was blessed on leaving the Garden of Eden with the title of 'handmaid of the lord,' like Mary, with whom she seemed to share the distinction of a virgin birth' (*Style* 16). The dead woman perversely resembles a Madonna, posed with a dead child at each of her breasts.

It is tempting to read 'Edge' against 'Wintering' and its oracle of spring rebirth, now unveiled as deceptive in its promise. Indeed, the lines

> Her dead
>
> Body wears the smile of accomplishment,
> The illusion of a Greek necessity
> Flows in the scrolls of her toga
> (*CP* 272)

would seem to confirm the fatal denouement veiled in an oracular riddle. What was intended as a 'cleansing flight' and cathartic 'taste' of the Christmas rose for the bee poet of the 'Other *Ariel*' ends instead with death. In conversation with herself, then, Plath is already writing beyond her ending. The question must remain, however, whether Plath's decision to create definitive closure in 'Edge,' where there was only an open-ended oracle and unanswered riddle in 'Wintering,' also authorizes Ted Hughes's decision to alter the ending of the 'Other *Ariel*.' As we have seen, Hughes at times expressed uncertainty about whether the volume might not have more coherence without the addition of the 1963 poems, and openly stated that these later poems were part of a new volume.

With the publication of *Birthday Letters*, however, Hughes appears to have arrived at his own interpretation of the allegory in the bee poems, and it tends to confirm once again the overall sense he has of Plath's poetic trajectory as fatal and doomed. In dialogue with Plath's bee muse, Hughes's poem 'The Bee God' (*BL* 150–52) explicitly links her bee sequence with a nunlike wedding that joins her to her dead father as a god. When she took up beekeeping, she 'became the Abbess / In the nunnery of the bees' (*BL* 150). Hughes may also have in mind Dickinson's 'White Election' (no. 528) to her 'Father's breast – / A half unconscious Queen' (no. 508), in the protective veil and gloves, the 'white regalia' Plath wears that is also characterized as poetic garb; for when Plath marries Daddy, she is simultaneously wedded to a poetry of bees inherited from him as a Germanic king of the bees:

> Your page a dark swarm
> Clinging under the lit blossom.
>
> You and your Daddy there in the heart of it,
> Weighing your slender neck.
>
> I saw that I had given you something
> That had carried you off in a cloud of gutturals –
> (*BL* 150)[39]

Whereas for Plath the swarming and clustering motion of the hive invites the poet to 'tell the bees,' to brood and commune with the beehive and its muse in '*Ariel* kisses,' Hughes typifies the buzzing swarm as this 'cloud' of harsh

Germanic syllables, a 'cave of thunder,' and their language is the father's: 'the bees' orders were geometric – / Your Daddy's plans were Prussian.' Daddy's orders and plans are to execute him, with stings like 'volts' and 'thudding electrodes' in an electrical storm built from 'The thunderhead of your new selves' (*BL* 151).

'Then the script overtook us'

For Hughes as for Plath, the rituals of the hive and beekeeping are also points of allegorical convergence with Shakespeare's *Tempest*, but here, too, in Hughes's view, Shakespeare's plot goes terribly awry and Plath's allegory turns against itself. Instead of Prospero being in control of the action – and, even more important, in control of his own vengeful wrath – and instead of Ariel winning release from the pine, in *Birthday Letters*, Sycorax intervenes and Caliban usurps Ariel's role. As Hughes reinvents the Shakespearean plot Plath borrowed at times for the 'Other *Ariel*,' a bellowing beast instead of dainty Ariel is set free from Plath's writing desk, her elm plank. In *Birthday Letters*, the witch Sycorax, supported by her malevolent god Setebos, was always present offstage, watching Hughes and Plath. Biding her time, Sycorax prepares herself as a deus ex machina to destroy their peace. She enters with a tempest of her own and avenges her loss of the island to Prospero: 'She hurled / Prospero's head at me, / A bounding thunderbolt, a jumping cracker' (*BL* 133). As in 'The Bee God,' he is executed with a 'thunderbolt,' and the 'thunderhead of [Plath's] new selves' is transformed into the decapitated head of Prospero, hurled in wrath at Hughes. Prospero, the benevolent artist and magician who subdues his desire for vengeance, is sacrificed to Plath's fury. Hughes explains, 'Ariel was our aura' (*BL* 132) before Plath began writing the October poems, just as they were Ferdinand and Miranda until an ogre, a 'little god flew up into the Elm tree' ('The God,' *BL* 189) asking for blood and sacrifice, until 'Caliban reverted to type,' and Hughes

> heard
> The bellow in your voice
> That made my nape-hair prickle when you sang
> How you were freed from the Elm. I lay
> In the labyrinth of a cowslip
> Without a clue.
> ('Setebos,' *BL* 132)

These lines by Hughes interpret the release of Plath's *Ariel* persona – but no longer the 'tricksy spirit' Ariel – as a tragic reversal. For Hughes, it was not a pine but the elm that stood outside her window, 'inhabited by a cry' (*CP* 193), which inspired her and from which her muse was freed. It was also the elm plank on which she wrote, described by Hughes in 'The Table' as the entryway to her father's coffin. Ultimately, for Hughes, Plath failed to release 'dainty Ariel,' failed to assume the identity of poet as bee producing mellifluous and healing song. Instead, Hughes names as her muse a vengeful Caliban and minotaur, a bellowing beast, while he assumes the Ariel identity ('In a cowslip's bell I lie'), but an Ariel now lost, 'without a clue,' in a cowslip turned into King Minos' labyrinthine maze.

At least one dimension to *Birthday Letters*, then, is Hughes's extension of the allegory initiated by Plath in the bee sequence. In his adoption of the Ariel identity as his own, the poet-as-bee, Hughes simultaneously creates a poetic argument that Plath abdicated this identity when she dedicated herself and her voice to a poetry of vengeance and sacrificial grief. He does not blame her for this abdication so much as grieve for her as a victim of its unintended consequences. As I will demonstrate in my final chapter, Hughes offers an alternative poetry of mourning to

Plath's in *Birthday Letters* and attempts to restore to Plath her Ariel muse, her 'kindly spirit' and 'a guardian, thoughtful' (*BL* 198). He wants to remember her in his own way, and in doing so, significantly alter her portrait in literary history.

FOUR

Mourning Eurydice

Ted Hughes as Orpheus
in *Birthday Letters*

It seemed you had finessed your return to the living
By leaving me as your bail, a hostage stopped
In the land of the dead.

Ted Hughes, 'The Offers'

I see you there, clearer, more real
Than in any of the years in its shadow -
As if I saw you that once, then never again.

Ted Hughes, 'St. Botolph's'

As yet, critical reception of Ted Hughes's *Birthday Letters* has focused relentlessly on biographical issues. Published thirty-five years after Plath's death, these letter-poems addressed to his dead wife seemed to promise answers to the many questions biographers have asked about the circumstances of their marriage, his apparent desertion of her and their children in 1962 for another woman, and his feelings about her suicide. After a prolonged and obdurate silence, Hughes suddenly appeared ready to tell what was presumably his side of the story – what A. Alvarez calls 'scenes from a marriage, Hughes's takes on the life they shared' ('Your Story' 58). Not suspecting what might now be understood as the urgency of their dramatic appearance in January 1998, critics and reviewers did not know that the poems were published even as Hughes was dying.

Perhaps if they had, the response would have been more sympathetic. With few exceptions, reviewers were inclined to question both the emotional and factual veracity and objectivity of Hughes's account. Symptomatic of this preoccupation with biographical accuracy is Katha Pollitt's description of the dilemma for Hughes's readers: 'Inevitably, given the claims that these poems set the record straight, the question of truth arises.' And Pollitt, with several other reviewers, was not convinced that Hughes was capable of impartiality, or even a modest and limited personal truth, expecially not over the stretch of eighty-eight poems and two hundred pages of verse: 'That intimate voice . . . is overwhelmed by others: ranting, self-justifying, rambling, flaccid, bombastic. Incident after incident makes the same point: she was the sick one, I was the 'nurse and protector.' I didn't kill her – poetry, Fate, her obsession with her dead father killed her. The more Hughes insists on his own good intentions and the inevitability of Plath's suicide, the less convincing he becomes' ('Peering' 6, 4). In a blistering review for the *New Republic* titled 'Muck Funnel,' James Wood likewise denounced *Birthday Letters* as boringly repetitious mini-tantrums: 'His poems are little epidemics of blame' (31) that endlessly rebuke the dead Plath and her poems, and reading them is 'like listening to one half of a telephone call' (30).[1] The other side of the conversation is missing.

Even when a reviewer offered a more positive view of *Birthday Letters* as poetry rather than biographical truth or evidence of some kind, as in Jack Kroll's praise of Hughes's 'masterly arsenal of forms, rhythms and images' (59), the laurel was quickly withdrawn because Hughes was not as 'merciless to himself' as he should have been, did not submit himself to the 'deep self-examination' that would have provided answers to biographers who want to know 'Why did he leave? And what happened to drive Assia to exactly the same self-destruction as Plath?' (59). Similarly, even as Jacqueline Rose in her review forgave the omen- and portent-laden plot of *Birthday Letters* which other reviewers derided as evasive and 'borrowed from the most familiar dirty magics' (Wood 33), she reminded her readers of her own and other feminists' famous battles with Hughes and his sister Olwyn over interpreting Plath's work. She concluded her review by asking him to end this feud with Plath's partisan women readers, to retract his wrongheaded and self-righteous 'caricature' of feminists as hyenas feeding on Plath's corpse in 'The Dogs Are Eating Your Mother.'

As all this suggests, *Birthday Letters* has received very little interpretation based on literary values or on the critical effort to intuit Hughes's motives as a poet as well as a husband. He is addressing his tragically dead wife, and this is why we have come to eavesdrop – to discover whether he wants belatedly to admit his guilt for her suicide or to offer intimate glimpses into what seemed to be a closed chapter in his life. As Pollitt notes, 'The storm of publicity surrounding *Birthday Letters* has turned into a kind of marital spin contest, an episode in the larger war between the sexes' (6), and Alvarez complains that the volume was on the bestseller list 'for all the wrong reasons. It's the Oprah Winfrey element' (quoted in Mead). Reviewers did not wish to interpret poetry so much as inquiring minds needed to know all the gruesome and scandalous details. Nor were feminist critics persuaded to examine Hughes's portrait of *the poet* Plath in *Birthday Letters* as at odds and in continued argument with the woman poet they had conceived and celebrated for literary history.

In what follows I shift critical focus away from the supposed evidentiary relevance of *Birthday Letters* as true or false testimony by a husband concerning his dead wife and their marriage, and focus instead on its literary dimensions. There is a conversation going on here between Hughes and Plath, and it is as much about poetry as it is about their marriage. Hughes's letters are not simply the utterances of a bereaved husband invoking the haunting presence of a beloved spouse, but also poems addressed by one poet to another. In 'Sam,' for example, Hughes speculates that when Plath survived a ride on a runaway horse, it was the genius of poetry that saved her:

> What saved you? Maybe your poems
> Saved themselves, slung under that plunging neck,
> Hammocked in your body over the switchback road.
> (*BL* 10)

The poems she wrote in her final months, Hughes suggests here, needed her to live long enough to write them, and by saving her, 'saved themselves' from oblivion. She 'couldn't have done it. / Something in you not you did it for itself' (*BL* 10), and that 'it' was poetic destiny at work. Similarly, in 'Flounders,' he claims that 'we / Only did what poetry told us to do' (*BL* 66), as if their lives were predetermined and their agency was governed entirely by the muse of their poetic marriage. Such assertions have no claim to factual truth, and indeed have been castigated as strategies for 'fate playing' – manipulations by Hughes throughout *Birthday Letters* to escape responsibility and culpability for what happened in his marriage to Plath.

I would like to begin, however, by simply acknowledging the fictive nature of such assertions and then describing what I see as a consistent patterning of poetic statements that offers an invented truth. Hughes clearly regards the *Ariel* poems about their marriage as inventions by Plath, corresponding to a Freudian and psychoanalytic narrative she imposed on her life and work. As we shall see, Hughes borrows from other sources, even as he contests Plath's invention with his own. His '*Birthday Letters*' are embedded with myth, superstition, and folklore, with references to other poems, many of them by Plath, and they display an inordinate degree of literary self-consciousness. When Hughes is not borrowing titles outright from Plath's poems – 'The Rabbit Catcher,' 'Totem,' 'Apprehensions' – he is, as we have seen, engaging his wife's preoccupation with honeybees and Otto Plath, with the figure of Ariel and the other dramatis personae from Shakespeare's *Tempest*, and with Plath's overarching themes of death and rebirth, mourning and melancholia. '*Birthday Letters*' are both companion poems and adversarial poems, in conversation and argument with Plath as a fellow poet of grief and as the irretrievable wife, Eurydice to Hughes's Orpheus.

'The life you begged / To be given again, you would never recover, ever'

Throughout *Birthday Letters* there is an implicit analogy between Hughes and Orpheus as the poet who mourns for his lost wife, Plath/Eurydice, who repeatedly fails to retrieve her from 'Inside that numbness of the earth / [for] Our future trying to happen' (*BL* 8–9), and who eventually challenges Plath's grieving verse with his own poetry of loss. By opposing her, he also releases himself from the melancholic and doomed poetic identity of Orpheus to complete a normal mourning process, simultaneously bidding a last farewell to his dead wife. In 'A Picture of Otto,' one of the final 'letters,' Hughes addresses Otto Plath, giving his wife back to her father, thereby lifting the mask Plath imposed on him in her verse, where the 'ghost' of Otto Plath is

> . . . inseparable from my shadow
> As long as your daughter's words can stir a candle.
> She could hardly tell us apart in the end.
> (*BL* 193)

Mourning Eurydice

At least one of Hughes's motives for writing *Birthday Letters* is to 'tell' himself 'apart' from Otto Plath in his poetic version of their marriage. Instead of joining his dead wife in the underworld, as Orpheus joins Eurydice in Ovid's *Metamorphoses*, Hughes descends to make peace with Otto Plath, meeting him 'face to face in the dark adit / Where I have come looking for your daughter' (*BL* 193). The ghost of Orpheus in Ovid

> . . . found Eurydice
> And took her in his arms with leaping heart.
> There hand in hand they stroll, the two together;
> Sometimes he follows as she walks in front,
> Sometimes he goes ahead and gazes back -
> No danger now – at his Eurydice.
> (11.63–68; 250–51)

The figure of Otto Plath, however, stands between Hughes and Plath, making such a reunion impossible, except on Plath's poetic terms, which deny Hughes an identity separate from her father. What Hughes has come to understand and accept is that she will always be her father's daughter:

> . . . you [Otto Plath] never could have released her.
> I was a whole myth too late to replace you.
> This underworld, my friend, is her heart's home.
> Inseparable, here we must remain.
> Everything forgiven and in common.
> (*BL* 193)

To hold his wife 'in common' with her father is the fate Plath's verse imposes on Hughes. Hughes's final line in 'A Picture of Otto' compares the dead Plath with Wilfrid Owen in Owen's poem 'Strange Meeting,' like Owen 'Sleeping with his German as if alone.'[2] Plath, too, sleeps with her German father – her only companion the supposed enemy she kills in her verse. The cold comfort of her poetic immortality is an eternity 'as if alone' ('Strange Meeting') with presences she herself created for imaginary battles. As Owen is forever identified as the poet who died too young, a casualty of the Germans in World War I, so Plath is remembered as another poet who died too young, a casualty of her own obsession with the German daddy, Otto Plath.

What further suggests that Hughes has appropriated an Orpheus-like identity for himself in *Birthday Letters* are two classical texts interwoven with its narrative: the already mentioned *Metamorphoses* of Ovid and book 4 of Virgil's *Georgics*. Hughes does not translate Ovid's version of the Orpheus and Eurydice myth for his own 1997 *Tales from Ovid*, but the overstated narrative in *Birthday Letters* often seems ruled by mythic powers of transformation, inspired by an Ovidian 'ether' invoked by the poet Hughes to explain his wife's poetic immortality. Even Plath's face is described in '18 Rugby Street' as continually metamorphosing, a shape-shifting shell for the restless spirit inside:

> A device for elastic extremes,
> A spirit mask transfigured every moment
> In its own séance, its own ether.
> (BL 23)

Plath's face is elementally protean, 'a stage / For weathers and currents, the sun's play and the moon's,' and does not assume its final mask, 'the face of a child – its scar / Like a Maker's flaw' until her death 'that final morning' (*BL* 23).

In the glossary for Hughes's *Tales*, Orpheus is described as the 'Thracian bard, whose music could rouse emotion in wild beasts, trees, and mountains; son of the Muse Calliope by either Apollo or Oeagrus, a king of Thrace; husband of Eurydice; after her death he wandered through the mountains of Thrace, playing his lyre' (252). The wildness associated with Thrace and Orpheus' musical affinity for animals and nature are frequently attributed likewise to the rough countryside and moors of Yorkshire and its native son, Hughes, also a poet of nature. In 'The Owl,' a 'letter' in which he remembers an early episode in his marriage to Plath, Hughes fascinates her with his Orpheus-like gifts: he rouses a predatory owl to swoop down on him by sucking 'the throaty thin woe of a rabbit / Out of my wetted knuckle.' Perhaps like Orpheus wooing Eurydice, Hughes 'made my world perform its utmost for you' (*BL* 33).

Finally, although Hughes does not appropriate Ovid's framing narrative, which begins book 10 of the *Metamorphoses* with the story of Orpheus and Eurydice and ends with the story of Orpheus' death to begin book 11, he does rework the Thracian bard's longer tales as they appear in Ovid: the stories of Pygmalion, Myrrha, Venus and Adonis, and Atalanta also form a group in *Tales from Ovid*. Of these tales, the story of Myrrha's attempted suicide and incestuous affair with her father, Cimyras, is especially pertinent to Hughes's understanding of Plath's suicide and her incestuous love for her father. Myrrha's metamorphosis into a tree weeping myrrh converges with Hughes's interpretation of Plath's 'Elm,' where she assumes its voice to give figurative expression to her experience of shock treatments –

> I have suffered the atrocity of sunsets.
> Scorched to the root
> My red filaments burn and stand, a hand of wires.
> (*CP* 192) –

and to an anxiety that 'petrifies the will': 'I am terrified by this dark thing / That sleeps in me' (*CP* 193). Like Hughes's narration of the birth of Adonis from the bole of his tree/mother, Myrrha – 'It heaves to rive a way out of its mother' (*Tales* 119) – is his description of Plath giving birth to *Ariel*'s voice from the process of composing 'Elm': 'the voice of *Ariel* emerges, fully-fledged, as a bird, "a cry"';

'Nightly it flaps out / Looking, with its hooks, for something to love' (*WP* 475). Like Hughes's Adonis in the *Tales*, conceived by Myrrha after spending several nights with her father, Cinyras, Plath's *Ariel* persona is, in his interpretation, the fruit of an incestuous bonding with her father in a classical underworld, followed by a strange metamorphosis:

> Between the second of April [1962], when she entered her father's coffin under the Yew Tree [in the poem 'Little Fugue'], and the nineteenth when she emerged as a terrible bird of love up through the 'taproot' of the Elm Tree, she has made a journey of self-transformation from the Tree in the West to the Tree in the East. From a tree at one of the gates of the underworld in the sunset to a tree at another of the gates of the underworld in the dawn. As if she had travelled underground, like the sun in the night, from one to the other other. (*WP* 475)

Hughes further describes this transformative journey by Plath as 'the bereft love returning to life' (*WP* 475), as if Plath had revivified her dead father, but only by disinheriting an erotic attachment that leads inevitably to her own suffering and sacrifice. As Hughes understands Plath's plight in 'Elm,' 'The unalterable truth to this reality is the voice's deeper negative story. It explains why the bird in the Elm 'terrified' her with its "malignity"' (*WP* 480–81). This 'terrible bird of love' is 'the voice of *Ariel*,' but nothing like Shakespeare's Ariel, and although Hughes may be described as similarly engaged in returning his bereft love to life in *Birthday Letters*, ultimately he will reject an ethos of sacrifice. His own mourning poems for Plath will enact a counter-ritual for expressing grief, at times anti-Ovidian in their handling of metamorphosis.

The other classical influence on Hughes's *Birthday Letters* is probably book 4 of Virgil's *Georgics*, a text commonly read by English schoolboys of his generation, and one that specifically intertwines the craft of beekeeping with the myth of Orpheus and Eurydice.[3] Here Virgil implicates Aristaeus, the classical patron of bees and beekeeping, in Orpheus' loss of Eurydice. As Hughes blames Plath's father, Otto, the entomologist and expert on bees, in 'The Bee God' and several other poems, for taking his wife away from him, so in the *Georgics* Orpheus' wrath is directed at the shepherd Aristaeus, whose lusty pursuit of Eurydice inadvertently precipitates her death. Aristaeus is punished when he loses all of his bees through famine and disease. Baffled at his misfortune, Aristaeus seeks oracular advice from Proteus, who explains why he has suffered this loss:

> The anger that pursues you is divine,
> Grievous the sin you pay for. Piteous Orpheus
> It is that seeks to invoke this penalty
> Against you – did the Fates not interpose –
> Far less than you deserve, for bitter anguish
> At the sundering of his wife. You were the cause:
> To escape from your embrace across a stream
> Headlong she fled, nor did the poor doomed girl
> Notice before her feet, deep in the grass,
> The watcher on the bank, a monstrous serpent.
> (11.452–61; 139–40)

Aristaeus is advised by Proteus to make a sacrifice to 'The nymphs with whom [Eurydice] used to dance her rounds' (1.534; 142), who sent 'this wretched blight' (1.535; 142) on his bees. From the 'putrid flesh' (1.554; 143) of a bull Aristaeus batters with a mallet until dead, a swarm of bees emerges to refurbish the ravaged hives of Aristaeus. Sacrifice reverses his misfortune and renews the life of his hives. Hughes reiterates this configuration of symbols and characters in *Birthday Letters*, adding to it an incestuous bond between Plath/Eurydice and Otto Plath/Aristaeus. Like Orpheus, he must contend with another maestro of bees who comes between him and his youthful wife and with a 'monstrous serpent' that appears as a 'great snake' and 'a mamba, fatal' to their marriage, in 'The Rag Rug.' In other poems, Otto Plath is a roaring minotaur, recalling the bull sacrificed by Aristaeus to renew his beehives. Otto Plath is also a 'German cuckoo,' like that bird usurping another's nest to lay the egg that will hatch into the voice of *Ariel*, 'fully-fledged, as a bird'; or, as Hughes goes on to describe the father who cuckolds him in 'The Table,' 'While I slept he snuggled / Shivering between us' (*BL* 138) – a cold, dead figure who robs their marriage bed of warmth and Hughes of his wife's body. Finally, in 'Fairy Tale,' he is an 'ogre' and once again Plath is a fledgling who 'died each night to be with him, / As if you flew off into death' (*BL* 159).

Throughout *Birthday Letters*, Hughes reiterates and refashions the Virgilian theme of sacrifice to placate and appease. The figure of Orpheus/Hughes, however, stands in stark contrast to Aristaeus, to Plath's poetry of sacrifice, to her father's portrayal as a bellowing minotaur demanding human victims, and, finally, to the women who advised Plath in her final days – like the nymphs who are Eurydice's friends and want Aristaeus punished. Whereas for all these figures in Hughes's narrative sacrifice is a form of reparation – even an exchange of death for new life – Orpheus/Hughes's loss is depicted as irreparable, his grief implacable, and his longing unappeased by sacrifice. Only through the historical process of remembering important moments in their marriage and then permitting them to fade does *Birthday Letters* complete the process of healing grief.

'Step for step / I walked in the sleep / You tried to wake from'

The early poems in *Birthday Letters*, even as they move forward temporally – love at first sight, a whirlwind courtship, marriage, and honeymoon – are also frequently encoded both with narrative strands belonging to the Orpheus-Eurydice myth and freeze-frames or snapshots arresting motion and reminding readers of Orpheus' impulsive gaze at Eurydice the final time. Memory and loss are conceived of as moments of backward-looking, briefly and stunningly vivid, then fading. Hence, in 'St. Botolph's,' Hughes remembers their first meeting: ' – suddenly you. / First sight. First snapshot isolated / Unalterable, stilled in the camera's glare' (*BL* 15). Almost immediately, however, he leaps forward to the 'years in its shadow – / As if I saw you that once, then never again' (*BL* 15), where 'its shadow' must be her death, the darkness that enfolds his 'clearer, more real' poetic imagining of his first sight of her. As with so many moments of Plath's evocation in *Birthday Letters*, Hughes works with paradox, with absence that is palpable, with a 'once' that is so real its 'never again' seems impossible – as impossible to accept as Orpheus' loss of Eurydice.

Another early letter, 'Caryatids (I),' plays with the frozen animation of Greek statuary – the young virgins who are simultaneously the columns supporting a roof. Hughes is also looking backward at the first poem he read by Plath, where these maidens make their appearance. Because he 'disliked' the poem 'through the eyes of a stranger' (*BL* 4), he 'missed everything' he now recognizes that he was meant to see. He foolishly

> . . . made nothing
> Of that massive, starless, mid-fall, falling
> Heaven of granite
> stopped, as if in a snapshot,
> By their hair.
> (*BL* 4)

In these artificed maids he might have discerned the ghostly aura of his future wife, 'Fragile, like the mantle of a gas-lamp' (*BL* 4), where 'mantle' alludes to the caryatids' streaming sculpted hair as an architectural framing support, but also to the mantle of a gas lamp, a mesh bag that holds the burning gas of the lamp and instantly crumbles to powdery ash at the slightest touch. With his friends, too 'careless / Of grave life' (*BL* 5), he saw 'No stirring / Of omen' (*BL* 4) in the 'Heaven of granite' held up by such 'friable' creatures, a forewarning of the terrible fate also waiting to come down on Plath, whose glowing and vivid appearance belied her fragility. The pun in 'grave life' alludes simultaneously to Plath's extraordinary posthumous life, the poetic immortality Hughes has had to take extraordinary care of, and also to how serious and precious life is and, contrarily, how careless youth is about death. Neither Orpheus nor Hughes anticipated how brief their marriages would be.

'Fate Playing' is about an incident in Hughes's courtship of Plath – a planned rendezvous in London that almost went awry – and may also be read as a warning. The poem ominously enacts a version of the Orpheus-Eurydice myth. Fate disguises its oracular content by playfully reversing the roles of Hughes and Plath. As Hughes emerges from a train at King's Cross, it is as if he has been pulled out of a dark underworld by the force of Plath's desire, suggested by his repeated use of 'molten' to describe the intensity of her inner fire. On their wedding day he will see her 'Wrestling to contain your flames' (*BL* 35), and here, in 'the flow of released passengers,' he sees her

> . . . molten face, your molten eyes
> And your exclamations, your flinging arms
> Your scattering tears
> As if I had come back from the dead
> Against every possibility, against
> Every negative but your own prayer
> To your own gods.
> (*BL* 31)

Even the taxi she hired to bring her there is a 'chariot' driven by a 'small god,' and her 'frenzied chariot-ride' may recall Persephone's kidnapping by Hades in a wagon, her descent as a young maiden like Eurydice into premature death. The poem ends with a miraculous tempest, a thunderstorm in which Plath's joy at being reunited with her 'lost' husband is

> Like the first thunder cloudburst engulfing
> The drought in August
> When the whole cracked earth seems to quake
> And every leaf trembles
> And everything holds up its arms weeping.
> (*BL* 32)

The epic simile here invites us to read – to exaggerate – this minor skirmish with 'fate playing' as artifice, equal to mythic Demeter's restoration of fertility to the earth when she is joyfully reunited with her daughter Persephone, or the mingled tears of joy and sorrow in Shakespearean recognition scenes. Hughes as Orpheus may well feel comfortable using the expansive epic simile, since Orpheus' mother was Calliope, the muse of epic poetry. He similarly deploys this technique to describe Plath's emotional response to Spain, too much an underworld like the one that envelops Eurydice, a nightmare world of insubstantial spirits

> . . . you tried to wake up from
> And could not. I see you, in moonlight,
> Walking the empty wharf at Alicante
> Like a soul waiting for the ferry,
> A new soul, still not understanding,
> Thinking it is still your honeymoon
> In the happy world, with your whole life waiting,
> Happy, and all your poems still to be found.
> (*BL* 39–40)

Plath's Spain mimics Eurydice's limbo between the world of the living and the world of shades to which she will be ferried after all memories fade. Indeed, in 'Moonwalk,' Plath sleepwalks on their honeymoon through a landscape resembling a charnel house and speaks a language belonging only to the dead. She mouths hieroglyphs from 'tomb-Egyptian' in her sleep that are 'like bits of beetles and spiders / Retched out by owls. Fluorescent, / Blue-black, splintered. Bat-skulls' (*BL* 41). Hughes, like Orpheus gazing at his wife from the dimension of life and vital color, watches Plath wander through 'a day pushed inside out. Everything in negative' (*BL* 41). He dares not wake her, and 'could no more join you / Than on the sacrificial slab / That you were looking for' (*BL* 42). Plath's search in sleep for an altar – 'sacrificial slab' – presages her later desperate search for a god to whom she can dedicate her writing and, finally, her life.

The mythic Orpheus, famed for his ability to animate what is dead, to imbue nature with his song, is also famed as the poet who fails, who looks back at the crucial moment and loses Eurydice, who then fades, loses corporeality, and becomes a shade. Indeed, Orpheus might be defined as the poet who fails, whose verse is dedicated to a compulsion to repeat his failure, fixated as he is on the lyric moment when desire comes into being as longing and regret for what may never be. As Eurydice dies twice, so Plath figuratively dies many times in *Birthday Letters*, as if retreating from the vividly realized life Hughes as poet/Orpheus briefly restores to her, fading again into a dark underworld, dematerializing as Eurydice did into the shadows. Hence, in 'The Blue Flannel Suit,' Hughes relives her appearance and still concentration the first morning Plath teaches at Smith College, only to lose the memory of her in the shade of her loss: 'as I am stilled / Permanently now, permanently / Bending so briefly at your open coffin' (*BL* 68). The paradoxical rocking between 'permanently' and 'briefly,' between a 'now' and an implicit forever, is commensurate to the realization of loss as brief, even while its trauma is lasting. Even more moving is the ending to 'Daffodils,' a poem that returns to the first and only spring they would have in their English home:

> We had not learned
> What a fleeting glance of the everlasting
> Daffodils are. Never identified
> The nuptial flight of the rarest ephemera –
> Our own days!
> (*BL* 127)

As with 'The Blue Flannel Suit,' his memory of this lost summer is at once fleeting and everlasting, ephemeral and eternal.

In an Orpheus-like reversal of a trope that conventionally celebrates spring rebirth, the 'everlasting daffodils' come to haunt Hughes with her death and his loss, as 'On that same groundswell of memory, fluttering / They return to forget' (*BL* 129) her every year. Only the 'wedding-present scissors' they lost while cutting daffodils in the garden remember, but what they remember is her burial: 'April by April / Sinking deeper / Through the sod – an anchor, a cross of rust' (*BL* 129). For Plath, as for Eurydice, there is no Christlike resurrection; the scissors are a rusting anchor pulling her down and a symbol for a life prematurely cut short. As a symbol of the Plath-Hughes marriage, too, the scissors both contrast and complement the meaning of the daffodils. The scissors are about the burial of memory, its gradual submergence and the healing of an old wound, while the daffodils are 'Wind-wounds, spasms from the dark earth' (*BL* 128), keeping Plath's loss fresh in the poet's heart. Indeed, many of Hughes's 'Birthday Letters' may be read as 'wind-wounds,' with the wind as a familiar trope for poetic inspiration and wounds reminding the reader of lyric poetry's conventional relief of anguish through its expression.

This final epithet to capture daffodils also echoes Hughes's description of the birth spasms of the windflower from

Adonis' bloody wounds in *Tales from Ovid*: 'His blood began to seethe – as bubbles thickly / Bulge out of hot mud' (132). In the *Metamorphoses*, the 'minstrel's songs' of Ovid's Orpheus end with this tale of Venus and Adonis, and her mourning tribute to Adonis, another life prematurely cut short, but immortalized by her in the spring return of a flower blooming from his blood. Venus also promises,

> Memorials of my sorrow,
> Adonis, shall endure; each passing year
> Your death repeated in the hearts of men
> Shall re-enact my grief and my lament.
> But now your blood shall change into a flower.
> (10.27–31; 248)

As Hughes renders this episode in his *Tales*, he stresses the fragility of the windflower as a symbol of Adonis' rebirth in a natural form. Hughes's Venus tells her dead lover, 'The circling year itself shall be your mourner' (131) along with the 'bright-blooded' windflower and its brief bloom: 'Its petals cling so weakly, so ready to fall / Under the first light wind that kisses it' (132). The Orpheus of *Birthday Letters* also insists more on nature's forgetfulness than its memory in the daffodils, as if Hughes were engaged in a type of mourning that seeks release rather than Venus' enduring attachment to her dead father. The pathetic fallacy of Venus' windflowers is painfully acknowledged as a failure. Nature does not grieve; instead, it gradually buries what is lost in 'the deep grave's stony cold,' out of which 'odourless' daffodils emerge, 'As if ice had a breath – ' (*BL* 128).

Although Hughes may be adopting an Orpheus identity for many of his lyrics, then, he does not solicit Orpheus' fate. Indeed, it is precisely here where Hughes and Orpheus may be said to part ways. In Ovid, the melancholic Orpheus retreats from human company, especially women's, and ultimately incurs their wrath for ignoring their attentions:

> ... a frenzied band
> Of Thracian women, wearing skins of beasts,
> From some high ridge of ground caught sight of him.
> 'Look!' shouted one of them, tossing her hair
> That floated in the breeze, 'Look, there he is,
> The man who scorns us!' and she threw her lance
> Full in Apollo's minstrel's face.
> (11.7–13; 249)

Orpheus is sacrificed to the frenzy of these Maenads, torn limb from limb, his voice 'that held the rocks entranced' having no persuasive power over the scorned women. Though Hughes has not escaped the wrath of Maenad-feminists over the years, he portrays himself in *Birthday Letters* as at last freeing himself from a scene of poetic sacrifice originally conceived by Plath. In 'Setebos,' it is not he who is 'dismembered' but their poetic marriage as Ferdinand and Miranda, an idealized union with *Ariel* as their guardian and muse. Plath's grief for her father, 'King Minos, / Alias Otto,' transforms her poetic voice into 'murderous music' and 'bellowing song,' a conflation of Caliban and the Minotaur. To protect himself from being sacrificed, torn limb from limb as a victim of her verse, Hughes/Orpheus

> ... crawled
> Under a gabardine, hugging tight
> All I could of me, hearing the cry
> Now of hounds.
> (*BL* 133)

'You wanted / To be with your father / In wherever he was'

The Orpheus disguise permits Hughes to mourn Plath extravagantly and deeply, to remember all of the key moments in his marriage to her in mythic contexts that are purposely redundant in their figurations of loss and sacrifice. Ultimately, however, these poems move toward catharsis and dissolution of grief and in many ways correspond to what Freud described as the normal process of mourning:

> The task is now carried through bit by bit, under great expense of time and cathectic energy, while all the time the existence of the lost object is continued in the mind. Each single one of the memories and hopes which bound the libido to the object is brought up and hyper-cathected, and the detachment of the libido from it accomplished. Why this process of carrying out the behest of reality bit by bit, which is in the nature of a compromise, should be so extraordinarily painful is not at all easy to explain in terms of mental economics. It is worth noting that this pain seems natural to us. The fact is, however, that when the work of mourning is completed the ego becomes free and uninhibited again. (166)

The term 'cathexis' denotes an investment of emotional significance, while a 'hyper-cathexis' is an exertion of counter-energy, an effort to dis-invest and take back the energy given to the lost love object. As this applies to Hughes's poetic strategy in *Birthday Letters*, counter-energy is exerted most strongly in poems where he engages Plath's own mourning verse, which he understands as tending toward the other state described by Freud in his 1917 essay 'Mourning and Melancholia.' Because the melancholic cannot, but obviously must, give up the lost love object, the dead loved one who will never return, she or he narcissistically identifies with this person, and

> then hate is expended upon this new substitute-object, railing at it, depreciating it, making it suffer and deriving sadistic gratification from its suffering. The self-torments of

melancholiacs, which are without doubt pleasurable, signify . . . a gratification of sadistic tendencies and of hate, both of which relate to an object and in this way have both been turned round upon the self. . . . [T]he sufferers usually succeed in the end in taking revenge, by the circuitous path of self-punishment, on the original objects and in tormenting them by means of the illness. . . .

It is this sadism, and only this, that solves the riddle of the tendency to suicide which makes melancholia so interesting – and so dangerous. . . . [W]e have long known that no neurotic harbours thoughts of suicide which are not murderous impulses against others re-directed upon himself. (172–73)

In 'The Inscription,' Hughes offers a convoluted version of this wounding/self-wounding – the turning 'round upon the self' of blows intended for him – in his description of Plath visiting his flat in Soho after their separation and begging for his 'assurance' of his faith in her:

> Over and over and over and over he gave
> What she did not want or did
> Want and could no longer accept or open
> Helpless-handed as she hid from him
> The wound she had given herself, striking at him
> Had given herself . . .
> (*BL* 173)

There is an irony to choosing Freudian psychoanalysis to interpret Hughes both as he mourns his dead wife in *Birthday Letters*, and as he simultaneously responds critically to her poetry of melancholia. Irony, because Hughes often appears to blame psychoanalysis for providing Plath with a sadistic and suicidal narrative to play out in her verse, her conscious motive being love for a dead father, while her unconscious desire is to worship at the altar of 'Your Aztec, Black Forest /

God of the euphemism Grief' (*BL* 191). But Hughes found in his wife's journals the homage to 'Mourning and Melancholia':

> Ted . . . is a substitute for my father. . . . Images of his faithlessness with women echo my fear of my father's relation with my mother and Lady Death.
>
> How fascinating all this is. Why can't I master it and manipulate it and lose my superficiality, which is a careful protective gloss against it?
>
> Read Freud's *Mourning and Melancholia* this morning after Ted left for the library. An almost exact description of my feelings and reasons for suicide: a transferred murderous impulse from my mother onto myself: the 'vampire' metaphor Freud uses, 'draining the ego': that is exactly the feeling I have getting in the way of my writing: Mother's clutch. I mask my self-abasement (a transferred hate of her) and weave it with my own real dissatisfactions in myself. (*J* 278–79)

Here is the dangerous and vengeful mix of motives Hughes ascribes to Plath, and the desire to 'master it and manipulate it' in her poetry. Only by giving up her father, mother, husband, and finally herself to this narrative and its 'murderous impulse' does Plath presumably satiate her muse – no longer *Ariel* but a fiery little god. Hughes can only watch

> . . . everything go up
> In the flames of your sacrifice
> That finally caught you too till you
> Vanished, exploding
> Into the flames
> Of the story of your God
> Who embraced you
> And your Mummy and your Daddy –
> (*BL* 191)

Here Hughes indicts Plath for her inability to discriminate between grief and self-flagellation, between a normal mourning that gradually accepts loss and a suicidal depression with its inevitable component of murderous aggression.

As Hughes portrays Plath's so-called 'Grief,' it is born out of her fear that she has no story to tell but the one given to her by her psychiatrist Ruth Beuscher about an Electra complex:

> Beutscher [sic]
> Twanging the puppet strings
> That waltzed you in air out of your mythical grave
> To jig with your Daddy's bones on a kind of tightrope
> (*BL* 174)

In her *Journals*, she describes the 'deep things' she discusses with 'R. B.': 'dreams of deformity and death. If I really think I killed and castrated my father may all my dreams of deformed and tortured people be my guilty visions of him or fears of punishment for me? And how to lay them? To stop them operating through the rest of my life?' (299). For Hughes, the poetic strategy Plath chose for laying her guilt and fear to rest only served to resurrect her 'Daddy's bones,' and to feed the frenzy of maenad/feminists who hounded him over the years as a 'model' of 'Daddy.'

These Maenads find inspiration in a Plath described by Hughes as 'Catastrophic, arterial, doomed' (*BL* 197). His final poem, 'Red,' describes the bedroom he shared with Plath in Court Green as 'A judgement chamber' and 'A throbbing cell. Aztec altar-temple' (*BL* 197). It is another scene of sacrifice from which he seeks release not only for himself but also, in some ways, for Plath as she is remembered in literary history. His revulsion for Plath's poetic identity as a priestess of blood is evident in his description of the impact of her ghoulish appearance. Her skirt is 'a swathe of blood,' and

> Your lips a dipped, deep crimson.
> You revelled in red.
> I felt it raw – like the crisp gauze edges
> Of a stiffening wound. I could touch
> The open vein in it, the crusted gleam.
> (*BL* 197–98)

In these lines, Hughes is in dialogue with a Plath who claimed 'The blood jet is poetry, / There is no stopping it' ('Kindness,' *CP* 270); who thrilled to her cut thumb, 'Clutching my bottle / Of pink fizz' ('Cut,' *CP* 235); and who in 'Purdah' meets her 'bridegroom' in a boudoir that is similarly 'A judgement chamber,' as Clytemnestra greets the returning Agamemnon with vengeance: 'The shriek in the bath, / The cloak of holes' (*CP* 244).

Hughes ends *Birthday Letters* in flight from these bloodstained poems, mourning Plath's adoption of a muse that needed to be fed with bloody sacrifice, when 'Blue was your kindly spirit – not a ghoul / But electrified, a guardian, thoughtful' (*BL* 198). Hughes prefers to remember Plath's genial spirit as fertile and forgiving, a guardian who is a healer, not an 'open vein' and 'stiffening wound,' and a muse for a poet who chooses forgiveness over vengeance. Instead of the Aztec goddess bathed in red, Plath is pictured as a nurturing Madonna, whose 'Kingfisher blue silks from San Francisco / Folded your pregnancy' (198). Plath's true muse was a winged creature ('Blue was wings') like Shakespeare's 'dainty' Ariel, an agent for executing Prospero's revenge who also inspires the magician-priest to pity the enemies in his power. Prospero might easily punish them, but, in response to *Ariel*'s empathy, he muses:

> Hast thou, which art but air, a touch, a feeling
> Of their afflictions, and shall not myself,
> One of their kind, that relish all as sharply
> Passion as they, be kindlier mov'd than thou art?
> (5.1.21–24)

Like Prospero, who knows that 'The rarer action is / In virtue than in vengeance' (5.1.27–28), Hughes bids farewell to his wife with tenderness and regret, because 'the jewel you lost was blue' (*BL* 198). Instead of expressing rage and accusation, then, often regarded as the predominant emotions of Plath's grieving verse, Hughes doubles the loss, gazing backward as he has throughout these poems at his wife and fellow poet, knowing that she herself was a jewel he failed to keep safe.[4] Instead of a 'bereft love returning to life,' described by Hughes as Plath's inspiration for the *Ariel* poems, *Birthday Letters* ends with a 'bereft love' being laid to final rest.

Notes

INTRODUCTION

1. The British edition has forty poems, while the American edition has forty-three. The British edition does not include 'Lesbos,' 'Mary's Song,' or 'The Swarm.' For a full listing of the poems in the American edition of *Ariel*, see chapter 1.

2. See chapter 1 for a list of Plath's selected poems for *Ariel*. When two more volumes of Plath's poetry, *Crossing the Water* and *Winter Trees*, were published in 1971, A. Alvarez wrote a review that also raised questions about Ted Hughes's handling of how Plath was published. In a letter to the editor response to Alvarez, Hughes describes the *Ariel* Plath had in mind and also some of his reasons for altering its design. Despite this earlier description of Plath's version of *Ariel*, critical interest was not aroused until the publication of the *Collected Poems* ten years later.

1. A RARE BODY

1. A yellow pamphlet available at Smith College's Neilson Library describes the collection as 'containing approximately 4,000 pages of Sylvia Plath's manuscripts and typescripts. The most significant material is a group of 67 poems in successive drafts, the complete drafts extant of the major work now called collectively the *Ariel* poems, written during the last year of the poet's life.' These complete drafts do indeed provide 'the anatomy of the birth of the poetry' and are the centerpiece of the collection.

2. 'The Body of the Writing,' chapter 2 of Jacqueline Rose's book *The Haunting of Sylvia Plath*, begins with the same analogy between archival and actual bodies, but quickly turns to the latter: 'What is the body of Plath's writing? That is, what is the body that Plath writes? For if there is a body of

her writing – an archive edited, glossed and cut – there is no less, and no less crucially, a body in her writing, a body whose relationship to writing and representation of Plath's texts repeatedly comment on and speak' (29). Also see my chapter 'The Female Body of Imagination,' in Plath's *Incarnations: Woman and the Creative Process*, where I am similarly concerned with the body *in* Plath's writing.

3. One of the stranger moments I had in looking through the collection was encountering a scribbled note by Ted Hughes on 'The Applicant': 'Reverse: 3 unidentified play by T.H.: hand.' Does this mean Hughes cannot or will not identify the play Plath was recycling for page 3 of her manuscript for 'The Applicant'? Did he, too, sometimes find his handwriting illegible? Or, was this an aborted effort, long ago cast aside? The librarian did not know.

4. In "Rekindling the Past in Sylvia Plath's 'Burning the Letters,'" Susan Van Dyne describes Plath's 'permeable page' and the way in which the 'boundaries' between Plath's poems and Hughes's are 'fluid' (254). Also see my discussion of 'Burning the Letters' in chapter 2.

5. Aurelia Plath describes this practice in *Letters Home*: 'Her self-discipline and confidence were steadily developing. Following the instructions of Dr B., she charted each day, checking off as an item was accomplished – a practice she followed the rest of her life' (135).

6. Among these narratives I include my own in *Plath's Incarnations.* I don't think I ever went as far as some of the other critical narratives. That is, I do not elevate Plath aesthetically beyond recognition of the duress under which she wrote these poems. But I also feel that, without seeing the manuscripts, without a sense of the poems' precise dating and sequence of composition, I wrote about them as if they were composed *sub specie aeternitatis* and not as they were, in the emotional fury of a marital breakup that permeated Plath's existence. As Marjorie Perloff notes in her review of *The Collected Poems*, the impact of dating and completeness in the sequence of 'Terrible Lyrics' of 1962' is to 'see her as more than the schizophrenic whose earlier suicide attempts prefigure her final one. . . . Rather, she becomes the outraged wife, a modern Medea who gave everything and was nevertheless betrayed' (313).

7. Jacqueline Rose describes this collage in The *Haunting* (9): 'At

the centre, Eisenhower sits beaming at his desk. Into his hands, Plath has inserted a run of playing cards; on the desk lie digestive tablets ('Tums') and a camera on which a cutout of a model in a swimsuit is posed. Attached to this model is the slogan 'Every Man Wants His Woman On A Pedestal'; a bomber is pointing at her abdomen; in the corner there is a small picture of Nixon making a speech. A couple sleeping with eye shields are accompanied by the caption: 'It's HIS AND HER time all over America'. In the top left-hand corner of the picture, this news item: 'America's most famous living preacher whose religious revival campaigns have reached tens of millions of people both in US and abroad.'

8. Plath's practice of drafting material on the wrong side of pink Smith memorandum paper echoes her mother Aurelia's practice of drafting letters on the wrong side of her Boston University stationery, another way in which bodies-in-writing seem to be intimately related here.

9. According to the librarians, Olwyn Hughes has never seen Aurelia's annotations or drafts, only the 'exact copies' of the final letters. One senses that Aurelia Plath's preservation of all of these papers was meant to clarify her feelings towards both Ted and Olwyn Hughes for future biographers and literary historians. On the back of Olwyn's letter dated July 2, 1968, in which Olwyn tries a variety of rhetorical strategies to persuade Aurelia that *The Bell Jar* should be published (e.g., it will bring money for the children; the people satirized in the novel should be proud to have known Plath; other authors have been more harsh; and how can we deprive 'literary heritage' of these works), Aurelia writes, 'Have you ever known such horror that you couldn't eat or sleep, Olwyn? For months in 1963, then, again in 1966 I couldn't sleep or swallow solids,' and separately, 'For the sake of the children I pulled out.' Indeed, the impression left at times is that Aurelia felt she needed to remain absolutely silent and cordial 'for the sake of the children' – to maintain access to Frieda and Nicholas, who were sent to visit her during the summer months.

10. Gordon Lameyer's project is eventually vetoed by Olwyn, who writes to Aurelia about his manuscript that she regards it as a 'colossal mistake.' She also tells Aurelia that he is neither the writer nor the critic he fancies himself to be, and no gentleman (October 12, 1971). Apparently he wanted to

Notes

include all of Plath's amorous gushing during the period of their love affair and offended Olwyn immensely by dedicating his memoir to Plath and Hughes's children.

11. In the Roy Davids Catalogue of 1995, item 111 is a copy of *Pursuit*, described as no. 19 of one hundred copies, and including an autographed poem by Ted Hughes of eight lines. The first three lines are:

> A nest of hands
> Nursed the egg
> As cold as the Arctic

I have been unsuccessful in tracing the sale of this volume and recovering the final five lines of Hughes's poem. Roy Davids claim to have sold it to the Mortimer Rare Book Room at Smith, but the librarians did not acquire a copy of *Pursuit* until a year later.

12. Aurelia comments on *Pursuit* in an annotation to a copy of a letter she sent to Owlyn, dated July 30, 1974. She thanks her for sending a copy of the volume and describes it as 'handsome, indeed.' Next to this, however, is 'Truth: Has no Contents page. 'The Earthenware Head' poem is missing three stanzas, some incorrect lines. Very poor.' In a letter to Aurelia dated June 5, 1974, Olwyn mentions that she is trying to bring together a *Collected Poems* by Plath, and asks Aurelia to review a list of 'early' poems and requests copies if they appear in magazines or letters Aurelia still has in her possession. Among these juvenilia, however, is listed 'The Burning of the Letters,' with a request for a typed copy if Aurelia has one, since Olwyn has only a manuscript with revisions. Olwyn's request raises questions about her role in creating *The Collected Poems*, and also, more generally, about her competence as an editor of Plath's work, since, as Aurelia notes, small editions like *Pursuit* do not seem very well conceived. Next to the query about whether Aurelia has a typescript of 'The Burning of the Letters,' Aurelia writes 'No!'

13. Given Hughes's frequent expression of scorn for Plath scholars and critics, I wonder at times whether he is not having some fun at our expense. Here, is he punning on the useless 'appendix' that Plath indeed did have removed in the spring of 1961? Did he perform a therapeutic appendectomy by burning and losing her journals?

14. Hughes may be referring to an earlier version of 'Stings' which he includes in his notes (*CP* 293). He dates its composition August 2, 1962. Like 'Burning the Letters,' it was first published in the Rainbow Press volume *Pursuit* (1973) under the title 'Stings [2].' Hughes's remark about 'Stings' may also be a Freudian slip of sorts, reflecting his dislike for this poem, which casts him as a drone to Plath's queen bee in the nuptial flight. One way it has been read is as a revenge fantasy.

15. Hughes's title *Birthday Letters* implies that the poems were written to Plath on her birthday over several years. I would suggest, however, an alternative interpretation. The publication date, January 29, 1998, marks the thirty-fifth anniversary of Plath's transition – or birth – into the poetic voice Hughes regards as irrevocably suicidal. With the revision of 'Sheep in Fog,' he argues, she finally succumbed to the despair of 'a heaven / Starless and fatherless, a dark water' (*CP* 262). See Hughes's essay 'Sylvia Plath: The Evolution of "Sheep in Fog"' (*WP* 191–211).

16. It is not clear from Hughes's notes for the *Collected Poems* what decisions and choices he made in selecting which version of a poem to publish in *Ariel* or the *Collected Poems*, since there are several variants in what appear to be final typescripts for the *Ariel* poems, and especially in terms of Plath's use of exclamation marks, which are as habitual to her composition as Emily Dickinson's famous dashes. Marjorie Perloff's review of the *Collected Poems* castigates Hughes as an editor: 'And even now, when we finally have the whole poetic oeuvre before us, it appears in an edition that is curiously inadequate' (306). It is 'a sloppy edition' (307) in its inaccurate dating, its incompetent handling of original publication, and especially its scholarly annotation, which provides geography for 'Hardcastle Crags,' 'but when we come to poems that concern, not Plath's father but her mother, husband, children, friends, or 'the other woman,' there are no annotations at all beyond citations from Plath's own BBC commentaries, which have been available for years' (306).

17. As I noted in the Introduction. Vendler and Pollitt are among the few reviewers to notice the discrepancy, and neither delves into the issue. For *The Nation* (January 16, 1982), Katha Pollitt wonders only briefly, 'Would it have made a

Notes

difference to her reputation . . . if Plath's pattern had been preserved, with the last poems added as a separate section,' but she is confused about which poems Plath wanted. She does note that 'the way in which her work was presented to the public did little to bring about a better understanding of it' and criticizes especially the 'chronologically jumbled' publication of *Winter Trees* and *Crossing the Water* (52).

18. The poems he deleted that were immediately published include 'Thalidomide,' 'The Jailor,' 'The Other,' and 'The Swarm,' in *Encounter* (October 1963); 'Lesbos,' in *The Review* (October 1963); 'Stopped Dead,' in *London Magazine* (January 1963); 'Purdah,' in *Poetry* (August 1963); and 'Amnesiac,' in the *New Yorker* (August 1963). 'The Magi' was published much earlier, in *New Statesman* (October 1961). 'The Rabbit Catcher' had already been read by Plath on the BBC.

19. In a draft of a letter to Olwyn Hughes, dated July 9, 1968, Aurelia reminds her of her desire to exclude 'Daddy' from *Ariel*: 'Well, it was the only poem quoted in TIME and the American newspapers. My instinct was tragically correct for us here.'

20. In a draft of a letter to Olwyn Hughes dated June 22, 1968, she complains of the 'horrors and indignities that transpired as a result of the TIME article.'

21. As we shall see in chapter 3, Hughes has an elaborate reading of 'Sheep in Fog' that justifies its placement in *Ariel* as an early harbinger of the despair that would overtake Plath. He regards it, however, not as a 'much less personal lyric,' but as very revealing of Plath's interior state of being at the end of January 1963.

22. Once again, in *Birthday Letters*, Hughes modifies this heroic view of Plath's release of the *Ariel* voice. In 'The God,' the figure who 'flew up into the Elm Tree' (189) feeds on human sacrifice, and in its roaring, burning rage is less like Ariel than Caliban. I address these alterations in Hughes's views at the end of both chapter 2 and chapter 3.

23. See my reading of this poem in *Plath's Incarnations*, pp. 196–201.

24. Susan Van Dyne is similarly interested in examining the parallel textual bodies underlying the *Ariel* poems in her critical study *Revising Life: Sylvia Plath's 'Ariel' Poems*. She was the first to see the ways in which the underlying verso texts

were important for reading the *Ariel* poems. My focus, however, is very different, and often my interpretations of individual poems differ markedly from Van Dyne's. In addition, Van Dyne's title is taken from Adrienne Rich's famous essay '"When We Dead Awaken": Writing as Re-Vision,' and this notion of feminist re-vision and reevaluation informs her understanding of what Plath is doing by writing on the reverse side of her own and Hughes's manuscripts and typescripts. Van Dyne situates her work in terms of previous feminist readings of *Ariel*, and while she intermittently discusses Plath's original plan for the 'Other *Ariel*,' this is not the central concern of her book as it is of mine. I also do not see re-vision or 'revising life' as the primary motive for the creative process in what Plath is doing, and whereas Van Dyne restates and refines the feminist perspective which has dominated Plath studies, I want to multiply *Ariel*'s narratives and interpretive possibilities in ways not governed solely by that feminist tradition.

2. PRIVATE PROPERTY

1. The British edition also omits 'Lesbos' and 'The Swarm,' which do appear in the American edition. In addition, 'Mary's Song,' not included in the 'Other *Ariel*,' is printed in the American edition but not the British edition. In the interpretations of the manuscript drafts of poems, I use pointed brackets (<>) to indicate lines that Plath has crossed out which are still legible. There are also places where Plath has scribbled out entire stanzas, but within those stanzas she has also crossed out individual words. In those places, if I am quoting the stanza in its entirety, I use double pointed brackets (<<>>) to indicate crossed-out words within a stanza that has been rejected and indicated by a single pointed bracket (<>).

2. In conversation at a symposium sponsored by the Academy of American Poets (February 26, 1998, Cooper Union, New York City), Alicia Suskin Ostriker suggested to me that Hughes was alluding to the death of Jezebel (2 Kings 9:31–37). She is thrown from the window at the command of Jehu, 'and he trode her under foot' (33). Before he can have her buried, dogs eat her carcass, leaving only the skull, feet, and the palms of her hands. If Ostriker is right that Hughes

means to allude to Jezebel, King Ahab's wife, then this makes Plath a painted and evil woman, and a worshipper of a false god of sacrifice – for Jezebel, Baal, and for Plath, her father. In this reading, Plath falls victim to a justice she has earned through her wickedness. Of course, Hughes does begin the poem by saying, 'That is not your mother but her body,' thereby suggesting that it is not her true self but her textual corpus that has been cannibalized by voracious critics who 'batten / On the cornucopia / Of her body,' living off the richness of her art.

3. The 'Lib Lobby' (Stevenson, *BF* 336), as Dido Merwin refers to Plath's feminist 'hagiographers,' is regarded as responsible for the three times Plath's gravestone has been defaced. In the poem 'The Burying of Hughes,' the feminist Robyn Rowland proudly describes the vandalism she engaged in with four other women:

> . . . call it political, call it artistic, call it
> the act women do and redo
> to name themselves or take back their
> names, though some would call that
> desecration
> (557)

Both Linda Wagner-Martin and Jacqueline Rose are regarded by Olwyn and Ted Hughes as feminist troublemakers in their scholarly rendering of Plath. Many of the controversies over permissions to quote from Plath have been public interchanges in letters to the editor of the *Times Literary Supplement*, the *Independent*, and the *Manchester Guardian.* See Ted Hughes, 'The Place Where Sylvia Plath Should Rest in Peace,' letters to the editor, *Manchester Guardian*, April 20, 1989; Ronald Hayman, 'The Poet and the Unquiet Grave,' *Independent*, arts section, April 19, 1989; Ted Hughes, 'Sylvia Plath: The Facts of Her Life and the Desecration of her Grave,' letters, *Independent*, April 20, 1989; Ronald Hayman, 'Plath: A Poet Mourned by Bongo Drums,' review of *Bitter Fame* by Anne Stevenson, *Independent*, November 10, 1989; Tracy Brain, 'Ted Hughes,' letters to the editor, *Times Literary Supplement*, March 6, 1992; Olwyn Hughes, 'Ted Hughes and the Plath Estate,' letters to the editor, *Times Literary Supplement*, March 27, 1992; Jacqueline Rose, 'Ted Hughes and the Plath Estate,' letters to the editor, *Times Literary Supplement*, April 10, 1992; Ted Hughes, 'Ted Hughes and the Plath Estate,' letters to the editor, *Times Literary Supplement*, April 24, 1992.

4.   This is, of course, an answer to Plath's poem of the same title, where she contrarily depicts herself as Mary, pleading with an unfeeling God to spare his son Jesus from sacrifice. See my reading of this poem in Plath's Incarnations (174–77).

5.   In the 'Author's Note' to *Bitter Fame*, Stevenson describes Olwyn Hughes's 'contributions to the text' as making it 'almost a work of dual authorship.' In a note on the same page, she specifically cites Hughes as responsible for the text on several poems, including 'The Rabbit Catcher.'

6.   There is a discrepancy in the dating of the incident that inspired the poem between Stevenson's account, which specifies 'some months before' the Wevills' visit, and Hughes's poem 'The Rabbit Catcher,' which opens, 'It was May' (*BL* 144).

7.   In the poem 'Suttee' which follows Hughes's 'The Rabbit Catcher,' he depicts himself as a poetic midwife, 'Tending the white birth-bed of your rebirth, / The unforthcoming delivery, the all-but-born' (*BL* 147) new self that emerges with flood and consuming fire in the *Ariel* poems. In the 'new myth' of these poems, he is 'dissolved,' 'engulfed,' finally 'consumed' with Plath as her husband: 'And I was your husband / Performing the part of your father / In our new myth –' (*BL* 149).

8.   The Stevenson biography, for example, describes Plath as almost Othello-like in her determination to spy on Ted with Assia: 'Sylvia, in the front room with David [Wevill], heard Ted come in by the back door. She went into the corridor, slipped off her shoes, and went silently to the kitchen. She found Ted and Assia chatting amiably, though it was clear she expected something more compromising' (*BF* 243). Assia, though no longer alive to confirm or deny what happened, is said to have confided in a mutual friend that nothing more than "a current of attraction"' (243) had passed between her and Ted, and to Olwyn Hughes she 'remarked that she doubted whether the attraction between Ted and herself would ever have developed into an affair, as it later did, had Sylvia behaved differently' (244). In this context, 'The Rabbit

Notes

Catcher' becomes a virulent symptom of Plath's desire to construct a 'self-justifying and unforgiving case' against Ted Hughes (245).

9. Although not published until 1971, 'The Rabbit Catcher' was read by Plath along with several other poems for the BBC in October 1962. Hughes does say that keeping poems out of *Ariel* 'that were aimed too nakedly' turned out to be 'in vain': 'They were known and their work is now done' (*WP* 166). 'The Rabbit Catcher' may be one of these poems.

10. This is one of those 'rare books' on handmade paper created by Olwyn Hughes. According to Stephen Tabor, four hundred copies, 'plus a few for the copyright deposit' were printed. Of these 1–10 were vellum-bound and sold for £110 ($270); 11–100 were calf-bound and sold for £40 ($100); and 101–400 were bound in quarter leather and sold for £12.60 ($35). For a more complete description, see Tabor's *Bibliography*, A13 (31–33). The contents are 'A Winter's Tale,' 'Mayflower,' 'Epitaph for Fire and Flower,' 'Old Ladies Home,' 'Wreath for a Bridal,' 'Metamorphoses of the Moon,' 'Owl,' 'Child,' 'Electra on Azalea Path,' 'In Midas' Country,' 'Tinker Jack and the Tidy Wives,' 'Two Campers in Cloud Country,' 'The Rabbit Catcher,' 'The Detective,' 'On the Difficulty of Conjuring up a Dryad,' 'The Snowman on the Moor,' 'Widow,' 'The Other Two,' 'Gigolo,' 'Brasilia,' and 'Lyonnesse.' According to Tabor, 'Wreath for a Bridal' was published as a pamphlet in 1970 (A7, 23–24); 'Child' was published as a pamphlet in 1971, and 'depending on whether it preceded or followed *Lyonnesse* (June 1971), it is either a first edition or a first separate edition of this poem' (A16, 37); and 'Widow' was previously collected in *Crossing the Water* (1971).

11. This comparison is specifically argued against by Anne Stevenson in her preface to *Bitter Fame*, as if she anticipated Rose's claims: 'To assess her contributions to the feminist movement as being politically of the same order as that, say, of Adrienne Rich, is to misunderstand Plath with a degree of perversity equal to her own' (xiii).

12. Both Wagner-Martin and Rose are somewhat misleading in their quotations from lines in the early drafts, implying that they are citing 1a from the first draft of the poem and that it is more revelatory in its details about the Plath-Hughes marriage than the final version of the poem. The lines quoted

239

by Wagner-Martin (205) and Rose (141) actually come from draft 1b. Draft 1a ends on the same page where draft 1b begins, indicated by a line drawn to separate the two versions.

13. For a lengthier discussion of these episodes, see my chapter '*The Bell Jar*: The Past as Allegory,' in *Plath's Incarnations* (109–56).

14. In Hughes's 'The Rabbit Catcher,' he literalizes this situation, describing Plath's rage 'against our English private greed / Of fencing off all coastal approaches' (*BL* 144).

15. Ted Hughes's poem 'Astringency' (*BL* 80–81) speculated on the identity of Plath's poetic 'constrictor' in the context of her habitual blockage. When she delivers 'The sole metaphor that ever escaped you / In easy speech, in my company -' he asks how it managed to get

> Past the censor? Past the night hands?
> Past the snare
> Set in your throat by whom?

These lines simultaneously allude to the poem 'Daddy' and to Otto Plath's baleful effect on Plath's poetic utterance, and to an unconscious censorship – 'night hands' – that made poetic composition for Plath painful and slow. If Hughes acknowledges any responsibility for Plath's blockages as a writer, it is by proxy, by virtue of Plath's insistence that Hughes was a model of Otto Plath.

16. Hughes answers these lines with his own version, interpreting Plath's revulsion as directed at English customs, and only through this cultural lens at him: 'You saw blunt fingers, blood in the cuticles, / Clamped round a blue mug. I saw / Country poverty raising a penny, / Filling a Sunday stewpot' (BL 145).

17. Jacqueline Rose reads Plath's rivalry with Hughes as 'a struggle over different forms of imagination, a different register, for the main and for the woman, in the world of signs' (*Haunting* 179). While this might suggest a difference based chiefly on gender, what is of special interest to her is the playing out of this struggle in terms of high versus popular culture in Plath's prose fiction, with the masculine imagination and Hughes associated with high culture, and the feminine imagination and herself associated with the

vulgar and the popular. See her reading of Plath's 'Wishing Box' (179–82).

18. The first version of 'Stings' does not appear in The *Collected Poems* but is included in the limited edition of *Pursuit* (1973). According to Edward Butscher, on Olwyn Hughes's authority, it was written in either July or August 1962. In *Method and Madness* (320), he says it is one of the two poems Plath wrote in August; on the next page he says, 'In July also came 'Stings (2),' which Olwyn Hughes has identified as "the first of all the bee poems."'

19. Plath neither read this poem in her BBC broadcast of new poems, nor does she appear to have sent the poem out to journals or ever planned for its inclusion in the 'Other *Ariel*.' What this suggests to me is that she knew she was committing poetic sacrilege in this poem, mocking not only one of her husband's most prized poems but also, in some ways, her own standards for poetic beauty. It was not a poem, I suspect, on which she would stake any claims for greatness, even though it offers a defiant version of poetic 'immortality.'

20. See Judith Kroll's elaborate reading of the fox's immortality in *Chapters in a Mythology*, based on her belief that Plath 'was more than superficially acquainted with Hinduism and Buddhism. (Her familiarity with these literatures was confirmed by Ted Hughes, in conversation)' (n. 37, 275–77). My reading directly contradicts Kroll's in the sense that she chooses to elevate what I describe as the literal-mindedness of the poem to an extraordinary symbolic height. I am also skeptical of the way in which Hughes authorizes her reading of the poem, which may be seen as a strategy for obscuring the wounds Plath inflicts on his 'Thought-Fox.'

21. See Jon Rosenblatt's commentary in *Sylvia Plath: The Poetry of Initiation* (107).

22. For a more detailed account of this conversation with the Comptons, see Elizabeth Sigmund, 'Sylvia in Devon: 1962' (104).

23. Alexander cites an interview with Clarissa Roche as contradicting her earlier statement that Assia's name was revealed in the fire: 'Plath told Roche that the name 'Dido' was written on the charred scrap of paper, not 'A——,' as appeared in the Roche memoir. . . . According to Roche, Butscher changed the name . . . to make the scene more dramatic' (378–79). If so, then Plath did as well in her poem,

since 'patent-leather gutturals' alludes to Assia Wevill's German accent, and 'Sinuous orchis' fairly hisses out her name.

24.   The visual image is reminiscent of Gulliver in Lilliput:

> The spider-men have caught you,
> Winding and twining their petty fetters,
> Their bribes –
> So many silks.
> (*CP* 251)

25.   According to a note in *Bitter Fame*, 'This account is from Dido Merwin, to whom Hughes confided it in the autumn of 1962, after his breakup with Sylvia' (206).

26.   Hughes does not name the person who gave him a new Oxford Shakespeare, but the wound its inscription inflicts on Plath suggests that it came from either Assia Wevill or Dido Merwin, both considered rivals by Plath.

27.   One of the stranger essays in Hughes's collection *Winter Pollen* is 'The Burnt Fox' (1993), an account of a dream Hughes claims to have had as a student reading English at Cambridge in the early 1950s. While trying to write one of his weekly critical essays, he falls asleep and is visited by a 'figure that was at the same time a skinny man and a fox walking erect on its hind legs. It was a fox, but the size of a wolf. As it approached and came into the light I saw that its body and limbs just now stepped out of a furnace. Every inch was roasted, smouldering, black-charred, split and bleeding. Its eyes, which were level with mine where I sat, dazzled with the intensity of the pain. It came up until it stood beside me. Then it spread its hand – a human hand as I now saw, but burned and bleeding like the rest of him – flat palm down on the blank space of my page. At the same time it said: 'Stop this – you are destroying us.' Then as it lifted its hand away I saw the blood-print, like a palmist's specimen, with all the lines and creases, in wet, glistening blood on the page' (9). One senses allegory at work, the medieval scholar-dreamer visited by a figure representing the English canon and warning him that his critical pedantries are 'destroying' literature. The anti-critical sentiment echoes many of Hughes's other statements about, for example, 'the hundred thousand Eng Lit Profs and graduates who . . . feel very little in this case [of Plath's life] beyond curiosity of quite a low order, the

ordinary village kind, popular bloodsport kind, no matter how they robe their attention in Lit Crit Theology and ethical sanctity' (see letter to Stevenson in Malcolm 141). The same 'bloodsport' is rending the body of Hughes's fox-man. In addition, though, one is tempted to read this as yet another self-critical allusion to 'The Thought-Fox,' an animal that also comes at night, but leaves behind not its bloody handprint on the blank page, but the neat prints of the poem's writing. The self-criticism may also extend to a comparison once again with Plath's bleeding fox in 'Burning the Letters,' making its appearance in the charred ruins of her husband's letters.

28. This poem, 'The Error,' is to be distinguished from the poem 'Error' in *Birthday Letters*. The latter poem describes Hughes's 'error' of moving to Devon, more specifically of transporting his American wife into an alien English countryside ('my land of totems') and bringing to an end Plath's 'flashing trajectory' in a 'dead-end' and unpromising 'red-soil tunnel' (*BL* 122).

29. In Hughes's 'Dreamers' (*BL* 157–58), he twice uses the word 'soot' to descibe Assia Wevill. Her voice is 'Edged with a greasy, death-camp, soot-softness,' and 'She sat there, in her soot-wet mascara.' The imagery of Hughes's poem recalls Plath's link of *Assia-ashes* and her own burning of Assia's letter-body in 'my little crematorium,' but also tells the reader that Assia came into their lives trailing clouds of gas and smoke from Hitler's crematoria.

30. In 'Trophies,' Hughes alludes to this passage in Plath's *Journals* from 1956:

> After forty years
> The whiff of that beast, off the dry pages,
> Lifts the hair on the back of my hands.
> The thrill of it.
> (*BL* 18)

As with so many of the poems in *Birthday Letters*, this one evokes Plath's ghostly power to move him. What Hughes also does, however, is to transfer the identity of the panther Plath meant to be him. In 'Trophies,' Plath is the predator who stalks and attacks him, numbing him 'Into drunken euphoria' (*BL* 19) and carrying him off.

31. For a complete description of the volume, see Tabor (A17,

38–39). The contents of *Pursuit* are as follows, with my inclusion of dates of composition: 'Dark Wood, Dark Water' (1959), 'Resolve' (1956), 'Temper of Time' (juvenilia), 'Words Heard, by Accident, over the Phone' (July 11, 1962), 'Stings [2]' (August 2, 1962), 'Spider' (1956), 'The Fearful' (November 16, 1962), 'The Rival [2]' (July 1961), 'A Secret' (October 10, 1962), and 'Burning the Letters' (August 13, 1962).

32. Plath tells Aurelia in a letter dated September 23, 1962, that Hughes left her, 'saying he was going grouse-shooting for the day with a friend' (Lilly Library). Stevenson, on the testimony of Richard Murphy, implies that Plath herself asked Hughes to leave so that she could be alone with Murphy (256). Alexander claims that it was a paranormal experience that urged Hughes to leave: 'After his night at the Ouija board, Ted was walking along a hallway in Murphy's cottage when he saw the face of a portrait suddenly change. He read this paranormal transformation as a sigh he should leave the cottage – indeed Cleggan [Ireland] – at once' (293). Wagner-Martin adds to the possibilities, suggesting that 'the two had an irreconcilable argument' (214).

33. Because Plath had already submitted 'The Jailer' to magazines, it was published very early in England, in *Encounter* 21 (October 1963) with several other poems (45–52): 'Death & Co.,' 'The Swarm,' 'The Other,' 'Getting There,' 'Lady Lazarus,' 'Little Fugue,' 'Childless Woman,' 'Thalidomide,' and 'Daddy.' I surmise that Robin Morgan must have seen the poem here and then reprinted it in her *Sisterhood Is Powerful: An Anthology of Writings from the Women's Liberation Movement* (New York: Random House, 1970). As the title suggests, this even further politicizes Plath's abject body for the feminist movement.

34. In 'Cut,' the speaker suffers similarly from a 'thin / papery feeling' (*CP* 235) as a result of a wound to her thumb. That Plath regarded composition as a form of violence to the blank white page that is literalized as a body may be seen in an early angry in her *Journals*: 'The virginal page, white. The first: broken into and sent packing. All the dreams, the promises: wait till I can write again, and then the painful, botched rape of the first page' (July 15, 1957, 161).

35. Although Ted Hughes's *Crow* was published in 1970 after Plath's death, critics Margaret Dickie (Uroff) and Keith Sagar

view his investment in the crow voice and trickster figure as older. See especially Dickie (201–12) and Sagar (113–15).

36. It is not until Typed Copy 3 that Plath revises the title from 'The Courage of Quietness' to 'The Courage of Shutting-Up,' from what is often conceived of as a feminine virtue to the internalization of what is usually a command by another.

37. According to Stevenson, Plath is probably thinking of her trip to Ireland, when Richard Murphy showed 'them his birthplace, a decayed eighteenth-century mansion called Milford. . . . It was here that Sylvia noticed the Rangoon prints that appear in her poem "The Courage of Shutting-Up"' (255).

38. 'The Swarm' is not included in the British version of *Ariel*, but Plath herself seems to have been in doubt about its inclusion. In her table of contents 'The Swarm' is parenthesized, as if she had not yet made up her mind about it.

39. The entire series is as follows: 'A Secret' (October 10), 'The Applicant' (October 11), 'Daddy' (October 12), 'Eavesdropper' (October 15), 'Medusa' (October 16), 'The Jailer' (October 17), 'Lesbos' (October 18), and 'Amnesiac/[Lyonnesse]' (October 21).

40. Note the way Plath's lines in 'Daddy' seem directly to converse with Hughes. She describes her condition in 'Daddy' as living in a 'black shoe' and 'Barely daring to breathe or Achoo' (*CP* 222).

41. In 'Error,' in Hughes's *Birthday Letters*, a poem in which Hughes chastises himself for bringing Plath to make a home in the provincial isolation of Devon, he describes the place as Lyonnesse, and says, 'Remembering it, I see it all in a bubble: / Strange people, in a closed brilliance' (123).

42. I wondered if it might not be wallpaper after seeing Stevie Smith's response (letter of November 22, 1962, Smith Rare Book Room) to a fan letter Plath wrote to her. After listening to a Harvard recording of Smith in which she alluded to the then out of print story by Charlotte Perkins Gilman 'The Yellow Wallpaper,' Plath wrote to Smith and specifically inquired where she could find a copy of the Gilman story. Plath also seems to have been a fan of Ingmar Bergman's films and probably saw Through a Glass Darkly, in which the heroine, Karin, hallucinates the presence of figures waiting for God in the wallpaper. The poem 'Mystic' and the reference

in a draft of 'Snares' to the 'silence of God' echo the film, which Plath is probably alluding to in a letter to Aurelia of December 21, 1962: 'Got in my old Doris, who loves the children, so I could see a marvellous new Ingmar Bergman movie' (*LH* 491). Bergman's *Brink of Life* also directly influenced *Three Women: A Poem for Three Voices* (*LH* 456).

43. Plath frequently attacked Hughes in conversations and letters for supposedly not wanting any children, but also for being particularly hostile toward the birth of a son. She persuaded a local midwife, Winifred Davies, who assisted in the birth of Nicholas, of this antagonism. Davies writes to Aurelia that Hughes 'has taken such a dislike to Nicholas, jealousy of the male' (letter of September 22, 1962, Lilly Library), and in another letter Plath writes to Aurelia that Hughes was too cowardly to tell her earlier that he did not want children. His vanity permits him to enjoy the flattery of Frieda, and Plath thinks, given that Assia is incapable of having children, he might want custody of Frieda (September 23, 1962, Lilly Library). Of course, Plath's belief that Assia was infertile proved false.

44. The Leonard Baskin drawing that accompanies 'A Secret' in the Rainbow Press volume *Pursuit* is of a hunched-over male figure, half-human, half animal, his mouth a grotesque O, his penis and scrotum dangling between four stout legs with three-clawed feet firmly planted. Baskin, I believe, is inspired by Plath's emphasis on an ugly and masculine sexuality in the poem – like the 'dirt' levered out of filthy fingernails in one stanza.

45. For my feminist reading of this poem, see *Plath's Incarnations* (220–24).

46. These lines echo an earlier disillusionment with Hughes in the *Journals*. At the end of teaching for a year at Smith, she sees him with a woman student and suspects the worst:

I made the most amusing, ironic and fatal step in trusting Ted was unlike other vain and obfuscating and self-indulgent men. . . . What I cannot forgive is dishonesty – and no matter what, or how hard, I would rather know the truth of which I today had such a clear and devastating vision from his mouth than hear foul evasions, blurrings and rattiness. I have a life to finish up here. But what about life without trust – the sense that love is a lie and all joyous sacrifice is ugly duty. I am so tired. My last day, and I cannot sleep for shaking at horror. He is shamed, shameful and shames me and my trust, which is no plea in a world of liars and cheats and broken or vanity-ridden men. Love has been an inexhaustible spring for my nourishment and now I gag. Wrong, wrong: the vulgar heat of it. (233)

47.   In her *Journals*, Plath understands her first suicide attempt through Freud's essay 'Mourning and Melancholia': 'An almost exact description of my feelings and reasons for suicide: a transferred murderous impulse from my mother onto myself: the 'vampire' metaphor Freud uses, 'draining the ego': that is exactly the feeling I have getting in the way of my writing: Mother's clutch. I mask my self-abasement (a transferred hate of her) and weave it with my own real dissatisfactions in myself until it becomes very difficult to distinguish what is really bogus criticism from what is really a changeable liability' (279). While Plath's emphasis is on her mother here, in other places it is grief for her father's death, his loss, that figures prominently in her sense of fraudulence and her murderous self-criticism. See my psychoanalytic reading of *The Bell Jar* in *Plath's Incarnations*.

48.   Hughes is also, I believe, alluding to one of Ovid's *Metamorphoses*, which he translated, and published only a few months before *Birthday Letters*. In *Tales from Ovid* he translates the story of Myrrha, whose incestuous desires for her father, Cinyras, are fulfilled. She is discovered attempting suicide by her nurse, who then helps to trick Cinyras into giving his disguised daughter a place in his bed for several nights of passion. When he discovers the ruse and threatens her with death, the pregnant Myrrha takes flight and eventually metamorphoses into a tree that 'weeps' myrrh (104–19). Plath's mother, Aurelia, was also maligned – 'sacrificed' – in favor of an incestuous love for Otto Plath which Plath regarded as the motive for her first attempt at suicide.

49.   Hughes, I believe, is suggesting that Plath was encouraged to be 'matricidal' by her psychiatrist, Ruth Beuscher. In her *Journals* she quotes Beuscher as saying, 'I give you permission to hate your mother,' and feels 'terrific' about this 'sanction' for expressing a hostility that is socially illicit (265).

50.   Hughes's poem also takes issue with Plath's poem 'The Detective,' where the fingers of a killer, 'tamping a woman

into a wall' (*CP* 208), belong to the woman's husband, not her father.

51. *Howls and Whispers* is a limited and unpaginated edition of eleven poems by Hughes, accompanied by etchings by Leonard Baskin for each poem. Only 110 copies of the volume were printed by the Gehenna Press in the spring of 1998. The copy I looked at is number thirteen and resides at the Rare Book Room at Smith College.

52. This may reflect Hughes's feeling that he had been hounded by the press concerning Plath's suicide.

53. In *Bitter Fame*, Stevenson and Olwyn Hughes identify the serpent that undermined the marriage as follows: Court Green 'was, as Sylvia declared, a veritable Garden of Eden. Yet it came complete with a serpent. Sylvia herself identified it the following April, jotting hastily on a draft of her poem 'Elm': "the stigma of selfhood"' (223). If it is Ted Hughes's similar intention in 'The Rag Rug' to blame a failed marriage on Plath's self-absorption, the poem does not delineate the serpent as entirely her responsibility, but rather depicts it as nurtured by both of them.

54. A 'cradle' is also a term used to describe the type of cell in a beehive where the queen bee larvae are nurtured and fed royal jelly. They resemble cradle-like outgrowths from the hexagonal cells in which worker and drone bee larvae are fed.

3. A LATE WINTER MIRACLE

1. After Plath recovered from her first breakdown and suicide attempt in 1953, she returned to Smith in the spring of 1954 and decided to bleach her hair and wear it in a Veronica Lake pageboy, deeply parted and falling seductively over one eye. As her mother notes in Letters Home, 'It was more than a surface alteration; she was 'trying out' a more daring, adventuresome personality' (*LH* 138). After a 'platinum summer' (*LH* 143) living with three other Smith students in Cambridge, Massachusetts, which Nancy Hunter Steiner also describes as a period of sexual experimentation for Plath in her memoir *A Closer Look at Ariel*, she dyed her hair brown again in her senior year, telling her mother, 'My brown-haired personality is most studious, charming, and

earnest. I like it and have changed back to colorless nail polish for convenience and consistency. I am happy I dyed my hair back, even if it fades and I have to have it touched up once or twice more. I feel that this year, with my applying for scholarships, I would much rather look demure and discreet' (*LH* 141, 144). More than one acquaintance reports that Plath was a manipulator of her image, a woman of many masks or personae, and there is the testimony of Hughes that he 'never saw her show her real self to anybody – except, perhaps, in the last three months of her life' (Foreword, *J* xii).

2. In 'Remission,' Hughes describes the pregnancy and birth of Frieda as offering Plath only a remission, as in some deadly form of cancer, from 'The death who had already donned your features' (*BL* 110). For Hughes, the pregnant Plath was 'the you / You loved and wanted to live with,' the earth mother she so often celebrates in her letters and Hughes identifies as 'The inmost, smiling, solid one, the joy-being, / Venus of Willendorf or the Wyf of Bath' (*BL* 109).

3. Broe chooses to include this early poem because the nature of her study is developmental and not focused on Plath's original plan for *Ariel*.

4. Both of these generic titles, if Plath had kept one of them, would have imposed a singular identity on the speaker as a human beekeeper.

5. On February 4, 1963, Plath writes to her friend Marcia Plumer that while she is in London with Frieda and Nicholas, Hughes visits regularly, loaded down with gifts like an 'apocalyptic Santa Claus'; but she fears when she returns to Devon, 'months and years will go by with no visits from their father' (Smith College Library, Mortimer Rare Book Room).

6. In his poem 'Red,' Hughes describes Plath's devotion to red frighteningly as a bathing of their environment in blood, as if Plath were a goddess of human sacrifice. Their bedroom, particularly, is 'A throbbing cell. Aztec altar – temple' and 'A judgement chamber' with completely red furnishings – curtains, cushions, window seat, walls, and a 'carpet of blood' (*BL* 197). This particular detail suggests that Hughes's poem is in dialogue with Plath's 'Purdah,' where she claims kinship with Clytemnestra and the fatal red carpet she rolled out for Agamemnon on his return from Troy.

7. The money sent by Olive Higgins Prouty was intended for new clothes. The idea of a 'makeover' – new hairdo, new

makeup, and new clothes – to make a new woman, or restore a housewife to her original beauty before marriage, is a cliche in American popular culture. Plath is clearly trying to be attractive to men, or perhaps to rekindle Hughes's passion. From London she writes to her mother about a new haircut: 'It looks fabulous. . . . Ted didn't even recognize me at the train station! My morale is so much improved – I did it on your cheque. Men stare at me in the street now; I look very . . . fashionable' (November 7, 1962, *LH* 479). In terms of her restored 'royalty,' Plath's description of the hair-styling as preserving 'my long coronet in back' refers to the 'crown' of braided hair atop her head, even though 'from the front I look to have short hair' (*LH* 479). Prouty's best-selling novel, made into the Bette Davis film *Now, Voyager*, depends heavily on the emergence of the heroine Charlotte Vale from ugly duckling to swan as the result of a similar makeover.

8. There is no evidence of a second bride flight for the queen bee. Once the queen has mated, she begins laying eggs two days later, and, in Maurice Maeterlinck's words, 'begins her veritable life' (88). She will leave the hive only to swarm, not to mate, and continues to lay eggs on the basis of this one union with drones until the approach of death.

9. Hughes indicts the fairy godmothers in Plath's life for an interference that 'jammed all your wavelengths / With their criss-cross instructions' (*BL* 174). His 'Night-Ride on *Ariel*' is about the suicide itself – 'That Monday' – and he blames women advisers, including 'Beutscher' (sic), for 'Hauling your head this way and that way' in a confusion 'that tipped your heart / Upside down and drained it' (*BL* 175). At the February 26, 1998, symposium on *Birthday Letters*, Fran McCullough suggested that Hughes's misspelling of Beuscher's name in this poem is a Freudian slip, conflating her name with the biographer Edward Butscher's, and betraying his dislike for both of them. Both names also sound like 'butcher.' In the title poem of *Howls and Whispers*, Hughes blames Beuscher for keeping them apart sexually: 'And from your analyst, "Keep him out of your bed. / Above all, keep him out of your bed."' Aurelia is similarly blamed for Plath's obsession with money and is linked with Iago, that great provocateur of the 'green-eyed monster, jealousy': 'Your mother wrote: 'Hit him in the purse.' / Reiterated it, like Iago.' An unnamed 'confidante' and 'professional dopester'

(possibly Suzette Macedo) is also described as an Iago dishing dirt to Plath: 'She squatted at your ear. / She was the bug in my bed. / Pretty, innocent-eyed, gleeful Iago.' Hughes clearly blames these women for Plath's death. What they plugged in her ears 'had killed you by daylight on Monday.'

10. As Taylor describes bumblebees, they are 'primitive in comparison with honeybees': 'Instead of complex and beautiful combs, they construct crude waxen pots as receptacles for honey and pollen and as cradles for their young. Compared to the sixty thousand or more honeybees that can be found in a normal hive, the bumblebee colony never exceeds a few hundred, and in the fall all perish except the queen, who survives to begin a new colony, singlehandedly, in the spring' (3).

11. Later in this chapter I develop the metaphorical analogy between the labor of bees and poiesis. The musical 'humming' of the virginal hive anticipates this allegorical development.

12. Van Dyne points out that this line is drafted on the reverse side of a page from chapter 6 of *The Bell Jar* 'which contains Esther's devastating comment that Buddy's proud display of male flesh reminded her of a "turkey neck and turkey gizzards"' (*RL* 102).

13. Dennis Austin, the Vermont beekeeper I consulted, regards this as a common practice to prevent swarming. The reasoning is that a colony will not tolerate more than one queen, and because the old queen wishes to avoid duelling with emergent princesses, she will choose to leave the hive and swarm, taking a large number of the colony with her. Literature on the subject, however, goes against the folk wisdom and argues that the queen does not determine if and when a hive will swarm. 'There is really no certain way to *prevent* swarming, as distinguished from *controlling* or inhibiting swarming.' It is, however, true that

Colonies with old queens – three years or more – are first to swarm. One with a new queen, that is, one born the preceding fall or since, is unlikely to swarm unless positively goaded into it.

Beginners determined to prevent swarms by whatever means sometimes try to accomplish this by destroying queen cells. This is almost always futile. . . . Bees determined to swarm rebuild queen cells very quickly and then swarm without waiting for them to be capped, sometimes within six or seven days of their being started. The beekeeper's work has then gone for nothing and, worse yet, in the likely case he fails to see the swarm come out, he will not realize it has swarmed and cut out all the queen cells once more, thereby rendering the colony helplessly queenless. (Taylor 85).

14. This is highly unlikely, given beekeeping practices. To prevent the queen from flying too far or high, her wings are usually clipped.

15. In 'Error,' Hughes describes a situation like this one developing between his wife and the locals in Devon. Plath is perceived as foreign and 'royalty,' like an alien queen bee in a new hive, and the locals, like worker bees, sniff at her suspiciously (*BL* 122).

16. Plath's sense of being in a life-threatening situation, however implausible or paranoid, was real enough to her psychologically. Letters written the week following composition of the bee sequence are filled with accusations against both Hughes and Assia Wevill. These are also letters she claims to have written while feverish and delirious with the flu, and overcome with a sense of loss and neediness: 'I am as bereft now as ever . . . I must have someone I love . . . to protect me, for my flu with my weight loss . . . has made me need immediate help' (letter to Aurelia, October 16, 1962, *LH* 469). In this same letter she writes that Ted and Assia are hoping she will kill herself and mocking her with her earlier suicide attempt (Lilly Library). She begs her mother for 'someone from home. A defender. . . . I have a fever now, so I am a bit delirious' (October 16, 1962, *LH* 470). To her brother Warren she writes on October 18 – only two days later – that Hughes is urging her to kill herself and sordidly 'playing on my nervous breakdown' (Lilly Library).

17. As translated by Sir John Sandys, the passage reads, 'For the blossom of these hymns of praise flitteth, like a bee, from theme to theme' (293). The classical scholar Meredith Hoppin tells me that throughout this passage, Pindar's wordplay intertwines *meli* (honey) with *melissa* (bee) and *melos* (melody). Such wordplay is typical of Greek poetry (e.g., Plato in the *Ion*), but Pindar extends the associative cluster with *melena*, a word meaning 'an object of care, a

beloved object, a source of care, anxiety,' specifically in relation to the Muses who are invoked as gracing his song with this melodic-loving attention.

18. Karen V. Kukil, associate curator of rare books at Smith College and editor of Plath's *Unabridged Journals*, found the Oesterreich book in the Neilson Library collection. She noticed that the citation was underlined and asterisked in the distinctive manner in which Plath often marked passages of significance to her.

19. The story of Aristaeus that concludes book 4 of the Georgics links the 'craft' of beekeeping with poetry and song through the story of Orpheus and Eurydice. As we shall see, this association of the story of Orpheus and Eurydice with the art of beekeeping is extremely important in Hughes's *Birthday Letters* and *Tales from Ovid.*

20. Susan Scheinberg has an extensive list of poets who 'represent themselves and other poets as bees': 'Bacchylides calls himself 'the shrill-voiced island bee.' Aristophanes refers to Phrynichus as a 'bee . . . feeding on the fruit of ambrosial songs.' Lucretius asserts that he approaches the teachings of Epicurus *floriferis ut apes in saltibus omnia libant.* . . . Later commentators commonly call Sophocles a bee. Xenophon, whose speech Cicero called *melle dulcior,* is the 'Attic bee.' Likewise, Sappho and Erinna are compared to bees in the *Palatine Anthology* (24–25; see Scheinberg's essay for her sources).

21. In homage to his wife's 'deft, practical touches,' Hughes poetically celebrates the 'winged life' of Plath's 'Fingers' (*BL* 194), which, in turn, are remembered in her daughter's fingers: 'In everything they do. / Her fingers obey and honour your fingers, / The Lares and Penates of our house.' Simultaneously these lines echo Plath's delight in her own dexterity, her practicality.

22. I refer to *Ariel* as 'he,' both for convenience and based on the memoir of Laurie Levy, one of Plath's fellow guest editors at *Mademoiselle.* In 'Outside *The Bell Jar,*' she reports an entry in her diary that suggests Plath regarded *Ariel* as masculine: 'Re-read *Tempest.* S.[ylvia] thinks *Ariel* – animal power, fiery depths. I said air, heaven, female' (46).

23. Illustrations for *The Tempest* occasionally portray Ariel as a bee, as in the lovely pastel Edmund Dulac created for an edition published by Hodder and Stoughton.

24. Plath also struggled with this word. Before finally choosing

'appals,' she tried 'terrifies,' then 'appals,' then 'alarms,' and 'dismays' (draft 1, 1).

25. For discussion of this folk custom of 'telling the bees,' see the final section of this chapter on 'Wintering.' What should also be evident from my argument here is that, unlike most of the other critics on the bee sequence, I do not see the birth of a singular or isolate selfhood from its allegory.

26. It should be mentioned in this context that the relationship between Prospero and Caliban has been similarly politicized in recent criticism. Prospero is the colonial white man to Caliban's native inhabitant and promptly enslaves him, additionally forcing him to learn his language and customs in an effort to 'civilize' a supposedly 'inferior' being.

27. Other types of swarming include 'hunger swarms,' which occur as a result of lack of food; 'absconding swarms,' when bees are dissatisfied with a new abode; and 'nuclei' swarms, which leave with a young queen when she takes her mating flight (Root 65).

28. In Flora Thompson's *Lark Rise*, swarming is regarded as a potential loss for a beekeeper if the swarm is not brought down on his or her property: 'Where they settled, they belonged' (82). This means that the laws governing bees favor possession over original ownership.

29. When Plath went hunting for a flat in London, she sought the assistance of Hughes, who then 'took me round looking at places.' As Plath waits for the approval on her lease for the London flat to go through, she writes to her mother, 'Now he sees he has nothing to fear from me – no scenes or vengefulness' (November 7, 1961, *LH* 478). The beekeeper mistakenly reads the essentially peaceful migratory behavior of the swarm as threatening to him, while Hughes is eventually reassured that Plath is not moving to London in order to 'sting' him with her jealousy. Plath even writes, later in the same letter, 'I may even borrow a table for my flat from Ted's girl – I could be gracious to her now and kindly' (479).

30. It is not hard, however, to trace the poem back to the incident in June when 'Ted had only put a handkerchief over his head where the hat should go in the bee-mask, and the bees crawled into his hair, and he flew off with a half-a-dozen stings' (letter to Aurelia, June 15, 1962, *LH* 457).

31. The queen bee's stinger is longer, curved like a scimitar, and she uses it as a weapon. She does not lose it in battle.

Notes

32. One of my colleagues, knowing my interest in this tradition in beekeeping, gave me an article from our local newspaper by Mary E. Potter, titled 'Listening to the Bees' (*Berkshire Eagle*, June 8, 1999), in which she cites John Greenleaf Whittier as authoring a poem titled 'Telling the Bees,' 'based on the old superstition that if a member of the family dies, the bees must be told, or they will die or fly away. Books of folklore are filled with the elaborate customs of 'telling.' Some families, after actually speaking to the bees, would drape the hive with black crepe or leave a piece of funeral cake for the bees' consumption. Some went so far as to pin on the hive a formal invitation to the funeral.'

33. Pindar describes the 'unprompted utterance of the Delphic Bee,' who commands the suppliant Battus to establish a city in Libya, even though Battus has come to ask 'the oracle what release the gods would grant thee from thy stammering tongue' (205). In fn. 4 Sandys translates Herodotus 4.155 as Pindar's source for the allusion to Battus.

34. The drawing is reproduced as a frontispiece to *Crystal Gazer and Other Poems* (London: Rainbow Press, 1971).

35. The scenes from *The Bell Jar* manuscript on the reverse side occur in an all-women's New York hotel called the Amazon (Plath's turn on the Barbizon) where men are similarly not allowed beyond the lobby.

36. Plath and Hughes celebrated their sixth wedding anniversary in June 1962. In 'Daddy,' she claims to have been married to a model of Daddy for seven years, but this is a sadomasochistic marriage. In 'Wintering,' however, she may be alluding to the six good years of her marriage before the 'sweetness' and 'honey-making' ended.

37. An eerie echo of this passage may be found in Stevenson's description of how Plath was discovered on February 11, 1963: 'Forcing open the door to the kitchen, they found Sylvia sprawled on the floor, her head on a little folded cloth in the oven' (296).

38. It is too clever, I know, but when the bee maidens are not fed honey, they are unreliable soothsayers, and here Plath implies that the beekeeper is deceptive when she gives them sugar syrup 'To make up for the honey I've taken' (*CP* 218). How can they be expected to give an accurate divination when the heavenly food of flowers is replaced with 'refined snow'?

39. While the 'slender neck' here appears to be readying itself for

255

cutting, the earlier image of Plath in the wedding poem 'A Pink Wool Knitted Dress' as a 'slender' and 'nodding spray of wet lilac' (*BL* 35) celebrates her femininity, her delicacy and need for support.

4. MOURNING EURYDICE: TED HUGHES AS ORPHEUS IN *BIRTHDAY LETTERS*

1. Wood's title is taken from Plath's poem 'Words Heard, by Accident, over the Phone' (*CP* 202), discussed briefly in chapter 2.
2. In Owen's poem, the irony of the speaker's meeting with the German enemy in hell is compounded by the fact that his foe is a fellow poet, who also 'went hunting wild / After the wildest beauty in the world.' Hughes must also have been attracted to the lines that stress the grief, in the young German's words, of 'the undone years, / The hopelessness' of a promising life cut short (1846–47).
3. My colleague in the classics department at Williams College, Meredith Hoppin, is the source for this observation. She also provided invaluable assistance in my working through of the classical sources for Hughes's *Birthday Letters*.
4. In 'Robbing Myself' (*BL* 165–67), Hughes remembers his clandestine return to Court Green after Plath and the children had moved to London. He describes the house as a 'plush-lined casket,' 'From which (I did not know) / I had already lost the treasure.' As in the final 'Red,' he describes the aura through which he moves as 'snow-blue twilight, / So precise and tender, a dark sapphire,' and contrasts it with 'our crimson chamber.'

Works Cited

Academy of American Poets, A Public Symposium on Ted Hughes's *Birthday Letters* to Sylvia Plath (with A. Alvarez, Lynda K. Bundtzen, Michael Hofmann, Fran McCullough, and Alicia Suskin Ostriker; moderated by Bonnie Costello). Cooper Union, New York, February 26, 1998.

Aebi, Ormond, and Harry Aebi. *The Art and Adventure of Beekeeping.* Emmaus, Pa.: Rodale Press, 1975.

Alexander, Paul. *Rough Magic: A Biography of Sylvia Plath.* New York: Viking Penguin, 1991.

Alvarez, A. *The Savage God: A Study of Suicide.* New York: Random House, 1970.

——, 'Your Story, My Story.' Review of *Birthday Letters* by Ted Hughes. *New Yorker*, February 2, 1998: 58–64.

Aronson, Theo. *The Golden Bees: The Story of the Bonapartes.* Greenwich, Conn.: New York Graphic Society, 1964.

Boedeker, Deborah. *Descent from Heaven: Images of Dew in Greek Poetry and Religion.* Chico, Calif.: Scholars Press, 1984.

'The Blood Jet Is Poetry.' Review of *Ariel* by Sylvia Plath. *Time*, June 10, 1966: 55–56.

Broe, Mary Lynn. 'Plathologies: The 'Blood Jet' Is Bucks, Not Poetry.' *Belles Letters* 10 (1994): 48–62.

——, *Protean Poetic: The Poetry of Sylvia Plath (PP).* Columbia: University of Missouri Press, 1980.

——, 'Recovering the Complex Self: Sylvia Plath's Beeline.' *Centennial Review* 24 (1980): 1–24.

Bundtzen, Lynda K. *Plath's Incarnations: Woman and the Creative Process (PI).* Ann Arbor: University of Michigan Press, 1983.

Butscher, Edward. *Sylvia Plath: Method and Madness.* New York: Seabury Press, 1976.

——, ed. *Sylvia Plath: The Woman and the Work.* New York: Dodd, 1977.

Dickie, Margaret. *Sylvia Plath and Ted Hughes.* Urbana: University of Illinois Press, 1979.

Dickinson, Emily. *The Complete Poems*. Ed. Thomas H. Johnson. Boston: Little, Brown, 1960.

Ferrier, Carole. 'The Beekeeper and the Queen Bee.' *Refractory Girl* 3 (Spring 1973): 31–36.

Fitzgerald, F. Scott. *The Great Gatsby*. New York: Scribner, 1980.

Freud, Sigmund. 'Mourning and Melancholia' (1917). Trans. Joan Riviere. In *General Psychological Theory*. Ed. Philip Rieff. New York: Macmillan, 1963. 164–79.

Gilbert, Sandra M., and Susan Gubar. *The Madwoman in the Attic: The Woman Writer and the Nineteenth-Century Literary Imagination*. New Haven: Yale University Press, 1979.

Gluck, Louise. 'Education of the Poet.' *Proofs and Theories: Essays on Poetry*. Hopewell, N.J.: Ecco, 1994. 3–18.

Hardy, Barbara. 'Enlargement or Derangement? 'In *Ariel Ascending: Writings about Sylvia Plath*. Ed. Paul Alexander. New York: Harper, 1985. 61–79.

Hayman, Ronald. *The Death and Life of Sylvia Plath*. London: Heinemann, 1991.

The Homeric Hymns. ('To Hermes.') Trans. Apostolos. N. Athanassakis. Baltimore: Johns Hopkins University Press, 1976. 31–47.

Hughes, Ted. *Birthday Letters* (*BL*). New York: Farrar, Straus and Giroux, 1998.

——. 'The Burnt Fox.' In *Winter Pollen*. 8–9.

——. 'Capturing Animals.' In *Poetry in the Making: An Anthology of Poems and Programmes from Listening and Writing* (1969). London: Faber, 1982. 15–21.

——. 'Collecting Sylvia Plath.' In *Winter Pollen*. 170–76.

——. *Crow*. New York: Harper and Row, 1971.

——. 'The Error.' *New Yorker*, June 26 and July 3, 1995: 156–57.

——. Foreword. In The *Journals* of Sylvia Plath. Ed. Ted Hughes and Frances McCullough. New York: Dial, 1982. xi–xiii.

——. *Howls and Whispers*. Etchings by Leonard Baskin. Hadley, Mass.: Gehenna Press, 1998.

——. Introduction. In The *Collected Poems* by Sylvia Plath. New York: Harper and Row, 1981. 13–17.

——. Introduction. In *Johnny Panic and the Bible of Dreams* (*JP*) by Sylvia Plath. New York: Harper and Row, 1979. 1–9.

——. Letter: 'The Place Where Sylvia Plath Should Rest in Peace.' *Manchester Guardian*, April 20, 1989: 18.

——. Letter: 'Sylvia Plath: The Facts of Her Life and the Desecration of Her Grave.' *Independent*, April 20, 1989: 23.

Works Cited

———. 'Publishing Sylvia Plath.' In *Winter Pollen*. 163–69.

———. Reply to letter of Jacqueline Rose: 'Ted Hughes and the Plath Estate.' *Times Literary Supplement* (*TLS*), April 25, 1991: 15–16.

———. 'Sylvia Plath and Her Journals.' In *Winter Pollen*. 177–90.

———. 'Sylvia Plath: The Evolution of "Sheep in Fog."' In *Winter Pollen*. 191–211.

———. 'Sylvia Plath's *Collected Poems* and *The Bell Jar*.' In *Winter Pollen*. 466–81.

———. *Tales from Ovid*. New York: Farrar, Straus and Giroux, 1997.

———. 'The Thought-Fox.' In *The Hawk in the Rain* (1957). London: Faber, 1964, 14.

———. *Winter Pollen*: Occasional Prose (*WP*). Ed. William Scammell. New York: Picador, 1994.

Jackson, Laura Riding. 'Suitable Criticism.' *University of Toronto Quarterly* 47 (1977): 74–85.

Kamel, Rose. 'A Self to Recover': Sylvia Plath's Bee Cycle Poems.' *Modern Poetry Series* 4 (1973): 304–18.

Kinzie, Mary. 'An Informal Check List of Criticism.' *The Art of Sylvia Plath*. Ed. Charles Newman. Bloomington: Indiana University Press, 1970. 283–304.

Kroll, Jack. 'Answering Ariel.' Review of *Birthday Letters* by Ted Hughes. *Newsweek*, February 2, 1998: 58–59.

Kroll, Judith. *Chapters in a Mythology: The Poetry of Sylvia Plath*. New York: Harper and Row, 1976.

Levy, Laurie. 'Outside The Bell Jar.' In *Sylvia Plath: The Woman and the Work*. Ed. Edward Butscher. New York: Dodd, 1977. 42–48.

Longgood, William. *The Queen Must Die and Other Affairs of Bees and Men*. New York: Norton, 1985.

Lowell, Robert. Foreword. In *Ariel* by Sylvia Plath. New York: Harper, 1965.

Maeterlinck, Maurice. *The Life of the Bee*. Trans. Alfred Sutro. New York: Dodd, 1904.

Malcolm, Janet, *The Silent Woman: Sylvia Plath and Ted Hughes*. New York: Knopf, 1994.

Mead, Rebecca. 'Poesy Department: For Better and For Worse, It's the Ted and Sylvia Show.' *New Yorker*, March 16, 1998: 27.

Morgan, Robin. 'Arraignment (I)' and 'Arraignment (II).' 'Conspiracy of Silence against a Feminist Poem.' *Feminist Art Journal* (1972): 1–2.

Newman, Charles, Ed. *The Art of Sylvia Plath*. Bloomington: Indiana University Press, 1970.

Oesterreich, T.K. *Possession Demoniacal and Other among Primitive Races, in Antiquity, the Middle Ages, and Modern Times.* London: Kegan Paul, Trench, Trubner & Co., 1930.

Ovid. *Metamorphoses.* Trans. A.D. Melville. New York: Oxford University Press, 1986.

Owen, Wilfred. 'Strange Meeting.' In *The Norton Anthology of English Literature.* Ed. M.H. Abrams et al. 6th ed. 2 vols. New York: Norton, 1993. 2:1846–47.

Perloff, Marjorie G. 'On the Road to *Ariel*: The 'Transitional' Poetry of Sylvia Plath.' In *Sylvia Plath: The Woman and the Work.* Ed. Edward Butscher. New York: Dodd, 1977. 125–42.

——. 'Sylvia Plath's *Collected Poems*: A Review-Essay.' *Resources for American Literary Study* II (1981): 304–13.

——. 'Sylvia Plath's 'Sivvy' Poems: A Portrait of the Poet as Daughter.' *Sylvia Plath: New Views on the Poetry.* Ed. Gary Lane. Baltimore: Johns Hopkins University Press, 1979. 155–77.

——. 'The Two *Ariel*s: The (Re)Making of the Sylvia Plath Canon.' In *Poems in Their Place: The Intertextuality and Order of Poetic Collections.* Ed. Neil Fraistat. Chapel Hill: University of North Carolina Press, 1986. 308–33.

Pindar. *The Odes of Pindar Including the Principal Fragments.* Trans. Sir John Sandys. London and New York: William Heinemann and Macmillan, 1915.

Plath, Sylvia. *Ariel.* New York: Harper, 1965.

——. *Ariel* Poems. Manuscript and typescript. Sylvia Plath Collection. Smith College Library Mortimer Rare Book Room, Northampton, Mass.

——. *Ariel* typescript. Sylvia Plath Collection. Smith College Library Mortimer Rare Book Room, Northampton, Mass.

——. BBC interview with Peter Orr, London, October 30, 1962. In *The Poet Speaks: Interviews with Contemporary Poets.* Ed. Peter Orr. New York: Barnes and Noble, 1966. 167–72.

——. *The Bell Jar.* New York: Bantam, 1971.

——. *The Collected Poems* (CP). Ed. Ted Hughes. New York: Harper, 1981.

——. *The Colossus and Other Poems* (1962). New York: Vintage, 1968.

——. *The Journals of Sylvia Plath* (J) (1982). Ed. Ted Hughes and Frances McCullough. New York: Ballantine, 1983. One citation from the 2000 edition edited by Karen V. Kukil. London: Faber and Faber.

Works Cited

———. Letters. Manuscript and typescript. Sylvia Plath Collection. Smith College Library Mortimer Rare Book Room, Northampton, Mass.

———. Letters. Mss. II, Box 6. Sylvia Plath Manuscript Collection. Lilly Library, Indiana University, Bloomington.

———. *Letters Home (LH)*. Ed. Aurelia Plath. New York: Harper, 1975.

———. Lists. Manuscript and typescript. Sylvia Plath Collection. Smith College Library Mortimer Rare Book Room, Northampton, Mass.

———. *Lyonnesse*. London: Rainbow Press, 1971.

———. 'Pair of Queens.' Review of *Josephine* by Hubert Cole. *New Statesman*, April 27, 1962: 602–3.

———. *Pursuit*. London: Rainbow Press, 1973.

———. Tablet Diary 1962. Sylvia Plath Collection. Smith College Library Mortimer Rare Book Room, Northampton, Mass.

Plato. *Ion*. Trans. Paul Woodruff. Indianopolis: Hackett Publishing Co., 1983.

Pollitt, Katha. 'A Note of Triumph.' Review of The *Collected Poems* by Sylvia Plath. *Nation*, January 16, 1982: 52–55.

———. 'Peering into *The Bell Jar*.' Review of *Birthday Letters* by Ted Hughes. *New York Times Book Review*, March I, 1998: 4, 6.

Rackham, H., trans. *Pliny: Natural History*. Vol. I. Cambridge, Mass.: Loeb Classical Library, 1979.

Roche, Clarissa. 'Sylvia Plath: Vingettes from England.' In *Sylvia Plath: The Woman and the Work*. Ed. Edward Butscher. New York: Dodd, 1977. 81–96.

Root, A.I. *The ABC and XYZ of Bee Culture*. 38th ed. Medina, Ohio: A.I. Root Co., 1980.

Rose, Jacqueline. *The Haunting of Sylvia Plath*. Cambridge, Mass.: Harvard University Press, 1991.

———. Reply to letter of Olwyn Hughes: 'Ted Hughes and the Plath Estate.' *Times Literary Supplement (TLS)*, April 10, 1982: 11.

———. Review of *Birthday Letters* by Ted Hughes. *Observer* Review, February I, 1998: 15.

Rosenblatt, Jon. *Sylvia Plath: The Poetry of Initiation*. Chapel Hill: University of North Carolina Press, 1979.

Rowland, Robyn. 'The Burying of Hughes.' In *Radically Speaking: Feminism Reclaimed*. Ed. Diane Bell and Renate Klein. London: Zed Books, 1996. 557.

'Russian Roulette.' Review of *Ariel* by Sylvia Plath. *Newsweek*, June 20, 1966: 110.

Sagar, Keith. *The Art of Ted Hughes*. Cambridge: Cambridge University Press, 1975.

Scheinberg, Susan. 'The Bee Maidens of the Homeric "Hymn to Hermes."' Harvard Studies in Classical Philology 83 (1979): 1–28.

Shakespeare, William. *The Tempest.* In The Riverside Shakespeare. Ed. G. Blakemore Evans et al. 2nd ed. Boston: Houghton Mifflin. 1656–88.

Sigmund, Elizabeth. 'Sylvia in Devon: 1962.' In *Sylvia Plath: The Woman and the Work.* Ed. Edward Butscher. New York: Dodd, 1977. 100–107.

Steiner, Deborah. *The Crown of Song: Metaphor in Pindar.* New York: Oxford University Press, 1986.

Stevenson, Anne. *Bitter Fame: A Life of Sylvia Plath* (BF). Boston: Houghton Mifflin, 1989.

Style, Sue. *Honey: From Hive to Honeypot.* San Francisco: Chronicle Books, 1992.

Tabor, Stephen. *Sylvia Plath: An Analytical Bibliography.* Westport, Conn.: Meckler, 1987.

Taylor, Richard. *The How-To-Do-It Book of Bee-keeping,* 3rd ed. Interlaken, N.Y.: Linden Books, 1977.

Thompson, Flora. *Lark Rise.* London: Oxford University Press, 1939.

Van Dyne, Susan R., '"More Terrible Than She Ever Was": The Manuscripts of Sylvia Plath's Bee Poems.' In *Stings: Original Drafts of the Poem in Facsimile* Reproduced from the Sylvia Plath Collection at Smith College. Northampton, Mass.: Smith College Library Mortimer Rare Book Room, 1982. 3–12.

——. 'Rekindling the Past in Sylvia Plath's "Burning the Letters."' Centennial Review 32 (Summer 1988): 250–65.

——. Revising Life: Sylvia Plath's '*Ariel*' Poems (RL). Chapel Hill: University of North Carolina Press, 1993.

Vendler, Helen. 'An Intractable Metal.' Review of The *Collected Poems* by Sylvia Plath. *New Yorker,* February 15, 1982: 124–38.

Virgil. *The Georgics.* Trans. L.P. Wilkinson. London: Penguin, 1982.

Wagner, Erica. *Ariel's Gift.* London: Faber and Faber, 2000.

Wagner, Linda W. 'Plath on Napoleon.' Notes on Contemporary Literature 15 (March 1985): 6.

Wagner-Martin, Linda. *Sylvia Plath: A Biography.* New York: St. Martin's Press, 1987.

Wood, James. 'Muck Funnel.' Review of *Birthday Letters* by Ted Hughes. New Republic, March 30, 1998: 30–33.

Index

Index

Index

Index

Index